# Looking Beyond Neoliberalism

# Looking Beyond Neoliberalism

French and Francophone Belgian Cinema and the Crisis

**Martin O'Shaughnessy**

EDINBURGH
University Press

Edinburgh University Press is one of the leading university presses in the UK. We publish academic books and journals in our selected subject areas across the humanities and social sciences, combining cutting-edge scholarship with high editorial and production values to produce academic works of lasting importance. For more information visit our website: edinburghuniversitypress.com

© Martin O'Shaughnessy, 2022

Edinburgh University Press Ltd
The Tun – Holyrood Road
12(2f) Jackson's Entry
Edinburgh EH8 8PJ

First published in hardback by Edinburgh University Press 2022

Typeset in Arno and Myriad
by Manila Typesetting Company, and
printed and bound by CPI Group (UK) Ltd,
**Croydon, CR0 4YY**

A CIP record for this book is available from the British Library

ISBN 978 1 4744 4862 8 (hardback)
ISBN 978 1 4744 4863 5 (paperback)
ISBN 978 1 4744 4864 2 (webready PDF)
ISBN 978 1 47444865 9 (epub)

The right of Martin O'Shaughnessy to be identified as the author of this work has been asserted in accordance with the Copyright, Designs and Patents Act 1988, and the Copyright and Related Rights Regulations 2003 (SI No. 2498).

# Contents

List of figures .......... viii
Acknowledgements .......... xi

**Introduction** .......... 1
   Looking sideways at the Crisis .......... 3
   Chapter outline .......... 6

**Chapter 1: Audiard's triumphant neoliberal subjects** .......... 11
   Between conservatism and radical destabilisation: Audiard
      and his critics .......... 12
   Heroes and prophets: Audiard's prototypical neoliberal
      subjects .......... 15
   Neoliberal subjectivity .......... 22
   Escaping precarity: Audiard's happy endings .......... 26
   Gendering the neoliberal subject: Audiard's violently
      vulnerable men .......... 29
   Audiard's flexible families .......... 34
   Conclusion .......... 37

**Chapter 2: Subjects in the chains of debt** .......... 40
   *Le Silence de Lorna* and indebted citizenship .......... 41
   *L'Emploi du temps* and debt's disciplinary reach .......... 45
   *Le Père de mes enfants* and the indebted image .......... 49
   Debt, governance and subjectivity .......... 54
   Cruel optimism and impasse .......... 57
   Film and theory in dialogue .......... 59

|  |  |
|---|---|
| Indebted variations: the narrative of impasse or the impasse of narrative? | 63 |
| Conclusion | 68 |

## Chapter 3: The desperate search for the exit    70
|  |  |
|---|---|
| The death of the worker: Brizé's hidden and spectacular suicides | 71 |
| Subjective, symbolic and systemic violence | 77 |
| Working men dead and dead men working | 80 |
| The death of the trader | 83 |
| The murderous violence of the corporation | 86 |
| The Dardennes' ethical exits | 89 |
| Finally, the exit? Kervern and Delépine's anarchic departures | 92 |
| Conclusion | 96 |

## Chapter 4: The deconstructive materialism of Sciamma and Kechiche    98
|  |  |
|---|---|
| The materialism of the encounter | 99 |
| Kechiche's vitalist materialism: *La Graine et le mulet* | 102 |
| The mobile body of the Black Venus | 108 |
| *La Vie d'Adèle* and its troubling encounters | 111 |
| Sciamma's embodied becoming | 115 |
| *Tomboy*, or what a body can do | 116 |
| Women on fire and under water: what cinema can do | 120 |
| *Bande de filles*: mutability and material limits | 125 |
| *Bande de filles* and the limits we do not see | 129 |
| Conclusion | 130 |

## Chapter 5: The Dardennes' unwitting gifts    132
|  |  |
|---|---|
| *La Promesse*: Finding a way to live in a new world | 133 |
| Theorising the gift | 139 |
| Finite gifts, infinite debts and mutable objects | 144 |
| Poisonous and ethical gifts | 147 |
| Generous gifts | 150 |
| The reconnective power of the gift | 153 |
| Conclusion | 158 |

## Chapter 6: Machinic enslavement and cinema's machinic powers    160
|  |  |
|---|---|
| Centred subjects, machinic margins and ex-centric looks | 161 |
| Lazzarato and machinic subjection | 167 |

Cinema's semiotic pluralism 171
Besson's Lucy: a cog with superpowers 174
Sylvain George and the power of montage 178
George's Benjaminian machinery 182
Filming the occupation and its plural semiosis 186
Conclusion 190

**Conclusion** **192**

Bibliography 195
Filmography 201
Index 204

# Figures

| | | |
|---|---|---|
| 1.1 | Disrupting the narrative: young Albert expresses his older self's elation (*Un héros très discret*, Jacques Audiard, 1996) | 16 |
| 1.2 | Malik arrives in prison as a blank slate (*Un prophète*, Jacques Audiard, 2009) | 18 |
| 1.3 | Albert learning new skills (*Un héros très discret*, Jacques Audiard, 1996) | 18 |
| 1.4 | The networked Malik looks upon the isolated and diminished César (*Un prophète*, Jacques Audiard, 2009) | 20 |
| 1.5 | Fred as unlikely debt collector (*Regarde les hommes tomber*, Jacques Audiard, 1994) | 31 |
| 1.6 | Forging a family (*Dheepan*, Jacques Audiard, 2015) | 37 |
| 2.1 | Lorna as indebted citizen and reliable payer (*Le Silence de Lorna*, Jean-Pierre and Luc Dardenne, 2008) | 41 |
| 2.2 | Claudy as a demanding bodily presence (*Le Silence de Lorna*, Jean-Pierre and Luc Dardenne, 2008) | 43 |
| 2.3 | The UN building as a space of mutual surveillance (*L'Emploi du temps*, Laurent Cantet, 2001) | 48 |
| 2.4 | Grégoire's first appearance, as if born of the urban circulation (*Le Père de mes enfants*, Mia Hansen-Løve, 2009) | 50 |
| 2.5 | The pensive stillness of Clémence (*Le Père de mes enfants*, Mia Hansen-Løve, 2009) | 54 |
| 2.6 | Visiting his mother in prison, the child's role in keeping optimism alive (*Une vie meilleure*, Cédric Kahn, 2011) | 68 |
| 3.1 | Walking away from an oppressive workplace (*La Loi du marché*, Stéphane Brizé, 2015) | 73 |

| | | |
|---|---|---|
| 3.2 | Apparent mobile phone footage of the hero's self-immolation (*En guerre*, Stéphane Brizé, 2018) | 76 |
| 3.3 | The trader subsumed by his job (*L'Outsider*, Christophe Barratier, 2016) | 84 |
| 3.4 | An inert body soon to become an object of symbolic struggle (*Corporate*, Nicolas Silhol, 2017) | 87 |
| 3.5 | The worker's over-identification with her disposability (*Deux jours, une nuit*, Jean-Pierre and Luc Dardenne, 2014) | 91 |
| 3.6 | Not Dead: living in negation (*Le Grand Soir*, Gustave Kervern and Benoît Delépine, 2012) | 94 |
| 4.1 | The crisis of the older worker and the failure of desire (*La Graine et le mulet*, Abdellatif Kechiche, 2007) | 104 |
| 4.2 | Rym's closely scrutinised body (*La Graine et le mulet*, Abdellatif Kechiche, 2007) | 107 |
| 4.3 | Adèle's head is turned by the encounter with Emma (*La Vie d'Adèle*, Abdellatif Kechiche, 2013) | 112 |
| 4.4 | Laure / Mickaël discovering what their body can do (*Tomboy*, Céline Sciamma, 2011) | 118 |
| 4.5 | Resisting social destiny: Héloïse signals her attachment to Marianne (*Portrait de la jeune fille en feu*, Céline Sciamma, 2019) | 122 |
| 4.6 | *Bande de filles*' utopian opening (Céline Sciamma, 2014) | 125 |
| 5.1 | The garage owner passing on skills to Igor in *La Promesse* (Jean-Pierre and Luc Dardenne, 1996) | 134 |
| 5.2 | The identical jackets that seem to seal Bruno's forgiveness in *L'Enfant* (Jean-Pierre and Luc Dardenne, 2005) | 147 |
| 5.3 | Sandra's insistent bodily presence (*Deux jours, une nuit*, Jean-Pierre and Luc Dardenne, 2014) | 149 |
| 5.4 | Strength and vulnerability; collaboration: two dynamics in the same frame (*Le Fils*, Jean-Pierre and Luc Dardenne, 2002) | 152 |
| 5.5 | The bike's connective powers in *Le Gamin au vélo* (Jean-Pierre and Luc Dardenne, 2011) | 155 |
| 5.6 | The connective gift of the waffles (*La Fille inconnue*, Jean-Pierre and Luc Dardenne, 2016) | 157 |
| 6.1 | Behind the human drama: the graphs and charts (*La Loi du marché*, Stéphane Brizé, 2015) | 162 |
| 6.2 | Human hands harnessed to the barcode scanner (*La Loi du marché*, Stéphane Brizé, 2015) | 163 |

| | | |
|---|---|---|
| 6.3 | The containers becoming abstract (*Ma part du gâteau*, Cédric Klapisch, 2011) | 166 |
| 6.4 | Lucy's semiotic superpowers (*Lucy*, Luc Besson, 2014) | 175 |
| 6.5 | The spontaneous montage of political tradition and present struggle (*Paris est une fête*, Sylvain George, 2017) | 185 |
| 6.6 | Capturing the occupation's rich semiosis (*Vers Madrid: the Burning Bright*, Sylvain George, 2012) | 187 |

# Acknowledgements

My warm thanks go to Gillian Leslie, Richard Strachan and Sam Johnson at Edinburgh University Press for their wonderful support and their patience at the different stages of the writing of this book, and to Fiona Screen, my copy editor, for her eagle eye and careful attention to detail. My thanks also go to colleagues at Nottingham Trent, especially Dave Woods and Patrick O'Connor, for letting me try out ideas on them and helping me chart my way through some of the theory. My thanks, too, to Angelos Koutsourakis, Thomas Austin, Kate Ince, Richard Rushton, Rosemarie Scullion, Chris Holmlund, John Marks, Ben Scott and so many others for their generous willingness to discuss the ideas developed here and to share their own thoughts and suggestions with me. And my thanks, finally, to all those, at different conferences, especially Film-Philosophy, who have helped me get my thoughts straight.

Some chapters of this book update, rework or expand upon my earlier work, all single authored. Chapter 2 develops and updates 'The Crisis before the Crisis: reading films by Laurent Cantet and Jean-Pierre and Luc Dardenne through the lens of debt' (*Substance*, 43: 1, 2014, 82–95). Chapter 3 updates 'Putting the dead to work: making sense of worker suicide in contemporary French and Francophone Belgian film' (*Studies in French Cinema*, 19: 4, 2018, 314–34). Chapter 5 updates and expands upon 'Beyond neoliberalism? Gift economies in the films of the Dardenne brothers', in Thomas Austin and Angelos Koutsourakis (eds), *Cinema of Crisis: Film and Contemporary Europe* (Edinburgh, Edinburgh University Press, 2020). Chapter 6 reworks 'Beyond language and the subject: machinic enslavement in contemporary European cinema' (*Studies in European Cinema*, 16: 3, 2019, 197–217).

*To Gloria, Ana, John and Michael*

# Introduction

In his discussion of violence, Slavoj Žižek warns of allowing our attention to be drawn too directly to the obvious transgressiveness of what he calls subjective violence (crime, riot, war) in a way that would blind us to the systemic and symbolic violences that have become normalised as the apparently peaceful face of the status quo. To see violence more adequately, he suggests, we need to look at it askew or sideways (Žižek 2008: 1–7). The same might be said about the crisis, with or without a capital C, which erupted in 2007 to 2008. If we look at it too directly, we may only see its disruptiveness and be blinded to its complex connection to the status quo, its instrumentalisation as a governmental tool and its 'outsourcing' to ordinary people who are either forced to bear its cost or live under its more or less permanent sway. This is why, although I will not ignore the cinema that came out after 2008 and responded more or less directly to the crisis and its fallout, I will engage with a broader body of films, some from before 2008, that will allow me to look at the crisis 'sideways'. In this, I follow in the footsteps of scholars like Berlant and Koutsourakis who adopt a similar procedure (Berlant 2011a: 10–12; Koutsourakis 2020: 60–1). I will consider films that engage with debt, austerity, the rationing of productive places and the murderous violence of competition as so many personalised crises already lurking within the neoliberal status quo. But I will also be drawn to less obvious films which help us, directly or indirectly, and more or less consciously, to look beyond neoliberalism, without necessarily seeing crisis as the *deus ex machina* needed to render some form of exit possible. To begin with, though, temporarily ignoring my own counsel, I will look at the crisis frontally.

In 2007, something often called the sub-prime crisis began to make itself felt. Initially associated with major American banks that found themselves holding mortgage bonds whose value was collapsing, and with other American institutions such as insurers caught up in the shockwave, the crisis quickly revealed its global nature as more and more financial institutions across different countries faced potentially catastrophic losses and economies tipped into recession. Governments around the world stepped in to save their banks and financial sectors from collapse but only at the cost of massive sovereign borrowing and deficit financing. Private financial debt was effectively transferred to populations who would be forced to pay for it through economic austerity and reduced social welfare spending. As celebrated Marxist geographer David Harvey notes, there have been many financial crises around the world since 1973, the time of the first oil crisis, compared to very few between 1945 and 1973. Yet, this one was much bigger (Harvey 2010: 6–8). It seemed to confirm that an economic model was broken. With wage growth stagnant in the West, even as the gap between rich and poor grew ever wider, borrowing had become the privileged way for many to maintain access to housing and consumption. American mortgages were sold to people who would struggle to pay them. They were then bundled up in complex derivatives, sold on through a globalised financial sector and speculated upon. Inflated by inequality, debt, deregulation and speculation, the bubble, at some stage, would inevitably burst. When it did, and when finance was bailed out at the expense of populations, political unrest grew. Occupy-style movements sprang up around the world in 2011 not simply in rejection of the existing financial system but in search of more participatory and horizontally organised ways of doing politics outside of traditional party structures that no longer seemed to offer a way forward. With only a small Occupy movement, France seemed relatively peripheral to the protest wave. It would have its own major occupations in the spring of 2016, in the form of the Nuit Debout (literally 'night standing') mobilisations. The most prominent of these were in Paris but they also took place across France and spread into other countries, notably Belgium. In the end, and in the face of police repression, both Occupy and Nuit Debout would peter out while a system whose days might have seemed numbered seems to continue relatively unscathed and perhaps reinforced. Discontent and mistrust of government are still prevalent but the nationalist and racist right, or parties of government moving in a similar direction, seem better able to direct it than the left.

This briefly outlined frontal look might seem to make the task of this book straightforward. It would give us an object, the crisis, to which we could seek cinematic responses, films that were either directly marked by it and its aftershocks or which sought to capture and prolong the spirit of Occupy and Nuit Debout as movements which responded to it and the austerity and rising precarity that followed it. But perhaps a more sideways theoretical and cinematic look will allow us to view the crisis and the context which produced it more productively. Cautioning against a frontal approach, theory asks us to stand back from the concrete and empirical and to question and justify the concepts and methods we use to approach a given problem or issue. Cinema takes raw materials from the world around it and probes and refines them, asking us to see afresh, finding new possibilities where none seemed to exist, making us question what we think we know, challenging us to think again. Theory works upon the conceptual and the abstract. Cinema upon the concrete, affective, sensuous and aesthetic. Cinema and theory cannot be collapsed into one another. Nor should one be used simply to illustrate the other. But they can and should be placed in productive dialogue, as this book seeks to do. And, in their difference and convergences, they can help us see afresh or sideways.

## Looking sideways at the Crisis

In 2013, in a dialogue in *Radical Philosophy*, and in the context of Greece's sovereign debt crisis and the Syntagma Square occupations that followed it, French philosopher Jacques Rancière and Paris-based Greek philosopher Maria Kakogianni discussed the notion of crisis and whether it makes sense to talk of the Crisis, with a capital C. Kakogianni argues that the meaning of crisis is subject to struggle and adds, 'there's no such thing as *The* Crisis. Our crisis is not theirs' (Kakogianni and Rancière 2013: 20, emphasis in the original). Rancière agrees about the contested nature and shifting meanings of the concept. He reminds us of its medical origins as the positive or negative resolution of a mortal challenge to health. He then notes the modern slippages of the term, the way in which it shifts from indicating a resolution of pathology to naming the pathological state itself. The question then arises as to whether the sickness is something beyond the normal functioning of contemporary capitalism, simply part of it, or instrumentalised by it. Apparently leaning towards the first interpretation, Rancière initially observes that, in what we call the Crisis, 'there is something excessively pathological, with its Ponzi schemes, its high-risk speculation and the bubbles or snowballs that grow and grow until they collapse'. But, leaning towards the second understanding, he adds that the normal operation of the system is itself pathological, 'because it causes suffering for such a great number of people' (Kakogianni and Rancière 2013: 19). Bringing the third understanding into play, he points to how the notion of crisis as systemic dysfunction enables 'the situation of exception which allows drastic measures to be taken to destroy everything that obstructs the competitiveness of labour'. Everyone is made to take responsibility for, and, by implication, pay the price of the economic sickness, including the poor who want to eat, own property or have access to credit (Kakogianni and Rancière 2013: 20). Anti-systemic voices can themselves reinforce the performative power of the notion of systemic crisis by allowing it to structure and dominate their thought. On the one hand (following a long-standing tradition in leftist thought), there are those who consider that the crisis must be deepened by radical forces to bring it to its tipping point. On the other, there are those who see the way in which systemic forces instrumentalise crisis as proof that 'the enemy is all-powerful, [and] everything we do ends up profiting them' (Kakogianni and Rancière 2013: 20). Despite the best intentions of those who put it forward, this fetishised understanding of the crisis thus tends to validate, as Rancière notes, 'the dominant description of the crisis and the radical changes that it obliges' (Kakogianni and Rancière 2013: 21). Similarly, rather than being seen as part of a longer and continuing history, attempts to live differently are understood as beneficial effects of the crisis, dependent on its effects and, by implication, its duration (Kakogianni and Rancière 2013: 20–1).

Despite their different theoretical grounding, other important contemporary thinkers agree about neoliberalism's instrumentalisation of crisis while refusing the idea of the crisis as something which simply occurred in 2007 or 2008. For example, Dardot and Laval, two important thinkers of neoliberalism who draw on both the Marxist and Foucauldian traditions, consider that the crisis signalled not an end to neoliberalism but a reinforcement and radicalisation of it. They conclude, like Rancière, that it has become part of the machinery of neoliberal governance. This, they argue, widening the timeframe, was already emergent at the end of the 1970s when governments used the 'difficult times' to justify 'courageous' policies, following up each apparently necessary but scandalously harsh measure with another, never allowing their opponents to take breath. This initial experimentation with punitive policies driven by the proclaimed urgency of the situation has hardened up into neoliberalism's preferred system of governance. Crisis has become a normalised part of a war machine wielded by the powerful to crush any opposition to neoliberalism and to severely restrict any margin of manoeuvre to which democratic states might pretend (Dardot and Laval 2016: 17–44).

In his *Governing by Debt* (2015), Italian philosopher and social theorist, Maurizio Lazzarato rehearses some similar arguments and shows some of the same hesitation about the timeline of crisis. He lists 'crisis' as one the key words of his book and initially specifies that, when he uses it, he means 'the crisis which began with the collapse of the American real-estate market in 2007'. He immediately comments, however, that the definition is too limited as the crisis has been ongoing since the 1973 oil crisis. Broadening his point, and converging with Rancière, he then suggests that neoliberal governmentality involves moving from one crisis to the next, creating a permanent and fearful sense of crisis. 'Crisis', he concludes, 'is the form of government of contemporary capitalism' (Lazzarato 2015: 10). Like Rancière, he then complicates his own argument as he moves to another key term, 'human capital or the entrepreneur of the self'. Explaining the evolution of this figure and pointing to a dimension of crisis that cannot simply be instrumentalised, he suggests that the crisis is not simply economic, social and political but is also and above all a crisis of the neoliberal subject. The project of replacing the Fordist worker with the individual entrepreneur of the self, he suggests, has collapsed in the subprime crisis (Lazzarato 2015: 14).

Dario Gentili also makes the connection between crisis neoliberalism and the crisis of the neoliberal subject, although not tying the latter specifically to debt as Lazzarato had done. Under conditions of neoliberalism, he suggests, the discourse of the market and what it demands 'controls conduct by means of the constant threat of "mortal danger" [. . .] This includes marginalization, poverty, unemployment – the risk of not surviving if one is not able to compete in the "meritocracy" of the market.' In the same way as neoliberalism uses a sense of crisis to drive through its policies at the macro level, it cultivates a constant sense of precarity, of individualised crisis management, to shape the behaviour of apparently freely choosing subjects. He comments, 'crisis as art of government forces decisions from individuals who want to survive in the market [. . .]

Precarity is first and foremost the form of life in the age of crisis as art of government' (Gentili 2021: xviii).

Pulling together lessons from these different thinkers, we can better see the complexity of the crisis as an object of analysis. Something undoubtedly happened in 2007–2008 that sent tremors, whose effects still continue, through the financial, economic and political systems and through our broader societies. However, we would do well not to focus on it too frontally at the risk of normalising what came before it and from which it arose, and of only seeking ways beyond it, neoliberalism or capitalism more generally, in the crisis itself and not in the many untold stirrings that already lie hidden in the folds of our societies, waiting to be brought into view and developed. This is the spirit which guides this book in its sideways approach to the crisis. It has two main foci. Taking its cue from Lazzarato and Gentili, it first probes filmic responses to the crisis of the neoliberal subject, a crisis that was certainly exacerbated by the financial crisis and its fallout but did not begin with it. It then explores film's crucial capacity to bring into view forms of being and relating that help us look past neoliberalism and thereby reawaken a sense of possibility.

## Chapter outline

The first three chapters focus on the crisis of the neoliberal subject. Placing the films of Jacques Audiard, perhaps France's most internationally successful filmmaker, in dialogue with key theorists of neoliberalism, Chapter 1 explores how, across a range of genres, Audiard's films repeatedly confront and contain crisis tendencies within neoliberal subjectivity by showing characters exposed to precarity in violently competitive worlds but prospering by becoming successful entrepreneurs of the self. The chapter also considers the 'queering' of the films' subjects and analyses how, in another form of containment, reinvented gender and familial relations are put to work for neoliberal flexibility. The next two chapters explore groups of films which refuse such a containment of the crisis of the subject. Chapter 2 considers indebted subjectivity. It brings Lazzarato's seminal work on debt (2011, 2015) into dialogue with Cantet's *L'Emploi du temps* (*Time Out*, 2001), the Dardenne brothers' *Le Silence de Lorna* (*Lorna's Silence*, 2008) and Hansen-Løve's *Le Père de mes enfants* (*The Father of My Children*, 2009), and a cluster of 'crisis films' from 2011, to explore how debt forecloses the entrepreneurial subject's future and erases the memory of past resistances, trapping them in the management of ongoing crises. Berlant's *Cruel Optimism* (2011a) is also called upon to probe the films' exploration of the gestural and affective economy of filmic debt. Radicalising the sense of foreclosed futures but also probing films' capacity to reveal an exit, Chapter 3 centres on the successful and failed worker suicides that have become increasingly common in Franco-Belgian cinema. Most of the works discussed postdate 2008 and include Stéphane Brizé's *la Loi du marché* (*The Measure of a Man*, 2015), the same director's *En guerre* (*At War*, 2018) and the Dardenne brothers' *Deux jours, une nuit* (*Two Days, One Night*, 2016). They are analysed using Žižek's account of the interplay of subjective, symbolic and systemic violences (2008) and Cederström and Fleming's essay (2012) on work-related suicide. I argue that, while the films very effectively use the embodied violences of suicide to force hidden systemic violences into view, they struggle to open ways out of neoliberal labour and are effectively trapped in a left moralism (Brown 2001: 18–30) or an ethics frozen in opposition to what it opposes. I finish the chapter by bringing together Kervern and Delépine's anarchic comedy, *Le Grand Soir* (2012), and Foucault's (2011) discussion of parrhesia to probe what a filmic exit from labour involving a killing of the worker in the self (and not the self in the worker) might look like.

The search for exits moves the book towards its second core focus, film's capacity to bring alternatives into view and reawaken a sense of possibility. The next two chapters pursue that task. In some ways encapsulating the core thrust of my argument, Chapter 4 places Louis Althusser's late essay on the materialism of the encounter (2006) and Catherine Malabou's reading of that famous text (2015) in dialogue with the films of Abdellatif Kechiche and Céline Sciamma, two of France's most important contemporary directors. It argues that the aleatory or deconstructive materialism discussed by the two thinkers speaks productively to the way in which the filmmakers pit the desiring encounters and embodied mutability of their characters against social and institutional contexts that limit their becoming. Through attention to constantly emergent possibilities and obstacles to their realisation, the films bring into view the contingency of the existing order and the possibilities bubbling away beneath its surface. Continuing this exploration of contingency, of nascent forms of being and relating repressed by existing contexts, Chapter 5 focuses on the largely unremarked upon gift economy that runs through the Dardenne brothers' films. Marcel Mauss's famous anthropological account of the gift ([1925] (2012))) has been criticised for the conditionality of the practices it discusses and how it would disqualify them as gifts (Derrida 1992). I argue here that it is precisely the conditionality of gifts in the Dardennes' films that allows them to generate social connections and open futures. I further argue that the films' gift economy renders visible the essentially social nature of human gestures and the plasticity of objects as, rescued from mere commodity status, they become embedded in evolving human relationships, shifting in meaning and function in the process. Of course, under current conditions, gifts are incorporated within the capitalist economy and serve as a sentimentalised supplement to it. But, giving something more to us, the Dardennes' gifts point to potentially different ways to relate to each other, our gestures and the object world around us.

Bringing together the book's two foci, its sixth and final chapter returns to the neoliberal subject but only to show it being shattered and made available for reimagining. Contemporary subjection, Lazzarato notes, drawing on Deleuze and Guattari, has two faces. On the one hand, it relies upon our subjectification, named subjects being necessary to anchor hierarchical relations, social and economic roles and property rights. On the other, through processes of machinic enslavement, it tears us apart, turning our gestures, intellectual capacities and affectivity into cogs of different machineries. If our subjectification requires the signifying semiotics of language, our machinic enslavement relies upon the asignifying semiotics of graphs, charts, accounts, algorithms and the digital more broadly. Ignored by much critical theory, the machinic is central to our contemporary condition (Lazzarato 2014: 13–17). It was also at the heart of the subprime crisis, when individualised debts and properties were bundled up, speculated upon and reworked as so many insignificant cogs in the machinery of global financial speculation. With its own machinic powers and plural semiotics, cinema might seem ideally placed to engage with this machinic enslavement. As Lazzarato notes, however, its machineries are typically subordinated to the production of centred subjects (Lazzarato 2014: 108). Looking at a range of films, from post-2008 social realist, crisis-related works, through *Lucy* (Besson, 2014), a contemporary French blockbuster, to Sylvain George's avant-gardist documentaries about migrants and contemporary protests, I will probe how they put cinema's machinic powers to work to engage with our subjection. I will firstly discuss how, if we read the social realist works ex-centrically, we can find the machinic around their edges, its marginalised presence an unacknowledged recognition of both its contemporary centrality and the difficulty that subject-centred mainstream cinema has engaging with it. Turning to *Lucy*, I will look at how, in its creation of a semiotically super-powered cyborg heroine, it foregrounds yet resolves the tension between centred subjects and disempowered human cogs while paradoxically mobilising cinema's digital powers to re-centre human perception. Finally, looking at George's films, I will discuss how they use cinema's plural semiosis to engage with the machinery of the Occupy and Nuit Debout demonstrations in a way which suggests cinema might become the self-consciousness of a new collective actor beyond the individual subject. I will also consider how, mobilising the machinery of montage to create collisions between past and present and between precarious migrants and European struggles against precarity, such films ask how we might reinvent our politics beyond a narrowly national frame.

Discussing filmed images of the different Occupy movements in an interview with *Cahiers du Cinéma*, Rancière suggests that they reveal the tentativeness of the people in them: a desire to be together but uncertainty as to what form that being together might take. He finds a similar tentativeness in Sylvain George's *Vers Madrid* (2012), his film of the Spanish *Toma la Plaza* (Take the Square) mobilisation and notes the parallel 'between the difficulty of finding political forms and the difficulty finding fictional forms' (Delorme and Zabunyan 2015: 87, my translation). This is a lucid summation of where we find ourselves. We are not at a moment where there is a cohesive political cinema which, drawing on a formal repertoire of presumed effectiveness, places itself in the service of established political movements. As Rancière suggests later in the interview, we are at a time where a more diverse body of films can provide aesthetic resources to stimulate thought. Certainly, there are many pre-formatted works which offer nothing new, but other works retain the capacity to propose gestures, looks, bodily movements and ways for bodies to relate that it falls to politics to incorporate (Delorme and Zabunyan 2015: 92–4). In a similar spirit to Rancière, this book seeks to bring into view resources that cinema offers us for rethinking our politics.

The book's unity comes from its two central thrusts: a probing of the crisis of the neoliberal subject, on the one hand; an exploration of film's capacity to reveal potentially new forms of life pressing against the containment of the status quo, on the other. The range of theorists used is varied but, hopefully, this variety is justified by the use to which they are put and the insights they help generate. Those brought into the discussion of neoliberalism and the crisis of the subject tend to come from a Marxist and / or Foucauldian tradition. Those used to tease out the films' capacity to explore emergent possibilities (Lazzarato, Mauss, Althusser, Malabou) are more eclectic but converge nonetheless on some form of aleatory materialism: machinic assemblages, including those of cinema, which bear a constant potential for reassemblage (Lazzarato); gifts which carry the potential for alternative forms of relation between people, gestures and things (Mauss); a materialism of the encounter (Althusser) or a deconstructive materialism (Malabou) which, refusing determinism, reopen a sense of historical openness. This shared sense of contingency speaks productively to the films' probing of possibilities and how they help us see something beyond the capitalist present.

# 1

# Audiard's triumphant neoliberal subjects

With two Césars (the French equivalent of Oscars) to his name and one Cannes Palme d'or, Jacques Audiard is one of France's most successful and exportable filmmakers. He is not typically considered a progressive director or even a political one and is therefore not an obvious choice for inclusion here. I nonetheless turn to him because, perhaps better than any other director, and possibly despite himself, he undertakes a relentless probing of shifts in subjectivity, gender roles and family relationships in the context of neoliberalism. I begin by exploring some of the debate around his work, partly to give a sense of how it has been perceived, but mainly to open lines of inquiry that I will draw upon. I then focus on two films, *Un héros très discret* (*A Self Made Hero*, 1996) and *Un prophète* (*A Prophet*, 2009), to show how, whatever their apparent themes (myths of resistance, in one case, prison survival, in the other), they track the emergence of a distinctly new kind of subject that one might qualify as neoliberal. Broadening the scope, I will show how characters in other Audiard films are haunted by a precarity indissociable from neoliberalism but from which they escape by remaking themselves as entrepreneurial neoliberal subjects. Bringing gender into the frame, I then focus on two early works to show how their reworking of subjectivities also requires a reshaping of gendered identities and relationships. Then, looking specifically at *De rouille et d'os* (*Rust and Bone*, 2012) and *Dheepan* (2015), two more recent films, I look at how Audiard's cinema increasingly figures not simply reworked subjects but refashioned families. Although the neoliberal subject is almost always discussed as an entrepreneurial individual, neoliberalism requires a remodelled family to secure its work of reproduction in a way that Audiard's films bring to the fore. I conclude by asking whether Audiard's films open real avenues of escape from neoliberalism or simply show characters who, despite their self-reinvention, essentially learn to live under its sway.

## Between conservatism and radical destabilisation: Audiard and the critics

Back in 2015, legendary French journal *Cahiers du Cinéma* brought out an issue taking aim at the 'political void' ('vide politique') of French cinema. The journal's then chief editor, Stéphane Delorme, particularly targeted a dominant strand of works, typified by Audiard, which used political situations as a mere backdrop for genre filmmaking (Delorme 2015a, 5). He developed a withering analysis of Audiard's newly released *Dheepan*, noting how the film was 'at the centre of a little constellation [of works] that is turning French cinema gangrenous' (Delorme 2015b: 6, my translation). With its courageous focus on Tamil refugees and its casting of two unknowns, it had initially raised his hopes. But, picking up on a fatalistic tradition running through French cinema since 1930s Poetic Realism, it suggested one cannot escape one's past or one's origins, effectively closing down any sense the world could be different. Worse still, Delorme noted that by building parallels between the Sri Lankan civil war and the French *banlieue* (suburbs), the film suggested that ethnically diverse, working-class areas of France were like a war zone, an image that would have the racist Front National rubbing its hands in glee. Defenders of the work might seek to excuse its recourse to the most reductive sort of cliché by noting that Audiard makes genre films but, retorts Delorme, stereotypes deployed in genre fictions are not innocent. He adds that Audiard's blindness on this score is more broadly symptomatic of the failure of French filmmakers to develop a genuinely original vision or a politics (Delorme 2015b).

Another contributor to the issue, Cyril Béghin, confirmed the journal's line. He castigated the way in which French cinema, as typified by directors such as Audiard or Kechiche, repeatedly shows characters responding to the ambient economic, social or racist brutality through individual flight or social revenge, neither pathway opening any broader political horizon. Focusing more tightly on Audiard, he noted the prevalence of either thugs or *petits malins* ('little smart arses') in his films. The former, like the bare-knuckle boxer hero of *De rouille et d'os*, are out-and-out brutes but avoid our condemnation either because of their lack of awareness or because they have no way out. They are effectively excused by the surrounding violence of which they are also a victim. The latter, the *petits malins*, neither accept humiliation nor become pure brutes but, by using their cunning, are able to develop individual survival strategies. Malik, the French-Maghrebi hero of Audiard's *Un prophète*, is given as the main example here. The film could have used Malik's rise in prison to mount a devastating critique of the twisted nature of French Republican integration in (neo)liberal times had it pushed his monstrosity to the limit and forced us to confront its ugliness. Instead, it cynically leaves us with a feeling of exultation at the character's success and no way to see beyond a devastated socio-political terrain (Béghin 2015).

Despite these variations, *Cahiers'* overarching judgement of Audiard is clear enough. His films connect to socio-political issues but tie themselves to regressive stereotypes and stale generic codes and therefore cannot open any fresh political horizons. The violence of the world is made plain but no way through it is opened up. Conformist subjects, his characters bow to, channel or negotiate with the ambient brutality without allowing any glimpse of forms that an oppositional political subjectivity might take.

This sense of Audiard as a fundamentally conservative director is given a specifically gendered dimension by noted feminist analyst Geneviève Sellier. The director, she suggests, buys into the theme of a 'masculinity in crisis', but finds no productive way through it. He shows men as victims of either their own inability to express their feelings and control their lives or the modern women who threaten their hegemony, but he is also fascinated by the energy of violent male characters for whom everything is subject to bargaining and power relations. All his films are variants of this same operation: violent males, of the type whose presence is authorised by genre fictions, are made to appear fragile and vulnerable – and therefore acceptable (Sellier 2016). Sellier's analysis is different to that of the *Cahiers* critics but she agrees with them that Audiard essentially fails either to open any positive way through the violence of the worlds he shows or generate a sense of the shape new forms of subjectivity might take.

A contrasting analysis of the films is developed across a rich series of texts by Julia Dobson who emphasises their interlinked capacities to disrupt formal and generic expectations and destabilise patriarchal models. Examining *Regarde les hommes tomber* (*See How They Fall*, 1994), for example, she observes how the film undercuts its own realist features (handheld camera, direct sound, naturalistic lighting) with a narrative that evokes myth and foregrounds intertextual references. The generic conventions of the road movie and the thriller, she notes, arouse expectation around character and narrative trajectories that the film deliberately fails to meet. Its chronology is decidedly non-linear and its spatial co-ordinates elusive. These formal, stylistic and generic destabilisations create the shifting terrain upon which the film's knowing disruption of gender archetypes can take place (Dobson 2008: 39–44). Rather than showing the faithful transmission of gendered subjectivities from fathers to sons, the films show filial figures adjusting to their vulnerability by forming new alliances and forging new identities (Dobson 2008: 57). Dobson's readings point to a rather more progressive, disruptive Audiard than the reactionary figure described by *Cahiers* and Sellier.

Audiard's own account of his work aligns with Dobson's vision of him as a filmmaker keen to challenge norms, especially but not only those relating to gendered subjectivities. One radio interview which condenses his views in this area was given to Géraldine Sarratia, a journalist from cultural magazine *Les Inrocks*, as part of a series exploring different personalities' attitude to gender. Audiard told her how much he hated the ridiculous masculine competitiveness he found in his all-male boarding school. He notes that his parents feared he might be gay and regrets he is not, as that would have annoyed his mother. He also explains how he is drawn to the seductiveness of male actors before announcing, not for the first time, that his male characters are in fact women, a remark presumably to be explained by the emotional fragility and neediness they display. Traditional virility, as he sees it, is a vulgar domination exercised over other people that was for a long time taken as simply the way things were but is now in crisis. His male characters, he notes, find themselves faced with the failure of a certain masculine code and must find a new one. His role as a director is to track this attempt to find new forms of masculinity (Sarratia 2018).

Taken together, these strikingly divergent views of Audiard point to a series of questions: about the newness of the gendered subjectivities found in his films; about whether contexts are engaged with seriously or simply evoked through regressive stereotypes or genre codes; about the capacity of the films to open up ways out of a world of precarity and violence; and, ultimately, about their underlying politics. Significantly, none of the different analysts accorded a particular place to neoliberalism, its violences and the reworking of subjectivity it requires. It could be that some of the disagreements between them will be at least partially smoothed out when neoliberalism is put back in the frame.

## Heroes and prophets: Audiard's prototypical neoliberal subjects

Audiard's *Un héros très discret* tells the story of Albert Dehousse a young man with no experience of life who, in the turbulent period of the Liberation of France from German occupation, masquerades as a member of the Resistance and achieves the rank of Lieutenant Colonel in the French army before denouncing himself as an imposter. In between times, he marries the daughter of a family of resisters, travels to Paris, is hired by Monsieur Jo, a man who has worked with Germans, collaborators and later the Resistance, is enrolled in the army, achieves rapid promotion and contracts a second, bigamous marriage. The director's *Un prophète* recounts the rise of Malik, a young Frenchman of Arab extraction, who is forced to kill another French Maghrebi, Reyeb, to avoid being killed himself by the Corsican gang, led by César, a violent patriarchal figure, which effectively controls the prison. By collaborating with other groups (Jordi, 'the gypsy', and his gang, the 'Egyptian' and his gang, the Muslim 'brothers') inside and outside the prison, Malek builds his own criminal network, outmanoeuvres César and becomes a powerful figure by the time of his release.

Both films align with Dobson's account of Audiard's disruption of formal and generic expectations. This is more obviously the case with *Un héros très discret*. It seems to exist somewhere between the historical fiction film, with its period props, settings and costumes, and the documentary, with its documentation (photographs, newsreel footage) and witness statements direct to camera. This blend could work to validate the on-screen world, with the documentary techniques adding an extra sense of authenticity to the fiction's period detail. But the film will not allow this to happen. Firstly, it draws attention to its status as fiction by periodically interrupting its narrative flow with non-narrative sequences such as the hero flapping his arms as if in elation (Figure 1.1) or a chamber ensemble playing the film's accompaniment. Secondly, its lead character is a fabulist who creates a false media profile by inserting himself into news photographs, newsreels and even the memories of those who think they recall him, in a way which immediately undermines any weight the documentary

**Figure 1.1** Disrupting the narrative: young Albert expresses his older self's elation (*Un héros très discret*, Jacques Audiard, 1996)

elements may carry. Thirdly, the film destabilises its central figure by splitting him into three: Albert, the boy; a young adult self, played by Mathieu Kassovitz; and an older narrator played by Jean-Louis Trintignant who seems keener to please his audience than to tell the truth. Finally, it knowingly condenses and reflects France's own self-mythologisation as a country that was for a long period in denial about its wartime collaboration with the Nazi regime. Nothing, not even the historical context in which the film roots itself, seems to possess any solidity. *Un prophète*, a prison film, seems a more stable genre vehicle. However, its hero represents, as Audiard himself put it, a 'new prototype', a fluid character very different from the more hard-boiled masculinity we might expect. Moreover, the customary hard-edged realism typically associated with the genre is disrupted by both Audiardian stylistic flourishes and sequences in which the ghost of Reyeb, the man murdered by Malik, speaks with him. In short, the two films destabilise general fictional and more specific generic conventions to provide a context in which their reinvention of subjectivities can make sense.

This instability also embraces the diegetic worlds. Malik in *Un prophète* encounters prison as an unfamiliar and terrifying place. The first sequence gives us a sense of a character plunged into a baffling and frightening world with its shouting, its disruptive editing and its partially obscured shots – all part of the film's stylistic excess. Malik's first experience of the prison yard is of having his training shoes stolen and being beaten. This is followed by the encounter with César and the Corsicans who offer him protection in exchange for murdering Reyeb. When Malik tries to speak to the governor, the guard informs the Corsicans who almost smother him. His challenge for the rest of the film is to learn how to prosper in a hostile world in which authorities to whom one might have turned (the prison staff and, beyond them, the state) can no longer be counted upon. The world of Un héros très discret is less obviously violent – the war having just ended – but no less unstable, with the Republic giving way to the collaborationist Vichy regime which gives way in turn to the Liberation. Political values shift, almost from day to day. Figures like Monsieur Jo, Albert Dehousse's employer, are enormously influential one day but arrested the next. Albert's own father, whom his mother had presented to him as a war hero, turns out to have been an alcoholic. Institutions and authority figures can no longer be relied on. Again, the hero has to work out how to survive in an unpredictable world from which symbolic moorings have been removed.

The main characters of both works are from the same Audiardian mould. Both are young men seeking to make sense of the adult world. Both are physically slight. Both are essentially blank slates without strongly marked traits that would limit their capacity to adapt to new contexts. This is most obviously the case with Malik in Un prophète. He has French-Maghrebi parents but has been brought up in a children's home free from his parents' influence. He arrives in prison with almost nothing and the little he has is taken from him by the guards (Figure 1.2). He is illiterate. He speaks French and Arabic but does not really identify as a Muslim. These characteristics, or this lack of characteristics, endow him with a flexibility that others in the jail lack. Albert Dehousse is similarly plastic. The film makes it clear from the start that all he knows of the world is derived from reading books or from observing others. With his father already dead and his mother left behind when he heads to Paris, he is effectively as abandoned as Malik.

Bearing little cultural baggage or experience, both young men are astonishingly open to learning from an eclectic range of sources and from the experience of others. As they learn, they remake themselves. Albert takes his first lessons from the books he reads. Having lived a fantasy life through adventure novels, he decides to reinvent himself as a writer. Finding he has no talent, he plagiarises existing works, the absence of

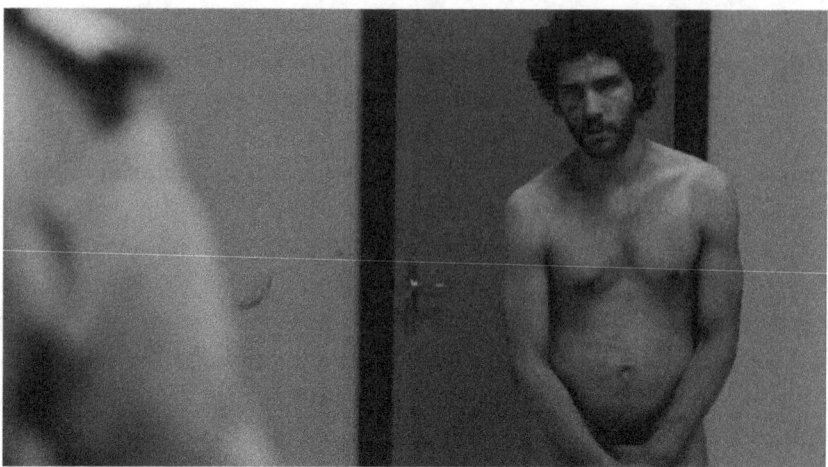

**Figure 1.2** Malik arrives in prison as a blank slate (*Un prophète,* Jacques Audiard, 2009)

originality underscoring the lack of a personal core which would limit his self-reinvention. His next mutation occurs when, to avoid forced labour in Germany's war economy, he learns to be a travelling salesman (Figure 1.3). He next becomes a beggar in Paris and is taught by the Captain, a gay resister, how to beg convincingly. Hired by Monsieur Jo, he works as a secretary, learning to cultivate an extensive network of

**Figure 1.3** Albert learning new skills (*Un héros très discret*, Jacques Audiard, 1996)

connections involving collaborators, resisters and the new authorities. Putting his acquired skills of fakery, networking and self-presentation to work, he teaches himself to be a resister, buying Resistance newspapers to familiarise himself with the different networks and insinuating himself into their reunions to absorb experiences that he can later pass off as his own. He teaches himself English so he can pretend he has been with the Free French in London. His acquired knowledge and skills open the path towards recruitment into the French army. Later, after release from imprisonment for bigamy, he adds a new career, as high-flying politician, to his collection.

Albert's flexibility and ability to absorb new knowledge is matched by Malik in *Un prophète*. Malik's first lessons on entering prison are on the dangers of isolation and the ability to kill, the latter taught to him in the kind of rehearsal scenes whose recurrence in Audiard's films underscores the importance of learned roles in his work. He attends class in prison and learns to read and write. He uses this new skill to learn Corsican from a dictionary so that he can listen in on the gang's conversations as he waits on them. Learning of his ability, César forces him to eavesdrop for him. He also has him meet up with a French Arab gang on his behalf when on day release. This role, effectively as a business intermediary, requires him to take a plane and wear a suit. Meanwhile, in prison, he has first learned to stitch denim jeans and then been assigned to deliver food to other inmates, the latter job helping him develop a drug-dealing business in the prison. By the time he leaves prison, he will have his own 'business' empire. This condensed overview of his career brings out how many skills or jobs he has learned and how flexible he has been. If work increasingly defines who we are, then he is defined more by mutability than by any specific profession. He is, as Audiard underlined, a new kind of man.

Central to Malik's success is the ability to form alliances and forge networks. He is able to do this for four reasons: firstly, his lack of a clearly defined identity that might tie him too closely to any one group; secondly, his communication skills and ability to move between languages; thirdly, his willingness to be of service, a skill honed while waiting on the Corsicans, as opposed to simply dominating; fourthly, a readiness to take calculated risks as he reaches out to new groups to whom he might appear as an enemy as much as a potential partner. The different alliances he builds allow him to outflank César, the Corsican gang leader, without needing to confront him face to face. By the end of the film, he has a powerful network inside and outside the prison while César has been isolated (Figure 1.4). An older, more rigid and hierarchical form of power has given way to a new one based on connectivity, communication, service to others and mobility.

Albert has a similar ability to move between groups, his lack of defined identity and flexibility endowing him with a chameleon-like capacity to blend in to different social contexts despite the constant risk of discovery. The Captain tells him how, during the Occupation, he had to maintain a number of identities, each entirely fictional. Albert imitates this lightness and fluidity. He acquires a knowledge of groups and people from his time with Monsieur Jo, but unlike his compromised employer, can move on untouched. His close study of the Resistance press ensures his knowledge of different networks. He worms his way into one network yet is seen as sufficiently detached from any particular group to be an ideal appointment at a time when inter-group rivalries are intense. Initially, he struggles to be accepted in the army, with at least some of those with real combat experience sniffing out his fakery, but he manages to win over almost everybody by his ability to read interrogatees and his generosity towards those less proficient than himself. Tellingly, his eventual downfall comes not because he is found out but because he himself cannot sustain an existence entirely based on lies. The first cracks appear when his second wife asks him if he loves her and he has to repeat his reassuring response several times before he gets the tone right. As his older persona played by

**Figure 1.4** The networked Malik looks upon the isolated and diminished César (*Un prophète,* Jacques Audiard, 2009)

Trintignant confides, he cannot convincingly express love when all the rest is a lie. He implodes more completely when he has to order his men to execute a group of compatriots who had volunteered for the notorious French SS Charlemagne Division. Faced with life-and-death decisions, he cannot sustain his purely superficial persona. In this, he is different to Malik who can move from the soft skills of alliance building to the hard skills of murder when it works to his benefit and enables him to eliminate a threat.

It is clearly not a major stretch to argue that a film like *Un prophète*, sitting as it does at the intersection of the gangster and prison genres, might constitute a coded engagement with capitalism and its violences. There is a critical tradition that sees the gangster film, especially the American one, in just such a way, with the gangster considered as either a general equivalent of the businessman, the boss of a company seeking to eliminate competitors, or a more specific evocation of the exclusion of ethnicised minorities (Italian-Americans or Latinos) from the American Dream and the temptation, typically punished, to achieve it through illegitimate means. The gangster film would then be a privileged place to look for cultural representations of shifts in capitalist subjectivities. Fredric Jameson, the great Marxist critic, for example, read *The Godfather* as a displaced account of a shift in capitalism from a more family-centred mode to a corporate one (Jameson 1979: 145–8). Clearly, it would make sense to read *Un prophète* along similar lines either as being about the broader emergence of a new kind of capitalism and the subjectivities associated with it or as a narrower comment on the difficulty minority groups have succeeding in French society despite the promises of French Republican universalism. Audiard was clear, as we noted, that Malik represents a new 'prototype'. Writing in *Positif*, Masson described the film's jail and its gangs as a stock exchange of competing companies (Masson 2009: 16). Foregrounding the apparent internationalism of the gangs in the film (the Corsicans, the Italians, the Muslim 'brothers,') and the way Malik triumphs because he can work at this international level, Oscherwitz (2015) analysed the film as a coded commentary on shifts in French capitalism in the era of globalisation. While not entirely convinced by this international dimension, the gangs all being tied to racialised minorities within France, I agree that the film represents a shift in French capitalism. But I would argue that Audiard's films more generally can be probed for their engagement with shifts in subjectivity driven by neoliberalism in a way that has not been recognised.

## Neoliberal subjectivity

Captured in recordings of his famous 'Birth of Biopolitics' lecture series, Foucault's account of neoliberalism was never fully developed but is possibly the most influential analysis of the topic. It returned to foundational texts by leading German Ordo-liberals and American neoliberals to probe neoliberalism and the subjectivities associated with it. What interested and some would say attracted Foucault in neoliberalism was its development of a mode of governance that apparently functioned not through constraint but through freedom, albeit a freedom equated with free exchange and, especially, competition in the market. Neoliberalism conceived society as being made up of 'enterprise-units' down to the level of the individual who was reframed as an 'entrepreneur of the self' whose choices with respect to healthcare, education, migration or even crime could be evaluated, in purely economic terms, as so many good or bad investment decisions (Foucault 2010: 225–9, 251). This extension of the market to all areas of life differentiated neoliberalism from earlier liberalisms as did its understanding of the role of the state. Rather than the function of the latter being to intervene as little as possible, as earlier liberalisms believed, it saw that its active involvement was required to promote and sustain a competitive environment. It was this work on the environment that explained how free individuals could be governed. By bringing action to bear on the context that structured decisions, neoliberalism could effectively govern freely choosing subjects (Foucault 2010: 270–1).

While Foucault's work provides precious general insights into the originality of neoliberal subjectivity and governance, it does not sufficiently flesh out its account of the former and can be usefully supplemented by other sources. Boltanski and Chiapello (1999) are helpful here, especially with respect to the qualities demanded of the apparently autonomous neoliberal subject and the resulting pathologies. Focusing on a different kind of text to Foucault, they probed evolutions in French managerial literature to analyse the new 'spirit' of capitalism. As they explain, capitalism has had three spirits or ethoses, each associated with a different kind of 'hero'. Its first spirit, dominant throughout the nineteenth century and into the twentieth, was typically associated with family businesses and the figure of the Promethean bourgeois entrepreneur. This figure gave way in the mid-twentieth century to the manager or *cadre*, the heroic driver of large, centralised, bureaucratic companies. In the 1960s and 1970s, capitalism moved into its third spirit, one which aligns closely with neoliberalism as discussed by other analysts. Faced with a two-pronged assault from, on the one hand, an 'artistic' critique of capitalist unfreedoms and inauthenticity coming from the libertarian left, and, on the other hand, a 'social critique' of capitalist egotism and inequality, two critiques which converged in the protests of 1968, it reinvented itself and outmanoeuvred its opponents. It overcame the 'social' critique that had been essentially borne by trade unions and the French Communist Party, the former being on the retreat and the latter in sharp decline by the 1980s. It effectively incorporated the 'artistic' critique of unfreedom as it broke up the large, hierarchical and bureaucratic organisations of the Fordist era and adopted the more fluid, mobile models associated with the outsourcing and off-shoring of production. This effectively meant offering apparently greater liberty to workers in exchange for lost security.

The new organisational forms in turn spawned a new kind of capitalist hero. While the old *cadres* were functional agents of bureaucratic structures, the new managers were visionaries able to lead a flexible response to a shifting and unpredictable environment and to assume risks previously managed internally by company career structures and externally by the welfare state. They were mobile figures who no longer needed rigid frameworks or a stable career to orientate or define themselves. They could work autonomously, leading teams in competition with other teams in the same workplace or responding directly to the demands of the market (Boltanski and Chiapello 1999: 119–29). They could shift from project to project and from network to network, pulling people together but also moving on to form new connections, their lightness in stark contrast to the weightiness previously associated with bourgeois figures (Boltanski and Chiapello 1999: 150–76, 234). Because they were expected to mobilise their affectivity, creativity and interpersonal skills, the traditional dividing line between the personal and professional lost its force. Their self was put to work as part of their professional competence (Boltanski and Chiapello 1999: 237). Inevitably, this new spirit came with its accompanying pathologies. The imperative to adjust to short-term projects meant that people struggled to project themselves into the future (Boltanski and Chiapello 1999: 506–8). The demand that the newly light, 'connexionist' persona mould itself to each new project and network inevitably entered into tension with any sense of a durable or resistant self. At the same time, the requirement to mobilise and adjust personal qualities for each new connection worked against the demand for authenticity and predictability in personal relations (Boltanski and Chiapello 1999: 560–3).

Dardot and Laval provide useful correctives to both Boltanski and Chiapello and Foucault. They accuse the former pair of taking managerial texts at face value and underplaying the disciplinary side of neoliberalism. They also judge Foucault's analysis to be too sanguine despite the considerable debt they owe to his work. When neoliberalism shapes the environment in which entrepreneurial subjects make their 'free choice', they note, it has a constant recourse to fear. It erodes existing statuses and cultivates precarity (of which more soon) and impoverishment as ways to stimulate (or compel) individual dynamism (Dardot and Laval 2010: 407–11). All the weight of complexity and competition falls on the individual, with the imperative to master the self being promoted in the absence of any possibility of shaping the world (Dardot and Laval 2010: 423–6). Rather than freeing the individual from bureaucracy, neoliberalism brings in a new, more individualised bureaucratic phase in which, enrolled for productivity, human subjectivity is subject to constant processes of scrutiny and evaluation (Dardot and Laval 2010: 411–13). The traditional institutional frameworks and symbolic structures through which the subject found a social place and an identity are subordinated to market norms, but the self is not freer as a result. Rather, with the enterprise becoming the measure of everything, the subject must internalise the entrepreneurial norms required to function efficiently in a competitive global environment (Dardot and Laval 2010: 419–20).

If we return now to the disagreement between the *Cahiers* version of Audiard and that developed by Dobson, we can begin to see how Foucault, supplemented by Dardot and Laval, can help us bridge it. The *Cahiers* critics essentially castigate Audiard for showing heroes who find ways to survive in a world that is no longer changeable. Dobson, in contrast, emphasises the capacity for self-reinvention and filial rebellion of the heroes. One could argue that these two accounts are looking at opposite sides of the same neoliberal coin. Because, in Foucauldian terms, neoliberalism is government through freedom, individuals can appear to be able to define themselves while in fact responding to an environment which conditions their decisions. Although Malik and Albert effectively become flexible entrepreneurs of the self, they do so in order to survive in chaotic or threatening environments which shape their every decision. Malik triumphs at the end of *Un prophète* and walks away a free man in control of his destiny: he can only do so, however, because he has internalised all that prison – a concentrated version of a violently competitive world – can teach him. Similarly, while his quasi-filial rebellion against the abusive patriarch, César, might seem to represent a form of self-liberation, it is in fact a conformist adaptation to a new status quo. The hollowing out of existing symbolic authorities and their subordination to the market, along the lines described by Dardot and Laval, can be seen in both films. In one, the prison authorities, the representatives of the state, are effectively for sale to the highest bidder. In the other, the nation has effectively been evacuated as a stabilising symbol. In both films, education, the archetypal French Republican value and the long-sanctified pathway to both successful social integration and induction into universal values, *seems* to be intact. Both young men are nothing if not ardent learners. But their learning has been entirely subjugated to instrumental ends and become an effective investment in the self and its entrepreneurial interests rather than a route to self-transcendence or any universal values.

The resemblances between the connexionist hero as described by Boltanski and Chiapello and the protagonists of *Un prophète* and *Un héros très discret* are just as striking. Audiard's characters mirror the light, flexible, networked individuals described by the two authors. Their expertise in moulding themselves to the demands and expectations of those they connect to and their capacity to respond in an agile manner to a chaotic world reflect exactly what the two authors describe. They are also subject to its dysfunctionalities. In the case of Malik, whose persona at the end bears little relation to that he entered with but embodies a response to the demands of the context, this remains implicit. In Albert's case, it is more explicitly thematised by his inability to sustain his mobile, depthless persona when faced with demands for durable commitment or life-and-death decisions. In short, despite their apparent thematic concerns, the films align uncannily with accounts of neoliberalism, the apparently unchangeable world that it creates and the subjectivities required to adapt to it, with all the accompanying pathologies that implies. But are the films as perfectly aligned with the status quo as it might seem? After all, they almost invariably engage with the enforced precarity which neoliberalism requires to stimulate its entrepreneurial subjects and point to the violences that follow neoliberalism like a dark shadow but are singularly neglected in accounts of its functioning by Foucault and Boltanski and Chiapello. These are issues to which we will now turn.

## Escaping precarity: Audiard's happy endings

With the neoliberal unpicking of the protections that used to be offered by stable Fordist employment and post-1945 welfare state regimes, precarity has become a word in increasingly common parlance. Perhaps for that reason, it risks being used loosely or ambiguously. To give it the necessary precision, my use of it here will mainly be guided by Isabell Lorey and Maurizio Lazzarato. Drawing on Judith Butler, Lorey makes a very useful distinction between what she calls precariousness and precarity. The former is ontological. Needing shelter, nourishment and care, life is intrinsically vulnerable. Although the highly gendered bourgeois model of the autonomous subject assumes mastery of oneself and one's property, human life necessarily depends on the nurture, labour and protection of others as well as complex, collectively generated infrastructures (Lorey 2015: 29–31). However, protection from this ontological precariousness is typically unevenly distributed: this is where precarity, the unequal social provision of protection from precariousness, comes in. For much of modern history, those who did not meet or who threatened the norms of autonomous bourgeois individualism, typically through lack of wealth or access to property, were exposed to precarity in this sense. Indeed, only in the twentieth century, especially the second half of it, was waged labour given the relative protection afforded by the welfare state. With the ascendancy of neoliberalism, however, unequal exposure to precariousness becomes normalised as a system of governance (Lorey 2015: 64). Along similar lines, Lazzarato suggests that, rather than establishing a sharp dividing line between those included and the excluded, neoliberalism establishes a striated system of differences moving through the unemployed, poor workers, those on short-term contracts, part-time workers, salaried workers and so on. No-one can feel their position is guaranteed. Individualisation and fragilisation affect everyone, albeit unevenly (Lazzarato 2008: 25–6). The ultimate aim is to undo collective protections, 'responsabilise' individuals and create a system of generalised competition.

Audiard's films do not, of course, attempt to develop a systematic account of how precarity works. Precarity and precariousness, as theorised by Lorey and Lazzarato, nonetheless run through them. When Malik enters prison in *Un prophète*, for example, he is doubly precarious: the guards remove his few possessions and he finds himself, an isolated individual, exposed to the violence of the prison yard. The system does indeed seek to some extent to reform him by teaching him to read and write, sew jeans in the workshop and to serve food to other inmates. He is also encouraged to learn car mechanics during his day release, although he puts the time to work very differently. Likewise, his closest ally, Ryad, is helped by an imam to get work in a call centre on release. This would seem to be the lot of the poor in the film: poorly paid, subaltern and almost certainly precarious labour or, if they fail to conform, prison to feed them back into the bottom end of the labour market. This is also the lot offered to Malik in the Corsican gang which uses him to do the dirty, risky work (murder) or wait upon the other gang members. He avoids this social destiny, as we explored above, by becoming a high-performing, networked neoliberal subject, a model entrepreneur of the self. It is ultimately this trajectory which, despite its apparently dark subject matter, gives the film its feel-good appeal. Essentially the same underlying dynamic, with variations, recurs in Audiard's other films. In *Sur mes lèvres* (*Read My Lips*, 2001) for example, Paul Angeli (Vincent Cassel) is recently released from prison. With a job sweeping up on a chicken farm lined up for him, he instead lies his way into work as an office temp, initially sleeping on the floor of the office storeroom. He must check in with his probation officer on a weekly basis to ensure he is behaving, with the threat of a return to prison if he is not. After a beating from a thug sent to collect on a debt to a crooked night-club owner, he is forced to work as a barman in the club, a kind of contemporary indentured labour. He escapes from this situation by forming an alliance with Carla (Emmanuelle Devos), the put-upon office receptionist who recruited him. Pooling their skills, they steal a large sum of money that the night-club owner and some violent crooks had earlier stolen.

Other Audiard films follow similar lines. The eponymous hero of *Dheepan* (Jesuthasan Antonythasan), a defeated soldier fleeing the Sri Lankan civil war, tries to integrate into French society by becoming a caretaker in the French banlieue. Yalini (Kalieaswari Srinivasan), the woman pretending to be his wife, is hired as a carer for the disabled father of a drug dealer who lives in the block opposite. Tellingly, one of the dealer's 'foot-soldiers' explains that he is paid by the day by the dealer, the criminal world also relying on unequally distributed precarious labour. As gang warfare erupts and increasingly threatens Dheepan and his adoptive family, he resumes his role as soldier to rescue Yalini. The film ends with them now a real couple, their new baby and their fake but now adopted daughter, Illayaal (Claudine Vinasithamby), in a suburban garden in London, somehow having escaped the social fate French society seemed to hold for them. Varying the pattern a little again, *De rouille et d'os* recounts the unlikely romance between Ali (Matthias Schoenaerts), a kick-boxer, and Stéphanie (Marion Cotillard), a killer-whale trainer, who, rather improbably, has had both her legs severed by one of the creatures. Unemployed and homeless, Ali has headed south to ask his sister to put him and his young son up. He has to look in bins on the train to feed himself and the boy. On arrival, he finds work first as a bouncer, then as a supermarket security guard but also makes money in unlicensed bare-knuckle fights. His sister is sacked from the supermarket where he works for taking food past its sell-by date to supplement her meagre wages after he unthinkingly participates in the installation of the surveillance cameras which trap her. His life turns around, firstly, when Stéphanie takes over as his trainer and secondly when his son nearly dies. This forces him to recognise his vulnerability and need for Stéphanie. The film ends with him as a successful professional boxer with her at his side.

Although Audiard's reputation is predominantly as a stylish and commercially successful director working at the interface of auteur and genre filmmaking, his films repeatedly foreground aspects of contemporary precarity that would not be out of place in committed social realist filmmaking. Debt, homelessness, disposable employees, in-work poverty, management surveillance, the role of prison in reinserting offenders at the bottom of the labour hierarchy: it all seems to be there. Layered over this social dimension, there is also a consistently intense focus on generically motivated violence, typically followed in close-up and with long tracking shots, as it impacts on individual bodies, reminding them of their precariousness. This violence generates a tangible sense that individuals are pitted in vicious competition with other individuals for survival. Taken together, these different elements could clearly provide raw materials for a fierce critique of contemporary precarity similar to that developed by Lorey or Lazzarato, one that showed how, with the withdrawal of collective protections and the cult of competition, a generalised precarity was set in place to which those at the bottom were most obviously exposed but from which no-one was safe. But the films do not articulate the elements in this way. As the *Cahiers du Cinéma* critics noted, both the violence and the competitiveness are naturalised rather than probed. Characters are forced to confront their individualised vulnerability but are not driven to a heightened political awareness or social solidarity by it. Instead, responding as true neoliberal subjects, they adapt to the threatening environment, make themselves flexible and forge alliances to outcompete apparently stronger adversaries. This triumph of the (conformist) underdog is what generates the satisfaction that the films' spectators are offered.

## Gendering the neoliberal subject: Audiard's violently vulnerable men

Thus far, we have considered the relationship between the Audiardian hero and neoliberalism without considering gender. Given that Audiard's heroes are overwhelmingly male, that he is knowingly engaging with the emergence of new kinds of male subject, and that important Audiard critics place gender at the centre of their analyses, this bracketing of gender cannot continue. Let us begin with the critics. For Sellier, as we saw, representations of masculinity in Audiard's films are essentially conservative. While male vulnerability might suggest some weakening of patriarchal authority, it mainly serves to make us sympathise with violent men. Dobson, as we also saw, viewed the films' representation of masculinity rather differently and placed greater emphasis on how the typically young male heroes break with older patriarchal figures and what they represent, find ways to reshape themselves and work collaboratively with others. My own suggestion was that, if we bring neoliberalism back into the frame, these apparently opposed positions can be bridged. I will now explain why, looking especially at *Regarde les hommes tomber* (*See How They Fall*) and *Sur mes lèvres*, Audiard's first and third films. In the process, I hope to show how finely Audiard's cinema probes the gendering of the neoliberal subject, an area of inquiry that is still underexplored, especially with respect to masculinity.

*Regarde les hommes tomber* is a relatively straightforward story told in a complex, elliptical and asynchronous way. Marx, an ageing, rootless gambler, finds that Frédéric, an equally rootless young man, clings to him. Marx owes money to a criminal. To pay off the debt, he and Frédéric firstly become debt collectors and then hitmen, a transformation reflected in their increasingly professional-looking clothes and acquisition of a smart car. A policeman, Mickey, is shot and left in a coma by Frédéric during one of their hits. Finding that the police invest too little time in finding the killers, Mickey's friend, Simon, a burnt-out travelling salesman who lives vicariously through his younger friend, vows to track them down and eventually finds them. He kills Marx and takes Frédéric, a replacement companion, under his wing. Tellingly, the film eliminates the more traditionally virile figures, Mickey and Marx, to arrive at the apparently softer pairing of Simon and Frédéric. This could be seen as signalling a transition from a hard masculinity to a softer one. Things are not that simple.

Marx is a loner, this autarky being a stereotypical male trait. When Frédéric attaches himself to him, Marx initially tries to drive the young man off, threatening to hit him. He often speaks brutally to him in their exchanges, telling him, for example, that he looks like 'une gonzesse' ('a girl') when he wears the hat that is part of his uniform in a pizza takeaway where he works for a period. Marx pays prostitutes for sex, an action that underscores both his heterosexuality and his instrumental treatment of women. Frédéric, in contrast, seems unable to live alone. He is uninterested in sex but wants to sleep beside Marx. Marx has a strongly defined character. Frédéric, a typical Audiardian young man, is completely pliable and changes his name to the more unequivocally masculine Johnny to appease the older man. The other male couple is marked by similar contrasts. Mickey is violent. Simon discovers, firstly, that his apartment is full of pictures of crime victims and pornography and, secondly, that he would routinely torture his informant. By contrast, Simon is both vulnerable (he unravels in the course of the film) and caring (he is repeatedly seen at his comatose friend's bedside). We also see him in a scene where, having picked up a young male prostitute, he quizzes him on his life with his partner as if trying to learn from him how to manage a relationship with another man. When, in the film's final scene, Frédéric asks to climb into bed with him, Simon agrees uncomplainingly. We might see this as a triumph of the sensitive men had their malleability not also allowed Frédéric and Simon to become violent. Tutored by Marx, Frédéric becomes an unlikely debt collector (Figure 1.5) but an efficient killer. Learning from Mickey, Simon tortures for information. Imitating Marx and Frédéric, he kills. He and Frédéric display the same malleability with respect to their gendered identity and sexuality: although Frédéric wants to get into bed with both Marx and Simon, there is no indication he is gay. He seems more like a child wanting to climb into bed with a parent. Simon has lost interest in sex with his wife and seems tempted by homosexuality but behaves as much like a parent towards Frédéric as anything else. When he effectively has a breakdown, his daughter takes him home and looks

**Figure 1.5** Fred as unlikely debt collector (*Regarde les hommes tomber,* Jacques Audiard, 1994)

after him, as if he had become the child and she the mother. There is a general queering taking place as sex, gender and family roles (of which more soon) lose their solidity.

How does this relate to neoliberalism and the new kinds of subjects it requires? Here, it is worth homing in on Frédéric, the first iteration of Audiard's malleable young men. As with Malik in *Un prophète*, it is as if he has no fixed identity at all. Crucially, this indeterminacy applies just as much to gendered identity as it does to work, as if one kind of flexibility called forth the other. In the course of the film, Frédéric goes from debt collector to pizza shop employee to hitman, changing his appearance on the way, and finding time in between to be a son-like companion to a landlady and to play piggy-back with the child of a man being threatened for non-payment of a debt. Like Albert Dehousse in *Un héros*, he rehearses new roles he needs to play, no role being an essential part of his being. Crucially too, and unlike Marx, at least when they first meet, he is driven to attachment and collaboration. At the same time, however, he can also lend himself to murderous violence without it seeming to rub off on him. This combination of extreme flexibility, interpersonal dependency and a capacity for ruthlessness suggests the emergence of a new kind of subject responsive to the neoliberal age, one that necessarily brings with it a reworking of gendered identities.

Audiard's second film, *Sur mes lèvres*, continues the same process. As we noted, it revolves around the unlikely but successful alliance between Paul, the ex-offender, and Carla. Carla has impaired hearing and is a skilled lip-reader. She works for a property developer, is very good at her job, but is stuck at the bottom of the office hierarchy and exploited by the men above her who talk insultingly about her. When describing to a recruitment agency the type of person she needs to assist her, she lists a series of features (male, young, with nice hands) that one would typically associate with online dating. The scene is undoubtedly comic but the significant point is the way in which, with personal qualities and emotions increasingly put to work, the private and professional inevitably blur. Paul, her recruit, does not immediately fit the bill. When she finds him somewhere to stay, he grabs her roughly, assuming she wants payment in kind. He does, however, prove useful to her. When a male colleague steals an important project from her, she gets him to break into the man's car and remove the vital paperwork he needs to present the work to the client. She delivers a successful presentation in his place. Later, when a local politician is holding up one of the company's projects, she has him step in with a criminal associate to beat up the man and make him toe the line in a way that again helps her look good at work. She, in turn, is recruited by Paul because of her unique skills. He persuades her to stand on a roof and lip-read meetings between the crooked night-club owner and a pair of criminals as they plot a major robbery. After the crime has taken place, her heightened attention to sound leads her to where the money is hidden when Paul fails to find it. Her lip-reading also allows her to communicate with him from a safe distance when the criminals capture him. In other words, her 'soft' communicational skills prove as essential to Paul as his 'hard' skills proved to her in her workplace.

Paul and Carla seem a much more traditional couple than any pairing in *Regarde les hommes tomber* but they also carry out a reworking of gendered identities and relationships for new times. In some ways, their partnership simply appears to underscore the competitive benefits of bringing together a stereotypical male capacity for violence and stereotypical female aptitudes for communication and cooperation in an androgynous alliance that defeats ruthless men in both the workplace and criminal activity, the two things in any case converging. Yet Paula and Carla do not simply collaborate. Each evolves in the process. Having been exploited by everybody in her office as long as she simply sought to help others, Carla adds a competitive ruthlessness, a borrowed violence, to her persona while Paul can only save himself and triumph through communication and collaboration, both demonstrating flexibility in the process. Paul's vulnerability does not simply make his violence more acceptable, as Sellier noted, it moves him towards a more collaborative and successful approach.

Between them, *Regarde les hommes tomber* and *Sur mes lèvres* set the pattern for Audiard's subsequent works. Some have central male protagonists who very much resemble the former film's Frédéric in their embodiment of a new, softer and extremely pliant masculinity (*Un héros très discret, Un prophète*). Others have heroes, like the latter film's Paul, who seem closer to traditional models of virile masculinity but are obliged by their vulnerability to turn to alliance and learn the required skills of negotiation and communication (*De battre mon coeur s'est arrêté/The Beat that My Heart Skipped*, 2005; *De rouille et d'os*; *Dheepan*). In the end, the two types are less different than they appear and converge in a shared flexibility that sees the less virile types, with the partial exception of Albert in *Un héros très discret*, learn violence and the more violent types, collaboration and compromise. What all the films then demonstrate is a reworking of masculinity for neoliberal times. While their male heroes do break with key elements of a more traditional masculinity (autarky, narrow instrumentalism, patriarchal authority) in favour of stereotypically more feminine traits (compromise, collaboration, communication, acknowledgement of vulnerability), this apparent softening in fact works to their competitive advantage by enabling them to form alliances.

In general, however, this renewal of male subjectivities is not paralleled by the reworking of female subjectivities that one might have expected. As Sellier noted, women in Audiard too often play minor, token or static roles. A few do have substantial narrative roles and undergo significant development. But, even in those cases, the films tend to reassert stereotypes before challenging them to a limited extent. Thus, for example, Carla in *Sur mes lèvres*, is linked to communicative skills and a focus on relationships, stereotypically feminine traits, before she adds competitiveness and (proxy) violence to her behaviours. Stéphanie in *De rouille et d'os* is a narcissist who relishes the desiring looks of men, a negative stereotype, before she loses her legs and has to reshape her subjectivity. It is as if the films could only show character evolution by first reasserting regressive gender representations.

## Audiard's flexible families

Some of the major analyses of neoliberalism by Foucault, Dardot and Laval or, although they do not name it as such, Boltanski and Chiapello, underplay not only gender but also the family. For example, Boltanski and Chiapello note that the family has become a mobile and fragile institution whose evolution adds a supplementary precarity to that generated by shifts in employment and the more general rise in insecurity, but show little interest in pushing this analysis further (Boltanski and Chiapello 1999: 24). More developed accounts of the question can be found in important analyses by Wolfgang Streeck (2009) and Melinda Cooper (2017). The former asks why there was not more resistance to the rise of 'flexible' labour and finds a partial answer in the parallel rise of what he calls the 'flexible family' (Streeck 2009: 5–18). The stable employment of the post-war period, the time of the Fordist / welfarist settlement, he notes, rested on the model of the nuclear family, the male breadwinner, and the family wage. With the rise in divorce and mono-parental families, declining birth rates, the second-wave feminist critique of the patriarchal family and the mass entry of women into the labour market, cultural and labour-market factors made the maintenance of the stabilised, Fordist-era family unsustainable. Happy to draw on the new pool of female labour, employers moved towards a flexible labour market while withdrawing security and no longer paying the family wage, now deemed unaffordable. Increasingly, families needed dual incomes if they were to cope (Streeck 2009: 15–22).

While agreeing with elements of Streeck's argument, Cooper criticises it for implicit anti-feminism and nostalgia for the Fordist family with its male breadwinner (Cooper 2017: 10–11). The neoliberal family arises, she argues, as the outcome of a political compromise between neoconservatives, on the one hand, who were deeply opposed to the countercultural forces unleashed by the 1960s and considered the primary role of the state to be to defend the family, and neoliberals, on the other, who were opposed to any form of redistributive welfare that might compete with paid employment as a pillar of individual and family security. The two forces were able to converge, not on a restoration of the Fordist family model, but on the reinvention of an older poor-law tradition of private family responsibility whereby the family would take up the slack left by the withdrawal of state protections (Cooper 2017: 21, 62–3).

This was not simply a return to the past: welfare was repurposed, along lines already discussed here, as a machinery of surveillance, incentivisation and discipline, while alternative family models incorporated gains made by the different liberation movements of the 1960s and 1970s but within a neoliberal socio-economic framework (Cooper 2017: 314–16). Cooper's account centres particularly on the United States. Streeck looks at the West in general and points to variations in it, with the USA typically being the country where state protections are least generous. Both argue, however, for a general if unevenly distributed shift that applies across different national frames.

While it would obviously be unwise to seek some direct equivalent of Cooper's or Streeck's analyses in Audiard's films, parallels between his flexible families and those described by the two theorists are nonetheless striking. In general terms, we might begin by reminding ourselves how Audiard repeatedly shows what Dobson calls filial challenges to inherited patriarchal models. We should also remember how, in their fluidity and flexibility, his characters, especially the male ones, refuse to be slotted into traditionally defined gender or familial roles. We might recall, finally, how a recognition of vulnerability repeatedly pushes his characters towards interdependence. This broader context in which a need for connectivity is reasserted but gendered identities are destabilised provides the grounds upon which a more explicit turn to the flexible family arises in the later films. The shift is initially announced in *Un prophète*. Malik's closest ally is Ryad. The latter is married and has a child but is dying of cancer. While on day release, Malik is welcomed into Ryad's family. At the film's close, and after Ryad's death, he is met at the prison gate by Djamila (Leïla Bekhti), Ryad's wife, carrying the child. Although several carloads of his criminal collaborators are there to pick him up, he waves them back and walks on with her, as if he were slotting into the place left by his dead friend and forming a new family as a source of stability in a world otherwise made up of competitors and instrumental alliances.

This turn to the family is more developed in Audiard's next film, *De rouille et d'os*. It begins with family failure and geographical relocation. Ali has broken with his unnamed partner, the mother of Sam (Armand Verdure), their child. He takes the boy to the south of France to live with his sister and her partner. Although the group form an improvised family unit of sorts, it is dysfunctional in several ways. Ali has no stable job. He neglects the boy and is rough with him. His thoughtlessness causes his sister to be sacked. There is the potential for him to form a family with Stéphanie once her accident has forced her away from her earlier narcissism and towards interdependence, and especially once she starts to manage his fights. But he treats their relationship in instrumental terms. He tells her, for example, that he can have sex with her when he is 'opé' (operational) and 'dispo' (available), as if he were making a business appointment. It is only after his son nearly drowns under the ice and he smashes his hands in the rescue that he recognises his vulnerability and emotional needs and declares his love. The final scene shows the couple and Sam leaving a smart hotel in the context of a high-profile, legitimate fight. In some ways, this looks like a conventional happy ending whereby the definitive establishment of the heterosexual romance or re-establishment of the previously broken family coincides with the successful conclusion of other plot elements (in this case, the fight story). What is different here is that the family is a flexible, entrepreneurial one rather than a biological one. It becomes the point of emotional and financial security in a world otherwise marked by precarity, violent competition (the fights) and opportunistic alliances. Tellingly, as elsewhere in Audiard, for this ending to be reached, the characters must re-learn how to relate to each other. It is as if, in a society given over to narcissism, instrumentalism and competition, people have forgotten how to maintain the durable emotional relationships that will guarantee its cohesion and reproduction.

The pattern is confirmed by *Dheepan*. Dheepan, Yalini and Illayaal have all been forced into the position of isolated individuals struggling to survive by the vicious Sri Lankan civil war. To escape the conflict and claim asylum, they form a fictive family (Figure 1.6). The two adults develop a partnership of sorts, a typical Audiardian alliance, when they both work to provide for the family's material needs. It is their 'daughter', Illayaal, who provides the initial impetus towards a more emotionally meaningful connection. She tells Yalini that she needs a mother. The latter has no experience of mothering but is advised by the girl to draw on her experience of caring for her brothers. She also asks her to kiss her goodbye at the school gate, like the other mothers do with their children. Dheepan, who has lost his own biological family, is no better at managing relationships than Yalini. When the gang violence initially breaks out in their banlieue and Yalini tries to leave, he hits her and confiscates her passport, only to return it later as he recognises that he cannot win her over through

**Figure 1.6** Forging a family (*Dheepan*, Jacques Audiard, 2015)

brutality. As elsewhere in Audiard, and as befits a world of flexible roles and fluid skill sets, the characters must learn and practise the behaviours required to be a family. The film's final sequence shows Dheepan driving a London taxi and arriving home to join Yalini, their recently born infant and Illayaal for a meal in the garden with friends. In some ways, this looks like a departure from the flexible families seen up to then and a conservative return to the biological family and the male breadwinner. It is perhaps better viewed as a compromise between traditional family models and the demands of new times, not dissimilar to the compromise Cooper notes between neoconservativism and neoliberalism around the flexible family. As in the other films discussed in this section, characters who, in one way or another, have been evicted from a world they knew, learn to survive in a new one. Faced with their precarity in a hostile, competitive environment, they forge alliances and renegotiate human bonds that straddle the uneasy border between the entrepreneurial and the personal. The recognition that individuals cannot stand alone might have signalled a renewed search for collective protections: instead, the need for human solidarity is contained within the renewed family unit.

## Conclusion

Audiard's cinema provides an excellent example of how mainstream cinema can pick up on deeply disruptive socio-economic shifts and feed off them to generate narrative tension and drive character development while shutting down any space they open for radical political re-imaginings. The director's films repeatedly foreground the malleability of the human subject, gendered identities and interpersonal bonds. But they contain it within limits entirely suited to the demands of the neoliberal economy with its need for flexible, collaborative and competitive individuals, and reworked families able to function as entrepreneurial units, take up the slack left by the withdrawal of state protections and provide a purely localised alternative to narrowly instrumental forms of human connectivity. It is this contained plasticity of subjects and bonds that helps explain the apparently irreconcilable judgements on Audiard's films. While some (the *Cahiers* critics, Sellier) point to the fundamental conservatism of the representations, others (Dobson, Audiard himself) place more emphasis on the reworking of subjectivities and relationships. As I suggested earlier, the conservatism and the flexibility can be seen as two sides of the same conformist coin.

The political limits of Audiard's cinema are encapsulated by *Un prophète*. The film offers us satisfaction in a story of triumph which is in fact a triumphant liberation into the status quo. In an article centred on Jean Genet, the great gay writer and filmmaker and repeated inmate of the French prison system, Michael Hardt suggests that the penitentiary, 'is not really a site of exclusion, separate from society, but rather a focal point, the sight of the highest concentration of a logic of power that is generally diffused throughout the world' (Hardt 1997: 66). Because the prison concentrates the disciplinary norms and routines that lie outside its walls, release from it represents not true freedom but an escape into a more diffuse unfreedom. Genet's response, as described by Hardt, is to recognise the fundamental entrapment of social existence and find fleeting moments of plenitude in passionate encounters with other prisoners. But such moments briefly suspend prison time rather than create a truly liveable alternative life, one that can only be founded and maintained through collective action of the sort which can blast open the continuum of a predictable temporality and create, for varying durations, an 'open, constituent history' (Hardt 1997: 72–9). Hardt comments, 'We do not break out of prison once and then remain free; our alternative existence must be a continuous project in perpetual motion' (Hardt 1997: 78). Neither showing a glimpse of an escape through the temporary suspension of prison time, nor looking towards the collective constitution of an alternative, *Un prophète* instead shows a character who adapts perfectly to the status quo, achieving freedom from prison by internalising its requirements. In concentrated form, this encapsulates the limitations of Audiard's broader output. As we move through the rest of this book, we will ask if other works can build on the mutability of human subjects and the need for interconnection and interdependency to imagine more genuine liberations.

# 2
# Subjects in the chains of debt

In the previous chapter, I looked at the positive construction of neoliberal subjectivity in the films of Audiard with their stories of triumphant underdog entrepreneurialism in a context of competition and precarity. In this chapter, I will consider how films frame the crisis of the entrepreneurial subject in the grip of debt. With the rise in the power of financial capital under neoliberalism, Maurizio Lazzarato suggests, the creditor-debtor relationship has replaced the capital-labour dynamic at the centre of social, economic and political life. The relationship has always been a profoundly asymmetrical one, with power concentrated in the hands of the lender rather than those in debt. The imbalance has nonetheless become particularly stark since the recent crisis and the austerity that came in its wake. This is why, for Lazzarato, the crisis is not only social, political or economic but is a crisis of neoliberal subjectivity. As he explains, 'the project of replacing the Fordist worker with the entrepreneur of the self, of transforming the individual into an individual enterprise that manages skills as economic resources to be capitalized, has collapsed in the subprime crisis' (Lazzarato 2015: 14). The dominant figure of the current moment is not the entrepreneurial self: it is the indebted man or woman.

To approach this figure, I will initially look at three important works, *Le Silence de Lorna* (*Lorna's Silence*, Jean-Pierre and Luc Dardenne, 2008), *L'Emploi du temps* (*Time Out*, Cantet, 2001) and *Le Père de mes enfants* (*Father of My Children*, Hansen-Løve, 2009). I will tease out their debt-related dynamics, before placing them in dialogue with two theorists, the already mentioned Lazzarato, a key voice on debt, and Lauren Berlant, whose *Cruel Optimism*, especially its discussion of the 'impasse', provides vital tools to engage with the affective, embodied and temporal dimensions of debt narratives. I will then move on to a cluster of films from 2011 that could clearly be labelled 'crisis films' in that they engage explicitly with either the impact of debt on individual lives or the behaviour of institutions (banks, courts) in relation to debt. These are: *De bon matin* (*Early One Morning*, Moutout, 2011), *Toutes nos envies* (*All Our Desires*, Lioret, 2011), *Une vie meilleure* (*A Better Life*, Kahn, 2011) and *Louise Wimmer* (Mennegun, 2011), the first three being star vehicles, the fourth, definitely not. While less obviously original than the first three films, these latter works allow us to probe how a broader cinema responds to the crisis of the indebted subject and to explore how the foreclosure of the subject's future might cause a wider crisis of cinematic narrative.

## *Le Silence de Lorna* and indebted citizenship

The Dardennes' films typically focus on bodies and gestures rather than character interiority. True to this pattern, *Le Silence de Lorna* begins with a close-up of hands counting money that they then pass through what looks like a bank counter window to another pair of hands (Figure 2.1). The camera tilts up to the face of the character we do not yet know to be Lorna (Arta Dobroshi) as she counts softly, along with the teller. Smiling, she informs the employee that she is acquiring Belgian nationality and

**Figure 2.1** Lorna as indebted citizen and reliable payer (*Le Silence de Lorna,* Jean-Pierre and Luc Dardenne, 2008)

would like to negotiate a loan. This is not the first time that financial debt has figured in a Dardenne brothers film: it is there in *La Promesse* (*The Promise*, 1996), in which the character Hamidou's real and invented debts play a crucial narrative role; it recurs in *L'Enfant* (*The Child*, 2005), where the hero finds himself forced to work for a criminal gang to which he owes money. But its role in *Le Silence de Lorna* is more central and has a greater symbolic resonance, as its presence from the film's opening indicates. Lorna, the film's eponymous heroine, is moving into a new world where indebtedness and citizenship simply seem to coincide, their blurring welcomed rather than resisted by the heroine. Her acceptance of debt is confirmed in the next scene where, in a telephone cubicle, still smiling, speaking Albanian, she tells a man we assume to be her boyfriend about both the borrowed amount and her love for him. As she leaves the cubicle and goes to pay, her mobile rings. This time, her tone is impatient. The caller has told her the same thing three times. She hangs up.

The underlying dynamics of the film are present in embryonic form. Between her new nationality, the loan and the love interest, Lorna seems to have mapped out a happy future, but a demanding person threatens to disrupt the smooth unfolding of her plan. This is a typical Dardenne brothers opening. Their films do not have plots in their conventional sense. They show characters who are torn between fundamentally murderous systemic logics and the ethical imperative not to eliminate the vulnerable Other. Typically, too, as befits a cinema that privileges the body, the Other is encountered, not as an idea, but as a demanding physical presence. *Le Silence de Lorna* is true to form. Lorna is involved in a deadly plot. She is working with a gang, led by Fabio (Fabrizio Rongione), which plans to sell on the Belgian citizenship Lorna has acquired through marriage to a recovering junkie, Claudy (Jérémie Renier). By eliminating him, they will free her up to marry a Russian who will thereby acquire Belgian nationality. The deal will help Lorna and her Albanian boyfriend, Sokol, pay for the little snack bar that is Lorna's dream. Despite the apparent warmth of this aspiration Lorna is tied into a series of coldly calculating investments and debts: the bank loan; the investment of time and money made by Fabio's gang; the mutually profitable bargain between Fabio's gang and the Russians. Lorna is a beneficiary from these deals but, an indebted subject, must also provide a return to the bank, Fabio and the Russians.

In these dealings, Claudy is a disposable pawn albeit a demanding one. While Lorna tries to keep their interactions to a minimum, he constantly asks for more from her, an importunate, vulnerable presence. His body is racked by withdrawal symptoms. He wants Lorna to help him and be with him, running errands for him or playing cards with him. He gives her his money to look after so he will not spend it on drugs. He curls up in pain and cries out for her help. He grabs her arm (Figure 2.2). Her response to this disruptive, physical presence is to develop a plan of her own: she will make it appear as if he is beating her so that she can obtain a quick divorce and eliminate the need to kill him. She bruises her arms and cuts her head to provide physical proof of the abuse inflicted on her. When he cracks and tries to buy drugs, she undresses and makes love to him to keep him in the apartment. This is not behaviour derived from a pre-ordained moral code, but a profoundly corporeal response to another human being's embodied vulnerability. Yet, even as Lorna tries to save Claudy, and in a way that is typical of the behaviour of the Dardennes' protagonists as they seek an impossible compromise between diametrically opposed ethical poles, she remains part of the different debt-driven deals she is involved in. In return, she is subject to scrutiny in a way that brings to the fore the capacity of debt to constrain behaviours and subjectivities.

In the opening bank scene, even before she contracted her debt, Lorna presented a version of herself as a reliable payer, a counting and calculating self. The requirement to produce such a subjectivity is affirmed in her dealings with Sokol and Fabio's gang. Both expect her to be instrumental

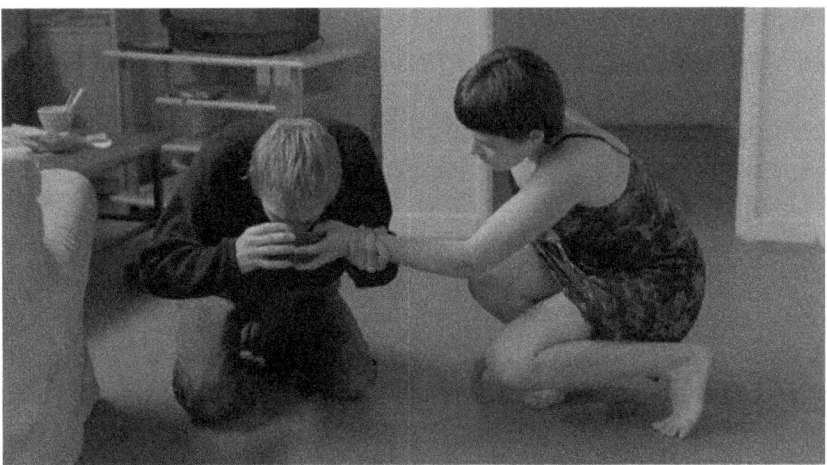

**Figure 2.2** Claudy as a demanding bodily presence (*Le Silence de Lorna,* Jean-Pierre and Luc Dardenne, 2008)

and ruthless. When they see her working to save Claudy, and thereby becoming unpredictable, they are concerned, as the following conversation underscores:

> Fabio: You're worrying me, Lorna
> Lorna: You don't trust me anymore?
> Fabio: I'm obliged to. It's my first job with the Russians. I don't want to mess it up.
> Lorna: Me neither. I want my money.
> Fabio: I recognise you now (My translation).

We see that Lorna must produce a self which reassures those who have invested time and money in her and need in turn to convince others that they are reliable, in a circle of mutual evaluation. After Claudy's murder, Fabio offers Lorna a bonus for having looked after him. Her attempted refusal of this payment arouses immediate suspicion: it makes it seem that she is no longer with the gang. The suspicion grows when she persuades herself that she is carrying Claudy's child and seeks to compensate for her failure to save him by protecting the unborn infant. Increasingly unpredictable, she loses the trust of Fabio, Sokol and the Russians, especially when a conversation at the hospital reveals that she has cancelled the bank loan and thereby lost the 7.000 Euro deposit.

The opening scene's integration of Lorna into indebted citizenship is progressively being undone. A brief scene at the bank sees her withdraw all her remaining money. The next scene sees first Fabio and then Sokol claim back any money they are owed, leaving Lorna with only one hundred euros. Her phone is taken away and she is told that she will be sent back to Albania, although we suspect that the gang in fact plans to kill her. This sequence of events provides an insight into the difficulty of exiting a debt economy. Not only is Lorna obliged to produce a calculating self that will pass inspection in the present, she also finds herself unable to escape her debt through repayment. Her future predictability, even if it comes at the cost of her disappearance or death, must also be guaranteed. Although we may or may not be convinced by the ethical escape route the film seeks to open from ruthless debt-driven behaviours, we cannot fail to be impressed by its rigorous examination of the power of the debt-surveillance nexus and the imperative it creates for the production of a particular kind of subject. Can we detect similar patterns in the other films?

## *L'Emploi du temps* and debt's disciplinary reach

Cantet is a very different filmmaker to the Dardennes. The latter make films driven by the overarching tension between systemic violence and an ethical commitment to the Other as it plays out in the closely tracked encounter of embodied individuals. Their films work towards a moment of ethical decision when a character finally realises that this tension cannot be bridged and an ethical choice must be made, as when Lorna effectively withdraws from her indebted subjectivity and the ruthless behaviours it dictates. Never starkly dichotomous in this way, Cantet's films are driven by at least two typically unresolved tensions: that between the individual, the group and the broader society; and that between conformist or oppositional utopias and the social and material obstacles to their realisation. Rather than moving us towards clarity, they question the characters' and our own certainties. The Dardennes have an easily recognisable style associated with the close tracking of bodies with an often highly mobile camera, the use of long takes and deliberatively interruptive editing. In contrast, Cantet's style is generally self-effacing with neither the camerawork nor the editing drawing attention to themselves. This is complicated in some of his films, including *L'Emploi du temps*, by recourse to a visual symbolism that responds to characters' psychological states or desires. One would still struggle to pin down a Cantetian style in the way that one can with the Dardennes. There are nonetheless interesting convergences between Cantet's *L'Emploi du temps* and *Le Silence de Lorna* with respect to their treatment of indebted subjectivity.

Vincent (Aurélien Recoing), the hero of *L'Emploi du temps*, is keeping the loss of his job with a consultancy firm secret from his friends and family. While they believe he is on high-powered business trips, he is driving around aimlessly and sleeping in his car. At the start of the film, he is far from unhappy. An early sequence sees him race a small train, clearly enjoying the playfulness of the moment. A subsequent sequence shows him happily singing along to his car stereo as he goes. We later learn that he in fact lost his job because he enjoyed the driving but not the arriving and tended to carry straight on, missing appointments as a result. This chosen path allows him to hold on to what he liked – the freedom of the road – and shed the rest. This is his escapist utopia, the one that the film – in typical Cantetian fashion – will test, not least as, again in a way typical of Cantet, Vincent finds himself exposed to the judgement of the group and the broader society. While the path to his utopia is an idiosyncratic one (it being unusual to cover up job losses), freedom itself, the capacity for the individual to define her or himself and to choose her or his own path, lies somewhere near the heart of neoliberalism's own utopian promise while the obstacles that Vincent encounters help reveal that promise's illusory nature.

The obstacles are essentially of two sorts: first, the pressure placed upon him by family and friends to demonstrate that he is maintaining his role as a high-flier; second, the need to remain solvent while unemployed. As we will see, the two pressures converge in that both expose Vincent to a surveillance that curtails his freedom and both demand that, like Lorna, he produce a specific type of entrepreneurial subjectivity that convinces other people of his ability to repay debts.

The first sequence of the film finds him asleep in his car, a people carrier that underscores his role as father rather than free agent. With the kind of symbolic use of the image that recurs in the film, the windows are steamed up, suggesting he is losing contact with the world. The ringing of his phone brings him sharply back to it. It is Muriel (Karin Viard), his wife, making contact. He tells her he has a meeting the other side of Marseille and will ring her back. Later, he calls her from a motorway picnic area where he is eating while reading the financial pages. His boss has set them an impossible timetable and he has to pick up the pieces. Later still, he drives on a darkened motorway, listening to stock exchange prices on the car radio. Finally, bringing the day to a close, he phones Muriel from a motorway service station before bedding down there. The boss of the company they are advising is being awkward. They have held a crisis meeting. He will not be home that night. On the plus side, the opportunity in Switzerland he has mentioned is becoming a real possibility. Bracketing the more ludic moments of freedom, these activities and conversations highlight how, even though unemployed, Vincent must produce the persona of a high-flier. While the open road seems to bring the freedom he seeks, his mobile phone plays a more ambiguous role. In some ways, it complements the car by enabling him to retain contact with his network when travelling. In other ways, it reins him in, forcing him to face scrutiny. The phone will work in this way throughout the film but with its capacity to exercise a decentred social surveillance coming increasingly to the fore.

Vincent raises money in two ways, each of which places him in debt and opens him up to inspection. Firstly, he persuades his father to lend him the deposit for an apartment he claims he is going to buy in Geneva for his invented UN development agency job. When he struggles to convince his father that this makes financial sense, Muriel chips in, 'we've done our calculations and we've seen that, with Vincent's accommodation allowance, we can pay everything back to you over two years. Therefore, when you add it all up, compared to staying in a hotel, this represents a saving' (my translation). The father is convinced but will later say, half-jokingly, that he should be able to visit the apartment when he likes, given the money he has invested in it. Vincent retorts that he will begin repayments the following month. Secondly, he comes up with a Ponzi scheme that he persuades his network of friends from business school to invest in. He tells them that his contacts in Switzerland have opened up the possibility for under-the-counter but highly profitable investments in the old Soviet Union. The opacity of the scheme starts to make the friends suspicious. As Vincent drives on a motorway, he is called to account by his old friend Fred, the mobility of his car again over-ridden by that of the mobile phone. He realises he will be forced to start reimbursing his investors, something he is only able to achieve by working for someone who smuggles counterfeit goods over the Swiss border.

This sense that Vincent is under constant scrutiny and must work to produce a version of himself that can sustain inspection is perhaps at its strongest when he goes to scope out the UN development agency in Geneva, the site of his supposed new job. Dressed smartly and with a briefcase, he attaches himself to a legitimate group. As he walks around the corridors, the glass-sided offices enable him to look in and the occupants to look out. A group in one meeting invite him in to join them. He clearly looks the part (Figure 2.3). Yet, when he installs himself at a table, he is seen on the CCTV by one of the security staff who invites him politely to leave. CCTV also finds him out on another occasion when he is spotted settling down for the night in his car in a hotel car park and is unceremoniously sent packing. Glass repeatedly recurs in the film's *mise-en-scène* as Vincent looks into his own modern house, offices or shops, or others look through windows at him. In some ways, in its capacity to work as a barrier, glass underscores his outsider status, his desire to escape the rules governing specific social spaces and groups. But, at the same time, through its transparency, it underscores the scrutiny he is repeatedly exposed to. Alongside the CCTV and the mobile phone, glass illustrates how socio-economic surveillance has become ubiquitous, decentred and mobile. It is worth mentioning too that the group that Vincent is invited to join in the UN building is discussing the rank order of African countries

**Figure 2.3** The UN building as a space of mutual surveillance (*L'Emploi du temps,* Laurent Cantet, 2001)

according to suitability for investment and the criteria (good governance, a predictable and transparent regulatory environment, social stability and the primacy of law) on which the ranking is based. The investment / repayment nexus and the surveillance that accompanies it stretches from the individual to the country level. With its focus on an unemployed man pretending to be a high-flier, a fiction within its own fictional narrative, *L'Emploi du temps* gives itself a grasp on the reach of debt that few more conventional fictions could match.

Following the inevitable discovery of Vincent's deception, the film's closing minutes suggest he may kill himself, just one of the worker suicides that have become so frequent in French and Franco-Belgian film and which will be discussed in the next chapter. He drives into the night, parks and walks away from his car towards a main road. Muriel's voice comes over his mobile telling him that she loves him. This intimate expression of genuine affection seems to deliver him into the next and final scene. He is interviewing for a job. Asked to explain his seven months of unemployment, he replies that he was looking for work that would satisfy him. His interlocutor is happy with this reply. His company is looking to make a significant investment in a new venture and would expect full self-investment in return. Vincent responds that he is not intimidated by the task but the way in which the camera tracks towards him to pin him in the frame suggests that he is once again trapped in a role not of his choosing.

There are several significant things of note here. One is the way in which, far from representing some pure outside or a space of refuge, the family, even in its most loving expression, is again figured as playing a major role in the monitoring and regularisation of behaviours, in the same way that Vincent's father and friends policed his capacity to repay debts contracted to them. Secondly, we see how the employment relationship is being reworked through the lens of the creditor-debtor relationship: the company *invests* in Vincent and expects him to provide a return through his own self-investment. Thirdly and relatedly, we again note the chronological reach of debt. Because the company requires repayment on their investment, they need reassurance concerning Vincent's reliability, just as his father and friends had; his future is no longer his own to define. But, worse still perhaps, he is required to erase even the memory of his escape attempt by framing it as a period when he was seeking the right job.

## *Le Père de mes enfants* and the indebted image

*Le Silence de Lorna* begins with the sound of what we retrospectively take to be the footsteps of the purposive, credit-seeking heroine as she moves towards the bank counter. *L'Emploi du temps* begins, as we noted, with the hero asleep in his car, temporarily free from pressure. Moving us back towards energetic movement, Hansen-Løve's *Le Père de mes enfants* begins with a montage of shots of busy Parisian streets, many of them with the signs of banks in prominent view. When the hero, Grégoire Canvel (Louis-Do de Lencquesaing) appears, marching briskly out of the Hôtel de Noailles, talking animatedly on the phone, it is as if he had been born from the relentless circulation of people, things and money. The remainder of the first sequence confirms this impression. In a series of shots, Grégoire walks towards the camera which then pans to show his retreating figure as he moves past it. He is always on the move and always on the phone, not in one, continuous conversation, but in a series of conversations (Figure 2.4). We learn he has been in a meeting with Georgians that has over-run, that accommodation for Korean filmmakers must be sorted out and that he wants work sent to his house in the country. As the sequence continues, he gets into his car, a family-man Volvo reminiscent of the people-carrier Vincent drives in *L'Emploi du temps*. His phone conversations continue throughout his drive home, but the editing pattern changes to show the people on the other end of the calls. A woman

**Figure 2.4** Grégoire's first appearance, as if born of the urban circulation (*Le Père de mes enfants,* Mia Hansen-Løve, 2009)

assistant in his office warns him of escalating costs on a Swedish shoot. Another assistant phones to update him about the human problems on the same shoot. His Italian wife, Sylvia (Chiara Caselli), comes through on a second phone and asks when he'll be home. His daughters tell him they are preparing a show that will cost him dear. His funds are limitless, he jokes. He asks them to tell him something nice. His wife responds, 'Ti amo'. Another call sees him talking to an unseen person about a script that the latter finds excessively wordy. How much does he owe his interlocutor, asks Grégoire, before responding, 'ah, no more than that?' laughing off what we assume to be a major debt. The final shots of the sequence are nocturnal. Grégoire is stopped by the police. He has been speeding and, in any case, has no points left on his licence. He is taken to the police station and must be fetched by his wife.

The sequence establishes, as openings typically do, underlying dynamics that will work themselves out in the rest of the film. Grégoire seems an exemplary entrepreneurial figure. A man of numerous projects, he appears to have the energy, confidence and connectivity to move between them, mobilising his charisma to pull people along with him and solve problems. He appears in control, his two phones allowing him to intervene over distance and his car permitting him to move between work and family. But, even at this stage, despite the confidence he projects, we sense a brittleness. The phones that empower him also channel demands to him, as they do with Vincent in *L'Emploi du temps*. Debt is already causing a pressing need to rein in expenses. The way in which his car is stopped encapsulates his position: he is having to go faster to meet commitments but, at the same time, his credit (the points on his licence) is used up. He needs Sylvia's love to keep his spirits up. Beneath the surface, the dynamic entrepreneur of the self is actually an increasingly hemmed in, indebted man. As the film proceeds, this latter figure becomes more prominent even as the veneer of confidence wears away.

Grégoire becomes increasingly constrained by debt and unable to control production costs. His Korean filmmakers turn up in greater number than expected. His lawyer tells him that the laboratory where their films are processed is moving towards foreclosure. The crew in Sweden threaten to go on strike unless they are paid. His contact at his bank tells him he may owe four million euros. His assistant tells him they are going under, that she is working herself into the ground. They have to hold on, he says. It is a question of time. But time is something he doesn't have. The sound studios refuse to work on his production. The bailiffs' arrival is imminent. The confident, energetic man of the start of the film is imploding before our eyes. He disappears into his office to escape and have a sleep. He walks in nocturnal Paris with Sylvia and tells her he can no longer manage and is a failure. She reminds him of all the directors whose career he has launched and of how much she loves him. In *L'Emploi du temps*, this kind of declaration pulls the hero back from the edge and reinserts him into alienating labour. Here, it is not enough. After burning some letters, presumably bills, and in a scene that we have anticipated but is still shocking in its abruptness, he shoots himself in the head. The act occurs in a quiet street away from the city centre. The energetic figure summoned forth by the urban bustle is no more, his movement never being sufficient to keep ahead of his debts, his future entirely foreclosed.

Sylvia's immediate reaction is to fight for his legacy and to complete all his company's productions. It is as if she were inhabited by his spirit, her body driven forward, trying to run ahead of debts, as his was. She tries to negotiate debt reduction with the laboratory. She goes to Sweden to negotiate a deal with Russian television that will rescue the shoot. She cannot, however, outrun the debts, any more than her husband could. The film distributors will not give any ground. The laboratory will not be flexible. The company is weighed under with twenty years of debt. The back catalogue is mortgaged. The debts far outweigh any assets. Not only does the company have no future. It no longer owns its past. Sylvia declares bankruptcy.

Hansen-Løve's films all tend to be about characters who, after a period of grieving or struggle, have to let go of a past self in a way that is not lived tragically but which opens a space of self-reinvention. Thus, for example, in the fittingly entitled *L'Avenir* (*Things to Come*, 2016), the heroine, a middle-aged philosophy teacher, has to deal with both divorce from her unfaithful husband and the death of her mother. The film refuses to frame this negatively but instead shows us a woman learning to live with a new-found freedom. Similar dynamics underlie *Le Père de mes enfants*. While it shows Sylvia and her children devastated by the sudden loss of their husband and father, it also shows them beginning to make plans for the future, especially after the company has been left to its fate. The eldest daughter, Clémence (Alice de Lencquesaing), shows a growing independence of mind and increasingly becomes the focus of the film. Sylvia talks of moving back to her native Italy and starting again. Tellingly, the closing sequence shows the mother and daughters in a car leaving Paris, even if only for a vacation, a movement away from the ceaseless circulation which had summoned the father into existence.

Neither Grégoire nor what he represents are abandoned, however. Early in the film, we saw him walking along the Loire with his wife and children before visiting a ruined church whose history he explained. After his death, Sylvia and the children repeat the walk and revisit the church to lay flowers, as if in tribute to him. By returning to locations in this way, the film constitutes its own internal memory. But, at the same time, and on a much more general level, it manifests a faith in the image to recall the past and capture the moment. In another scene towards the end of the film, his second daughter asks if she can take canisters of off-cuts from his films. His wife thinks the directors may have use for them but, when assured this is not the case, allows the girl to have them. This may seem trivial, or simply playful or touching, but is in fact crucial. That part of the films that has no commercial value escapes the temporal grasp of debt and has an afterlife.

The credit sequence of Jean-Luc Godard and Jean-Pierre Gorin's legendary 1972 film *Tout va bien* begins with anonymous male and female voices saying that to make a film one needs money. This triggers a montage of shots of a hand signing cheques for all the different aspects of a film's production, culminating in another intervention from the voices commenting that a film needs stars. Another shot of a cheque appears, this time with a percentage (23%). Two star names appear, those of Yves Montand and Jane Fonda, before the female voice says that they will need a story, typically about love. A final cheque appears. As it is torn away, it is replaced by a shot of Montand, with Fonda running to catch up with him on a riverbank. The film is telling us that the reverse shot of every shot in a conventional film is of money and that, whatever the shots show, they are all ultimately equivalent, all being 'money shots'. Although not a political film in the same way – *Tout va bien* issues directly from the mass worker and student protests of 1968 – *Le Père de mes enfants* updates its predecessor for new times. Debt, although implicitly there in Godard and Morin's work, each cheque being an investment demanding repayment, has now become the explicit reverse shot of every shot of every film, no matter how independent, reaching out to repossess the past of the images and own their future. In *Tout va bien*, the ultimate political redemption of the image can only come from collectively driven systemic change. In contrast, Hansen-Løve's film shows a perhaps idealistic faith in the image to exceed its capture through that within it which is not translatable into monetary equivalence or private ownership.

While Grégoire, in very masculine mode, believes he can reconcile the financial and artistic demands of multiple cinematic projects and keep his family happy, as if energy and charisma sufficed, Sylvia and the daughters suggest an alternative way forward, linked not to a heroic sense of human capacities but to a letting go. Their mourning for Grégoire expresses a liberation from the desire for control and heroic (masculine) autonomy that he embodies, a liberation also conveyed at the level of bodily movement and posture, and film form. This is apparent, for example, in the sequence in Sweden in which Sylvia is heading towards the shoot. Where Grégoire was seen talking on the phone and driving, Sylvia allows herself to be driven by another woman who is talking on the phone even as she herself gazes wistfully out of the window. The deliberate visual echo of Grégoire driving (the woman on the phone) underscores the difference of the shot. Rather than positioning us alongside a driven (driving!) masculine hero, it invites reflection and distance. Much the same could be said of other shots with Sylvia and especially those with Clémence who is repeatedly shown alone in close, static framings (Figure 2.5) that emphasise her elusive interiority rather than action in and upon the world (Wilson 2012: 277–82). Just as the film implied that the image could have a past and future that escaped the temporal reach of debt, there is a suggestion that images can open a space for reflection

**Figure 2.5** The pensive stillness of Clémence (*Le Père de mes enfants,* Mia Hansen-Løve, 2009)

and a distance between themselves and a purely instrumental relation to the world.

## Debt, governance and subjectivity

In his short but much-cited 'Postscript on control societies', Deleuze notes a transition from the disciplinary society famously analysed by Foucault across a series of works to something more diffuse and open-ended in its reach, which he called control society. In the latter, individuals no longer moved through a succession of disciplinary 'sites of confinement' (prisons, hospitals, factories, schools, the family), each of which imparted its own singular mould over a discrete time period. Instead, there was a continuous, open-ended modulation of individuals at the intersection of multiple institutions. This was a new, less bounded and more 'gaseous' capitalism, one centred on the firm and the circulating product not the factory, as site of enclosure, and production (Deleuze 1992). And, crucially, Deleuze adds, 'a man [sic] is no longer a man confined but a man in debt' (Deleuze 1992: 6). The remark is left undeveloped but there is a clear invitation to see debt as the key governmental tool for shaping the behaviour of mobile individuals as they move through social sites. This vision would inspire Lazzarato when, drawing on Deleuze, Guattari and

Nietzsche, he came to develop his own account of debt's power to constrain behaviours and shape subjectivities as part of his broader project of challenging accounts of neoliberalism that over-emphasised the freedom of the neoliberal subject (Lazzarato 2011: 72).

Nietzsche's *Genealogy of Morals* provides a cornerstone for Lazzarato's argument. While dominant traditions in political economy, anthropology and psychology made symbolic or economic exchange the paradigm of social relationships, Nietzsche gave precedence to the credit–debt nexus and the unequal power relations at its core (Lazzarato 2011: 13, 34). The social group's task, Nietzsche noted, was to engender humans able to promise to repay their debt through a mnemotechnics of cruelty that branded the spirit and the body (Lazzarato 2011: 37). This relied on the inculcation of a very particular kind of memory, one oriented to the future and thus with a vital forward-looking chronological reach. A healthy forgetting would leave the future open. Requiring predictable repayment, forcing a calculation and measurement able to establish equivalences between present and future behaviours, debt closes off the future as an opening to the new (Lazzarato 2011: 38–41). It thus appropriates not simply labour time (the work required to reimburse one's debt) but also time as action, choice, decision or wager (Lazzarato 2011: 45). Dependent on this latter time, a true living forwards implies a faith in the world and the creative possibilities it contains. But debt folds the possible back into the actual and shuts down the potential for radical change. The old disciplinary subject moulded by prisons, schools and factories was pushed towards passive acceptance of rules and roles. Now, the indebted individual is enjoined to be active, but, shorn of the power to shape the future, this is an empty activity (Lazzarato 2011: 109).

Debt has a history. While there are continuities in its functioning, Lazzarato argues, there are also deep shifts which must be considered if we are to understand the specificity of its functioning under capitalism in general and neoliberal capitalism in particular, especially since the crisis. In primitive societies, Lazzarato notes, drawing on Nietzsche both directly and filtered through Deleuze, finite debts circulate among social groups helping to maintain their cohesion. With the rise of monotheism, however, the debt to the all-powerful God became infinite, thus defying repayment, and was interiorised as a sentiment of moral guilt (Lazzarato 2011: 61–2). Capitalism, the new 'God', secularised this machinery of inescapable debt and culpability (Lazzarato 2011: 62–3). Money is often discussed as if it was a single object but, Lazzarato notes, drawing on Deleuze and Guattari (especially the former), this is profoundly misleading. Finance money (capital) seeks its own infinite expansion and monopolises the power to destroy and create and thus fashion the future. Payment money, the money of our salaries and purchases, is relatively impotent, limited as it is to the acquisition of what is being produced under existing conditions rather than having finance money's power to determine those conditions (Lazzarato 2011: 66–7). Financial capital has two faces. From the empowered perspective of those who control it, it appears as credit seeking a return. From the point of view of everyone else, it appears as debt. Finance invests in companies, lends to states or individuals and in return demands repayment with interest. This overarching creditor–debtor relationship is a deeply asymmetrical power relationship. Because it and the guilt associated with it are intrinsic to the functioning of capitalism, it cannot be escaped without an exit from capitalism itself. It is this history of debt that makes Lazzarato critical of David Graeber's famous tome, *Debt, the First 5000 Years* (2011). Lazzarato considers that Graeber's focus on the long-term alternation between cycles of credit money and commodity money obscures the specificity of debt's mobilisation by capitalism (Lazzarato 2015: 122–4).

The era of neoliberal hegemony gives free rein to the power of financial capital, with debt playing an increasingly central role in the governance of behaviours and the production of subjectivities. States transfer the power to create money to banks who issue it as loans to be repaid (Lazzarato 2011: 76). Cutting taxes or seeing their tax take diminish through corporate tax avoidance, states increasingly finance themselves through bond issues and thus subject themselves to the discipline of financial markets. The deregulation of financial flows gives a clear upper hand to financial capital over industrial capital, with share price and shareholder return on investment the principal measure of the success of firms (Lazzarato 2011: 79). Increasingly outgunned by capital on this new terrain, unions see their power and membership shrink and workers their relative share of national income diminish. They are increasingly obliged to borrow to maintain access to consumption, housing and other resources. The welfare state, a key pillar of the post-1945 social settlement, is shrunken but not simply abolished. Instead, it is repurposed in a way that enables a more individualised governance of behaviours. What were previously rights are now increasingly distributed as credits to be repaid not in cash but through a commitment to correct future behaviours and attitudes. Evaluation of the latter increasingly opens the individual up to moralising scrutiny (Lazzarato 2011: 85, 100–1). The heroic, self-defining neoliberal entrepreneur of the self gives way to a constrained subject. As Lazzarato acerbically explains, 'becoming an entrepreneur of the self only means having to manage, according to the criteria of the firm and of competitiveness, one's employability, one's debts, the reduction of one's salary and one's income and the reduction of social services' (Lazzarato 2011: 74 (my translation)).

With the more individualised relationship of inspection between citizen and state or between bank and borrower inaugurated by debt, one might think a more personal inter-relationship would develop. Instead, Lazzarato notes, credit, despite its semantic connection to belief, turns trust into mistrust, the borrower being forced to manufacture a version of the self that promises repayment, the lender inclined to disbelieve apparent reliability. He comments: 'In the conditions of generalised mistrust established by neoliberal policies, hypocrisy and cynicism are the contents of social relationships' (Lazzarato 2011: 103 (my translation)).

With the arrival of the crisis in 2007–8, governance through debt takes on a new amplitude and pervasiveness. States assume the debts of the banks, transfer moral responsibility for them to populations, and force them to pay for them through policies of austerity which further hack away at public health, welfare and education provision, and salaries (Lazzarato 2011: 88–9). This imposition of austerity as state policy underlines the unique transversal grasp of debt: it can operate at the level of the individual, the firm or the nation (Lazzarato 2011: 82–4).

## Cruel optimism and impasse

Lazzarato's account of debt provides precious insights for engaging with debt-related films but works at a general level and is usefully supplemented by a more fine-grained approach when one approaches specific cultural texts. It is here that Berlant's *Cruel Optimism* is especially useful. Picking up on Raymond Williams's notion of the 'structure of feeling' of a period, Berlant probes how affect and fantasy provide key elements of our 'shared historical time' (Berlant 2011a: 15). Engaging with a range of contemporary cultural texts, including works by Cantet and the Dardennes, she focuses specifically on the affects, temporalities, gestures and 'genres' that occur when, in the teeth of the neoliberal assault on the Fordist commitment to socio-economic inclusion, people remain perversely committed to a fantasy of the good life even though attachment to it actively impedes the fulfilment they seek through it (Berlant 2011a: 1). This notion of cruel optimism is particularly relevant for an analysis of most of the debt-related films I am discussing here. Genre is also a key term for Berlant but she does not use it in the way it might typically be understood by film scholars. Instead, she describes it as, 'a loose, affectively-invested zone of expectations about the narrative shape a situation will take' (Berlant 2011b: 2). The specific genre Berlant uses to describe how we relate to the neoliberal present is the 'impasse' (Berlant 2011a: 4), a paradoxical genre where narratives that allow one to inhabit the present comfortably or situate it in a meaningful, longer-term unfolding break down. Berlant develops this as follows:

> An impasse is a holding station that doesn't hold securely but opens out into anxiety, that dogpaddling around a space whose contours remain obscure. An impasse is decompositional – in the unbound temporality of the stretch of time, it marks a delay that demands activity. The activity can produce impacts and events, but one does not know where they are leading (Berlant 2011a: 199).

Although this sounds overwhelmingly negative, the final sentence opens the potential for an undefined opening to a future rather than mere entrapment. This nascent sense of possibility is confirmed when Berlant subdivides the impasse into three types. First, she notes, there is the impasse following a traumatic event or social catastrophe when 'one no longer knows what to do or how to live and yet, while unknowing, must adjust'. Secondly, she continues, 'there is what happens when one finds oneself adrift [. . .] without an event to have given the situation a name and procedures for managing it – coasting through life, as it were, until one discovers a loss of traction'. Thirdly, and more positively, 'there are situations where managing the presence of a problem / event that dissolves the old sureties and forces improvisation and reflection on life-without-guarantees is a pleasure and a plus, not a loss' (Berlant 2011a: 199–200). While the different types of impasse converge on a sense of lost bearings and an inability to see beyond the present, this disturbance can be lived as challenging, immobilising or potentially liberating. These variations will help us analyse the films to which we will now return.

## Film and theory in dialogue

Berlant's *Cruel Optimism* and Lazzarato's *La Fabrique de l'homme endetté* both date from 2011. The three films discussed so far all precede them and, in their different ways, anticipate key aspects of them. To begin with and perhaps most significantly, all three have central protagonists who move from being entrepreneurs of the self to indebted men or women and thus map the shift in neoliberalism from a more optimistic or triumphant phase to a more obviously punitive, austere and moralising one, the same shift that, again in different ways, drove Lazzarato and Berlant in their writings. Lazzarato stresses the movement from a disciplinary society of enclosed institutions to a less spatially circumscribed control society within which debt, with its decentred reach, plays a key role. Prefiguring this, and despite their attempts to control their own lives, the mobile protagonists of the three films, Vincent in *L'Emploi du temps*, Grégoire in *Le Père de mes enfants* and Lorna in *Le Silence de Lorna*, all find themselves unable to escape debt's pervasive governmental powers. The fundamental dynamics of the characters' movements are different. Vincent is running or driving away from neoliberal labour in search of the autonomy which it cannot give him but is hauled in by love (of which more below) intertwined with debt. Grégoire is desperately trying to run ahead of debt in pursuit of a dream of freedom but can never outstrip it. Lorna, more conformist, moves deliberately into debt as her path to social inclusion but is increasingly deflected from her calculating trajectory by the imperative ethical demands of the Other's vulnerability. Despite these differences, the three films underscore the reach of debt, its capacity to exercise control over mobile protagonists, and the shift to a more constraining vision of neoliberalism.

When analysing Audiard's films in Chapter 1, we noted the empowerment characters drew from networked connectivity. In the three films discussed here, we see that same networked connectivity mutating, when repurposed by debt, into decentred and individualised surveillance. This is most strikingly so in the cases of Vincent and Grégoire, the two male central characters. Both initially seem empowered by their ability to combine motorised mobility with the instant communication given by the mobile phone. Even as they move, they act at a distance, retaining contact with friends, family and associates. Yet, as both films progress, the phones increasingly negate the freedom of movement granted by the car, summoning one character, Vincent, to account for himself, and the other, Grégoire, to address his mounting debts. With less aspiration towards heroic individual mobility than the two male characters, Lorna is part of a broader circulatory flow within which movement still does not equate to autonomy. She must account for herself in a series of meetings, across a range of ad hoc locations (cafes, the street) or on the phone to Fabio, her gang leader, as he circulates in his taxi, to the Russian gang Fabio is dealing with, and to Sokol, her boyfriend, as he moves between Germany and Belgium. Audiard's films invite us to exult in the flexibility of characters able to shape themselves to respond to the demands of their networked connections. More in line with Lazzarato's account of a debt-governed world where mistrust and cynicism become the content of social relations, the films discussed here show characters who, in the face of networked inspection, produce personae they struggle to believe in and sustain. In the case of Hansen-Løve's and Cantet's mature male characters, this role fatigue manifests itself as an increasing loss of self-belief and, ultimately, an implosion. In the case of the Dardennes' Lorna, we see a character divided against herself: on the one hand, the ruthless debt-repayer; on the other, the person drawn by an ethical imperative to protect the vulnerable Other.

Lazzarato stresses the capacity of debt to reach into the past, shut off the future and work on multiple levels from the individual up the nation-state. Debt's chronological reach structures the temporal economy of all the films. Cantet's hero does not simply have to produce a conformist self who can promise reliable future repayment but must also erase the memory of his attempt to open up a time of idle possibility. Not only does Hansen-Løve's protagonist find his future closed down by debt but his past, and the aspiration for self-determination it contained, as expressed in his back catalogue of independent film productions, no longer belongs to him. Similarly, the Dardennes' Lorna has to produce a self that not only has been loyal to the gang but will continue to be so under implicit threat of elimination. Of the three films, Cantet's is perhaps best able to give an account of the scalar reach of debt. With its hero's invented account of working for the UN development agency, it invites us to draw parallels between how debt-exposed nations and individuals are governed. The UN agency building, with its CCTV cameras and glass-sided rooms, moves us into a surveillance space in which individuals as well as countries are subject to audit.

The films' foreclosed futures similarly anticipate Berlant's description of cruel optimism and impasse. Berlant describes, we remember, how a determination to nurture fantasies of an unattainable good life make us complicit in our own misery (2011a: 1). In their different ways, the heroes of the three films show just such a determination. Lorna remains perversely attached to a sentimental fantasy of running a snack bar with Sokol, even though the route to it lies through a murderous disregard for the Other and abandonment of her own status as an ethical human being. Grégoire maintains a dream of heroically independent film production in the face of the ceaseless pressure, stress and debt that eventually drive him to suicide. Vincent shores up the fantasy image of himself as prosperous high-flyer, even when his job has made him totally miserable and, as a newly unemployed man, he cannot sustain the lifestyle he and his family are used to. On a more abstract level, bringing Berlant closer to Lazzarato, we might say that all three protagonists cling to the neoliberal fantasy of entrepreneurial self-fashioning even when, in the era of a more punitive neoliberalism, this is manifestly out of their reach.

In many films, especially but not only Hollywood ones, children are sentimentalised and the family is presented as a loving refuge from an unfriendly world. Complicating these mythologies, Berlant observes how children and the family in Cantet's and the Dardennes' films are enrolled in the maintenance of fantasies of the good life and become complicit agents of a cruel optimism that affects not only the characters but also sucks spectators into its orbit. Discussing the Dardenne brothers' *La Promesse*, for example, she notes how its audiences feel obligated to 'side with the child's will not to be defeated', even though this simply means that we 'attach optimism for a less bad future to a blighted field of possibility' (2011a: 171). Young people in the brothers' films, she notes, keep alive 'the promise of familial love [as] the conveyance for the incitement to misrecognize the bad life as a good one'. Because their life still appears open, they protect (and demand protection of) a sense of futurity or what she calls 'the promise of the promise' (Berlant 2011a: 175). Commenting on the role of family members in Cantet's earlier *Ressources humaines* (*Human Resources*, 1999), she notes how 'these subjects of capital protect the fantasies of intimates by suppressing the costs of adjustments to labor's physical and affective demands' (2011a: 209), an observation which, with a little adjustment, could apply to *L'Emploi du temps*. Not only does the latter film's hero shore up appearances so that nothing changes for his children, but his wife works to maintain his optimism and, through her love, draws him back from the brink and helps return him to the work he loathes. In *Le Silence de Lorna*, as we have noted, Lorna's love for Sokol helps her sentimentalise their dream of owning a snack bar, no matter what the human cost.

Berlant's analysis can be extended. Family members and loved ones in the two films do not simply sustain each other's cruel optimism. They are active agents of surveillance in an economy of debt. Characters in *Le Père de mes enfants* are less obviously complicit. Certainly, Sylvia nurtures Grégoire's belief that his film production work is worthwhile, and she and the girls never question their comfortable lifestyle even as the company is going under. But they also demand Grégoire leave his work aside and spend unproductive time with them. While this does not constitute a directly political challenge, it preserves the sense of something not immediately recuperable by debt-driven labour in the same way as the film itself maintains a belief in the capacity of cinema to preserve something beyond its own debt-governed uses.

Berlant's nuanced discussion of impasse comes in useful at this stage. She distinguishes, we remember, between impasses emerging from traumatic events which force an adjustment, those where one simply flounders as old recipes break down, and those where improvisation in response to the breakdown of an order is experienced positively (Berlant 2011a: 200). These variations can be found in the films and help distinguish between them. In *L'Emploi du temps*, the trauma that forces adjustment, Vincent's job loss, occurs before the action begins. Temporarily, at least, he seems to be adjusting positively, enjoying empty time, (re)discovering playfulness. But, as the film progresses, we see that he is trapped, unable to leave his high-flying persona behind or to consolidate his more liberating gestures and behaviours, struggling to convince, losing confidence, growing tired, 'doggypaddling' in Berlant's words, even before he is definitively reeled back in. Trauma intervenes later for the Dardennes' Lorna. It comes when Claudy is murdered. Up till then, she had been stuck in an unstable holding pattern between ruthless instrumentalism and ethical commitment. After the death, as we saw, she moves towards a radical break with her indebted, calculating self as she dedicates herself to the protection of the unborn child. But, as we noted, the pregnancy is imagined, its lack of reality an inadvertent admission that her exit from impasse is incomplete and that an individual ethical commitment to the singular Other, no matter how radical, cannot constitute durable grounds for other ways of living. This has been the pattern in all the Dardennes' films since *La Promesse*. Characters mistake inclusion in a ruthless order for a good life (Berlant 2011a: 163–4) and are 'saved' as ethical beings when they recoil from symbolic or real murder. But this refusal to kill is simply the polarised reverse image of the current order and remains trapped in the same implicit individualism. When the brothers' films create a more promising route out of impasse, it is almost, as we will see in later chapters, despite themselves.

In *Le Père de mes enfants*, Grégoire is clearly trapped in Berlant's second kind of impasse. He persists with old behaviours but increasingly loses traction. Faced with his suicide, Sylvia initially declines the chance for radical re-evaluation that this trauma offers. It is only when she realises that the debts cannot be outrun and declares the company bankrupt that she creates an opening towards a potentially different future. This moves us towards Berlant's third kind of impasse whereby the failure of old gestures and behaviours, in this case around debts and their repayment, opens the possibility for experimentation that has not yet solidified into a new way of life. At the end of his discussion of debt and the neoliberal condition, Lazzarato underscores how the only way to escape the power of debt and reopen the future is not simply to annul debt or declare bankruptcy to break its grip but also to refuse the moral blackmail that accompanies it (Lazzarato 2011: 123–4). In Hansen-Løve's film, the exit from obligation is purely local but it points towards how the future, as a space of choice and possibility, may be reopened.

## Indebted variations: the narrative of impasse or the impasse of narrative?

The three films considered so far are particularly rich but relatively isolated instances of debt narratives. I will now look at a cluster of what one might see as more ordinary debt films from 2011–2012. Emerging in direct response to the crisis and the rise of a thematics of debt that it provoked, they look at the topic in more predictable ways, but it is their relative ordinariness, I would suggest, that makes them interesting. To the extent that they all narrate and attempt to contain crises of the subject and of futurity, they signal a broader crisis of conventional narrative as its core components come under increasing strain.

Three of the films are star vehicles: Moutout's *De bon matin*, Lioret's *Toutes nos envies* and Kahn's *Une vie meilleure*. Mennegun's *Louise Wimmer* is a distinctly less glossy production. Moutout's film stars Jean-Pierre Darroussin as Paul Wertret, a prosperous, fifty-something bank employee who comes to the end of his tether, murders two of his bosses and then kills himself. Lioret's film stars Vincent Lindon as Stéphane, an experienced but disillusioned magistrate who is enlisted by Claire (Marie Gillain), a younger, more idealistic but terminally ill colleague, to help her defend Céline (Amandine Dewasmes), a single mother who has contracted revolving loans whose interest payments outstrip her ability to pay. They win out through recourse to the European court just as Claire succumbs to her disease. Kahn's *Une vie meilleure* stars two major box-office draws, Guillaume Canet as Yann, a chef, and Leïla Bekhti as Nadia, a waitress and single mother. Yann uses multiple loans to buy a lakeside restaurant to refurbish but cannot keep up the payments and is swindled out of the property by a predatory local landlord. Nadia leaves for what seems legitimate courier work in Quebec but gets imprisoned when she is found to be carrying drugs. Yann waits for her release while looking after her son, Slimane (Slimane Khettabi). Mennegun's *Louise Wimmer* is very different from these star vehicles. Its eponymous divorcee heroine, played by Corinne Masiero, is unglamorous and middle-aged. Well-off before her divorce, she now lives out of her car and survives by working as a cleaner in a hotel and in people's homes. She owes money to a man who threatens to have her goods, including her car, seized, and to the bar owner who fills her flask with coffee, and is behind on payments for the lock-up where she keeps her remaining property. The film ends when, moved by her plight, someone in social services pushes her up the queue for an apartment.

The films could broadly be labelled as social realist despite considerable variation between them with respect to style, genre and narrative construction. Probably the most commercial of the four, *Une vie meilleure* is a love story with thriller elements (the hero robs the man who has swindled him to buy his air ticket to Quebec). With its heroine slowly dying, *Toutes nos envies* blends its social realism with elements of heart-tugging melodrama. *De bon matin* has elements of mystery and suspense but, probing the why of its murders not the who, is a dark social drama rather than a crime story. Devoting most of itself to an exploration of different layers of the past, it has a far more complex narrative structure than *Une vie meilleure* or *Toutes nos envies*, which are both linear narratives with straightforward causal chains. *Louise Wimmer* is also linear but is remarkable for the fragmentation and repetitiveness of its narrative line: the heroine is in day-to-day survival mode with no real forward movement until the allocation of an apartment provides respite. This focus on everyday activities gives the film a neo-realist feel that is augmented by its deliberately unpolished aesthetic.

Despite these and other differences, the films converge in suggesting a crisis of the subject and the difficulty of constructing a meaningful sense of self or a liveable life. *De bon matin* develops the nostalgia-tinged, before / after style narrative of capitalist evolution that we find in American films like *The Company Men* (Wells, 2010) or *Margin Call* (Chandor, 2011) (Toscano and Kinkle 2015: 164–5). Paul has been a confident, successful, hands-on banker, one who knows his business and local government clients and who supports them in productive ventures. We see him, for example, in animated conversation on a building site. We also see him and his wife engaged in voluntary work in Africa, work that they persuade the bank to support. Things go wrong when a new manager arrives at a moment which coincides with an announcement that the bank has made heavy losses by buying on the sub-prime mortgage market. The bank sees a growing number of debt defaults that the previously hands-on Paul is asked to take charge of. He realises that although the bank may sponsor development projects, it is using them to polish its image and will not desist from risky speculation. Too much part of the old regime and too outspoken, he is targeted for systematic harassment by the new management. The previously confident employee is now seen asleep at work, drunk at home or confessing his suffering and loss of a sense of self to a psychologist. His ageing and increasingly vulnerable body is more and more out of place in the workplace with its cold blues and greys and its hard, characterless surfaces. Made in the aftermath of the banking crisis, the film suggests that the shift in the bank's vocation from productive integration in the local economy to financial speculation and predatory treatment of debtors and employees finds its necessary prolongation in the crisis of the bank worker whose work loses any positive meaning.

Paul is more a creature of the old Fordist world, with its productive partnership between bank, state and productive economy, than a neoliberal entrepreneur of the self. Yann, the young chef in *Une vie meilleure*, embodies entrepreneurial subjectivity far better. The way in which his energy, ambition and risk-taking come up against and are defeated by debt repayments and predatory lending suggests not simply an individual defeat but the non-accessibility of a positive model of neoliberal subjectivity for those not already possessed of financial muscle. Less focused on entrepreneurial subjectivity as such, *Louise Wimmer* and *Toutes nos envies* show two separated or divorced women struggling to keep afloat in the face of debt. The eponymous hero of the former has been a prosperous member of the middle class. After her divorce, all she has are the decaying remnants of that identity as embodied in the possessions she keeps in her rented lock-up garage. Her ageing car, which is also her home, constantly threatens not to start. It is as if all those things that once signalled her social inclusion are giving way around her, leaving her in pure survival mode. Céline, the indebted character in *Toutes nos envies*, is a less major figure in the film than the two magistrates, Claire and Stéphane, who try to help her. She is separated from her partner, works part-time, is evicted from her apartment for non-payment of rent and cannot keep up the payments on debts whose initially low interest charges rise sharply. Like Mennegun's Louise Wimmer, she is in pure survival mode until Claire and Stéphane fight her case. The case is eventually won in the European courts because, by hiding its debt conditions in the small print, the loan company was deemed to be preventing fair competition among lenders. So, rather than somehow confirming that the French state or indeed Europe is on the side of citizens, the case confirms their abandonment.

This sense of subjects in crisis feeds off and into the loss of any meaningful opening to the future in the films. In *Toutes nos envies*, this is communicated by the awareness of the loss of the larger battle even as a loophole allows the smaller battle to be won. In *Une vie meilleure*, the characters survive but only by renouncing their ambitions for the better life evoked in the title. In *De bon matin*, the initial blind striking of the murders and the closing suicide underscore the loss of futurity. But that same loss is conveyed more conclusively by the layered flashbacks and looping, fragmented narrative structure of a film in which the beginning is already the end and what comes between is the breakdown of no longer effective habits and behaviours with no new ones arising to replace them. A similar temporal foreclosure is conveyed by the very different narrative structure of *Louise Wimmer*. There is no recognisable plot in the film, as the heroine's life is going nowhere. Instead, a limited range of scenes and sequences repeat themselves with small variations: Louise trying to start a car she cannot afford to maintain; Louise working in the hotel; Louise trying to keep herself presentable without access to facilities of her own; Louise pressuring social services for an apartment. The montage is fragmentary so that one scene does not build into the next. We simply move from one immediate present to another without any sense of forward movement. Films typically elide routine events (eating, sleeping, washing, working, travelling to work) unless they can be put in service of character or plot development. But, condemned to a stalled present, Louise has no access to a forward-moving plot and is effectively trapped in what would normally be the ellipses. Encapsulating this impasse, the stereo in her decaying car can only play one repeatedly heard song, Nina Simone's 'Sinnerman', with its own highly repetitive lyrics about a sinner with nowhere to run to. It is as if Louise were stuck in some nightmarish loop.

In this context of generalised impasse, untenable subjectivities and temporal implosion, it is hard to differentiate between the films' own attempts to shore up their cruel optimism and that of the characters. Along the lines described by Berlant, several of them foreground a commitment to children as a way to sustain their characters', their audience's and perhaps their own sense of a potentially liveable future in conditions that render such a thing impossible. In *Toutes nos envies*, Claire commits to helping Céline partly because their children are at the same school. Later, she lines up Céline as a potential mother substitute for her own children after her impending death. Stéphane, the grizzled older magistrate, recovers his lost sense of fight because of his younger colleague's determination. Outside his work, he coaches a rugby team, taking energy from the young men's commitment. It is as if everybody in the film needs somebody younger to keep their hopes alive. Similarly, in *Une vie meilleure*, Yann (and, through him, the film) keeps going through a commitment to look after Nadia's son and take him to be with his mother. The child's presence provides a note of optimism the film would otherwise lack (Figure 2.6). The heroine of *Louise Wimmer* is clearly committed to the daughter she rarely sees and encourages her to get back into education. But that film's cruel optimism rests more on the heroine's eventual escape from homelessness, an outcome that changes everything and nothing for her but gives the film an upbeat ending. With its future foreclosed by the hero's suicide, *De bon matin* is the darkest of the films. Yet the hero's farewell letter expresses his overwhelming love for the family around whom his moments of happiness in the film largely revolve. As his alienation grows, his family relationships also deteriorate. Rather than a cruel optimism, the film is perhaps better characterised by a cruel pessimism in that

**Figure 2.6** Visiting his mother in prison, the child's role in keeping optimism alive (*Une vie meilleure,* Cédric Kahn, 2011)

any positivity it offers is tied to an earlier period when work and family life were mutually sustaining.

## Conclusion

The films discussed in this chapter point to a crisis of neoliberal subjectivity as debt arrests the subject's capacity for autonomy and self-definition, turns networked connectivity into decentred surveillance, closes off the future as a space of choice and decision, and forces the erasure of memories of resistance. The temporal shift that occurs is expressed not simply at the superficial level of individual plot events but reaches into the deeper chronological structure of the films and their capacity to build any real sense of transformative onward movement or meaningful closure. This sense of impasse, of a stalled present, is there in all the films. In some, it is entirely without hope, a decaying of existing reflexes and gestures with no prospect of new ones arising in their stead. In others, where impasse is accompanied by some exit from debt's governing reach, individual actions and attitudes emerge as signs of resistance in the present and expressions of the potential for as yet undeveloped alternatives in the future. But where films insist on grafting happy outcomes onto contexts that suggest such things are impossible, it appears that they themselves are 'doggy-paddling', clinging onto habitual cinematic gestures that no longer bite upon the world they inhabit. In the end, the most interesting films are those that develop the most thorough and wide-ranging critique of the power of debt (*L'Emploi du temps*) or which limit themselves to foregrounding elements of human subjectivity or cultural production that resist its instrumentalising reach and remain opaque to its probing gaze (*Le Père de mes enfants*). In a similar way, the most perceptive works (*Le Silence de Lorna*, *L'Emploi du temps*) are those which, refusing the sentimentalisation of love, the family and especially children, show how interpersonal relationships can shore up the cruel optimism that sustains perverse faith in the status quo or act as devolved agents of debt's decentred modulation of subjectivities. Other, more conventional works enlist the warm glow of love and the future promise of children to both sustain and feed off our belief that true satisfaction can be found in a private life somehow unsullied by the increasingly ruthless world around it. But, in any case, this association of families and couples with cruel optimism, surveillance or retreat into the private is a significant move away from the flexible, entrepreneurial family units we found in Audiard and conforms a shift in subjectivity in the grip of debt.

# 3

# The desperate search for the exit

Our first chapter gave us a positive account of the entrepreneurial neoliberal subject as enacted in the cinema of Audiard. The second showed cinematic subjects enchained by debt and no longer able to shape themselves or their future. Radicalising this sense of a coming-into-crisis of neoliberal subjectivity but also seeking to look beyond it, the current chapter focuses on an important cluster of films that have successful or abortive worker suicides at their core. The chapter has two main thrusts. Drawing on Slavoj Žižek's tripartite typology of violences (Žižek 2008: 1–2), it gauges how productively the films connect the subjective violences (the suicides) to the systemic and symbolic violences that are built into the 'normal' functioning of the status quo. Supplementing Žižek, addressing workers' on-screen suicides more specifically, teasing out differences between them, it also draws on another tripartite typology, this time the suicide-related one deployed by Carl Cederström and Peter Fleming in their *Dead Man Working* (2012). If that book's title points towards the nightmare situation within which workers kill everything within themselves superfluous to the requirements of the neoliberal workplace, effectively becoming zombies, it also summons up the possibility that one might kill the worker in the self and open up an exit from capitalist labour. It is the films' capacity to develop the latter, more politically promising scenario that I probe as I move towards the latter stages of the chapter. To help me here, I draw on Foucault's discussion of parrhesia as a scandalous truth-telling that points the way towards another life within this life (Foucault 2011). I work through these questions in relation to some key worker-suicide films. I begin with the proletarian deaths of Stéphane Brizé's films *La Loi du marché* (*The Measure of a Man*, 2015) and *En guerre*

(*At War*, 2018) and move on to Christophe Barratier's *L'Outsider* (*Team Spirit*, 2016) and Nicolas Silhol's *Corporate* (2017), two films engaging with suicide in relation to the corporate and financial sectors where we might expect to find ideal neoliberal subjects. I will argue that, despite their differences, all these films bring us up against another impasse. They successfully force the violences of neoliberal employment and failure of neoliberal subjectivity into view but are trapped in a sterile left moralism or an individualist humanism that renders them incapable of looking beyond what they show. Their exits are blocked. Looking for a more promising escape route, I then probe the ethical exits of the Dardenne brothers' worker-suicide diptych *Rosetta* (1999) and *Deux jours, une nuit* (*Two Days, One Night*) (2014). Trying one final door, I turn to the anarchic comedies of Benoît Delépine and Gustave Kervern with their unemployable bodies and suicidal workers, looking especially at *Le Grand Soir* (2012).

## The death of the worker: Brizé's hidden and spectacular suicides

If, with its *Palme d'or*, Audiard's *Dheepan* made the biggest splash at Cannes in 2015, Brizé's *La Loi du marché* was also much talked about, not least because its star, Vincent Lindon, won the prize for best leading male. Lindon plays Thierry, a man who, having been committed to a hard-fought collective struggle to keep his workplace open, is now long-term unemployed and must rebuild his life at the age of fifty-one. The film has a documentary feel. Apart from Lindon, most of the performers are amateurs, often performing roles close to those they play in real life. As if emanating from the hero's restrained and taciturn performance, the action is generally de-dramatised. All the sequences relating to the search for work and, later, the workplace drew on considerable preparatory research. The use of a handheld camera that seems to follow rather than precede the actors, the deliberately unpolished framing and the apparent reliance on available light reinforce the strongly realist feel. Yet, counterbalancing this, the film declares itself as a fiction through its use of cinemascope and relentless focus on its charismatic star (Châtelet 2015). It follows the latter's character, Thierry, as he goes through a series of humiliating experiences: the interview at *pôle-emploi* (the job centre), where he discovers that his recently completed training course will not help him find work;

a Skype interview where he is told his expertise is outdated and his CV poor; a job application class where all the other (younger) participants dissect his self-presentation; a meeting between him, his wife and another couple during which the latter, knowing that Thierry needs money, tries to undercut the price agreed for their caravan; another meeting, this time at the bank, where he is told that he and his wife should consider selling their house, given that they are struggling to keep up with mortgage payments.

These scenes of relentless debt-driven humiliation give way to something apparently more hopeful when Thierry gets a job as a security man in a hypermarket, wins the bank's approval and takes out a loan for a replacement car. A scene showing the modest retirement party of a woman who has given many years to the company suggests he may even have arrived in a happy workplace. Yet, his experience soon takes a very different direction as the hypermarket reveals itself to be a place of surveillance, suspicion and no little oppression. Thierry is taught how to use the CCTV system to watch customers and learns that, once caught in the grainy images of its all-pervasive gaze, they are all seen as potential thieves. When those caught are shown in the store's interview room, it becomes clear that some of them, an old man taking meat he can't afford, for example, are driven to theft through sheer poverty. As the film proceeds, the surveillance cameras are turned on the hypermarket's own employees: not enough workers are taking early retirement and, to drive up profitability, the management is looking to sack people for disciplinary offences. Unwittingly complicit, Thierry finds himself in the interview room watching the humiliation of an older employee who has taken some coupons not picked up by a customer. There is no consensual retirement this time but a sacking. True to the film's deliberately restrained aesthetic, we only learn that the woman concerned, Mme Anselmi, has killed herself in her workplace when we see the staff gathered together to be briefed. The drama is passed off by a manager as a tragedy about which no-one should feel guilty. Life, he explains, is not only about work. There is also family life with its projects and disappointments. Mme Anselmi's son took drugs and she was having to support him. Only she knew the reason behind her act. We see Thierry at Mme Anselmi's funeral, her framed photograph on her coffin, but a brusque cut takes us back to the hypermarket and to hands passing the barcodes on goods in front of a scanner at a till (of which more in Chapter 6). The nature of the edit suggests that the dead woman's tragic end has been bracketed as a mere interruption of normal business and its impersonal mechanical flow. Thierry finds himself back in the interview room with another employee, this time a female cashier accused of scanning loyalty points a customer couldn't use onto her own card. Left to watch the woman, Thierry instead leaves the building, gets into his car and drives away (Figure 3.1).

The film ends with this departure, an individual act of refusal from which audiences can take satisfaction. Given the oppressiveness of the workplace conditions that he encountered and the complicity that was his inevitable lot if he continued to play the same role, Thierry had to walk away if he were to preserve his own existence as an ethico-moral being. But, extracting it from the temporal flow of the film, the definitive finality of his gesture rescues it from the inevitable question of what comes next. Thierry has walked away from a defeated collective struggle to preserve his peace of mind but his attempt to find an individual way forward has proven equally abortive. We might ask if the film is leaving us with a satisfying sense of moral outrage in lieu of a more properly political way forward.

We could easily have included this film in the previous chapter. With its story of the crisis of the fifty-year-old male evicted from previous certainties, forced to accept alienating labour by the governmental reach of debt and trapped in an impasse, it would certainly have fitted. But what is particularly interesting for our purposes here is its treatment of work-related suicide as an object of symbolic struggle. As we saw, the company circumscribes the death's symbolic resonance by making its cause opaque and presenting it as a purely private act linked to personal circumstances.

**Figure 3.1** Walking away from an oppressive workplace (*La Loi du marché*, Stéphane Brizé, 2015)

Within the diegesis, this account is not explicitly challenged. Implicitly, however, the film is suggesting something very different. All the evidence (the surveillance, the scene of humiliation) positions the suicide as a response to calculated managerial bullying of unwanted staff members. But, moving back from the individuals and the specific workplace, there is also a broader invitation to see the suicide as a condensation of a broader shift that sees workers once offered secure employment and a guaranteed future not only rendered disposable but made to take responsibility for their own disposability. We might remember Thierry's pre-history of eviction from stable employment and the humiliations visited upon him as an 'underperforming' job-seeker. The suicide thus emerges as an object of hermeneutic struggle, its meaning shifting according to whether one reads it in relation to a narrowly personal context, specific workplace malpractices or broader systemic shifts.

The symbolic resonance of the self-immolation that closes Brizé's later *En guerre* is more explicitly signalled. It could be seen as not so much a prequel to its predecessor as an alternate outcome where, instead of moving on from the losing struggle to defend his workplace as the protagonist of *La Loi du marché* does, the hero, Laurent Amédéo, again played by Lindon, pursues the collective fight to the bitter end. *En guerre* is different in other ways too. Where Thierry is taciturn, Laurent, a hardened union negotiator, is relentlessly talkative. Thierry is present very much as an individual only connected durably to his wife and disabled son. He is seen alone, a pensive figure, in a good number of shots. Laurent is driven by solidarity and surrounded by comrades, his body repeatedly framed by the camera as an organic part of a collective body in struggle. Despite these differences, however, the two films are stylistically very similar. Like *La Loi du marché*, *En guerre* is carefully documented, uses mainly amateur actors typically playing roles close to their real ones, relies on handheld cameras, and avoids over-neat framing and staging of action in a way that gives it a sense of documentary authenticity. It also incorporates staged television news reports that doubly underline its realist intent: there is not only the reality effect of the reports themselves but also the film's capacity to show a context, the negotiation scenes, for example, which exceeds and contests the more limited view of television reporting. At the same time, as in Brizé's earlier film, the use of widescreen and obsessive focus on the charismatic Lindon clearly signal the film's fictional status.

When the film begins, the workers' representatives form a relatively united front against a management that has reneged on a promise to guarantee continued production in exchange for sacrifices from the workforce. While the factory is profitable, the company, driven by shareholder value, does not consider its margins sufficiently high. In what is a familiar dramaturgy, the unions deploy all the traditional tools of worker resistance; the strike, the demonstration, the factory occupations that immobilise stock and safeguard machines. They pressure politicians and obtain their support. They go to court. They invade the headquarters of the MEDEF (the French employers' federation) to try to force the plant's German owners to agree to speak to them. Management also deploy the familiar weapons: they offer limited concessions; they make it clear that, if the workers fight on, their redundancy settlement will be less generous. Perhaps predictably, the different unions involved splinter due to these deliberately divisive tactics. While Laurent leads those determined to continue the struggle, others want to take the redundancy offer. This leads to bitter recriminations. In the end, the Germans are forced to the table but only to reaffirm their position and to block the possibility of the factory being sold to a competitor. At the end of their tether, some of the workers lose control and overturn the car of the German company president with him inside. This puts an end to negotiations and to any political support. Laurent travels to Germany, douses himself in petrol and sets himself alight in front of the German company headquarters (Figure 3.2). After his death, the company announces that it will restart discussions with the workers.

Although about a fictional company, the film draws on familiar stories about company behaviours and worker responses. The closure of factories not deemed to be sufficiently profitable is something seen multiple times over the years in France. Bitterly fought, drawn-out campaigns against redundancies involving companies such as Goodyear, Continental, Whirlpool and others, some of which have turned violent or involved 'bossnappings', have been familiar front-page stories. So too have been the notorious waves of work-related suicides, notably in enterprises such as the privatised France-Télécom and the still publicly owned La Poste (the postal service) (Waters 2020: 107–69). The film's capacity to evoke and condense these dramas obviously helps to ground the feeling of authenticity it seeks. But, beyond that, as noted radical economist Frédéric Lordon observes, it develops a lucid sense of the relative strength of the forces in play at the current time. Lordon explains that the film's hero is fighting to save jobs in a world deliberately structured to make their salvation impossible. Given neoliberal financial deregulation,

**Figure 3.2** Apparent mobile phone footage of the hero's self-immolation (*En guerre*, Stéphane Brizé, 2018)

the deliberate unleashing of shareholder power and the resultant ability of capital to move production to wherever regulation is weakest, wages lowest or profitability highest, the workers are objectively condemned to fail. Brizé's film is suffocating to watch, Lordon notes, unless we recognise within it the space hollowed out for an absent oppositional discourse that would assert the possibility of changing the structures that render alternatives impossible. More positively present though and as signalled by the film's title, *En guerre* is an account of the violence of the current order that positions the physical violence committed by the workers as a response to the prolonged and extreme structural violence, the class war, to which they are exposed. The tragedy of the film's hero, Lordon explains, is that he tries to absorb the violence of the situation as he struggles to contain his comrades' growing anger. He comments that there is a general economy of individual and collective violence that reaches turning points at which either one responds outwardly to externally inflicted violence or one turns it inwardly against oneself, as the hero of *En guerre* does. Ironically, this self-elimination of the worker is exactly the kind of violence that neoliberalism implicitly encourages even as it condemns externally directed violence (Lordon 2018).

Lordon's discussion of different kinds of violence in *En guerre* could usefully be extended to *La Loi du marché*. In that earlier film, we also saw violences we might describe as structural or systemic being turned inwards onto the individual and condensed and amplified in the process. This vital question of the articulation of violences will be developed below. Suicides in both films were born of despair but in one, *En guerre*, the act was spectacular and clearly sent a message, whereas in the other, *La Loi du marché*, the act sent no message within the diegetic world and its potential public resonance was deliberately shut down by the company. These contrasts in public visibility will also require analysis. Given that one of the two films showed how collective action in individual companies was doomed to failure and the other showed an attempt at individual salvation that also ended in impasse, we will also need to ask whether these suicide-related films are condemned to what Wendy Brown calls left moralism, an attitude which she explains as the kind of 'moralizing against history' that arises in the absence of and as a substitute for a more properly political project and a sense of history as 'a productive or transformative force' (Brown 2001: 30). Let us look at the question of violence first.

## Subjective, symbolic and systemic violence

Žižek begins his *Violence: Six Sideways Reflections* by identifying the three categories of violence – the subjective, systemic and symbolic – whose definition and interaction the rest of his work will explore. The first category, subjective violence, occurs when the 'normal' order of things is disturbed by acts of crime, terror, civil unrest or international conflict committed by a clearly identifiable agent. Our habitual reaction to such disruption is to be fascinated and horrified by it because of its challenge to the pacifying liberal tolerance that is the dominant norm in modern, Western societies. In a manner unsurprising to those who know his work, Žižek invites us to question this initial, unthinking reaction. Subjective violence is simply the most visible of the three types of violence, and, if, drawn to its disruptiveness, we look at it too closely, we are blinded by it. Instead, as the title of his book indicates, we need to look at it 'sideways', locating it in the context of the two forms of objective violence, the systemic and the symbolic, which constitute the ground from which subjective violence arises and against which it is typically defined (Žižek 2008: 1–10).

If subjective violence is characterised by its scandalous capacity to disrupt the status quo, systemic violence is inscribed within the status quo itself and relates to 'the often catastrophic consequences of the smooth functioning of our economic and political systems' (Žižek 2008: 1). Not a purely modern phenomenon, systemic violence nevertheless shifts under capitalism as, driven by capital's relentless drive to expand, it takes on a more impersonal form. Money seeks to make more money and speculative bubbles rise and burst, seemingly detached from real-world circumstances. But this abstraction of money, profit and speculation is a *real abstraction* that underlies real-life developments, catastrophes and harms (Žižek 2008: 11–12). As alternatives to capitalism have receded in more recent times, it increasingly seems to be the natural, peaceful state of affairs, the normalised background against which disruptive forms of subjective violence are defined.

Symbolic violence, the third member of the triptych, relates particularly to language. Language is neither a neutral, intrinsically peaceful, communicative medium nor some secondary distortion that reflects or adds to 'real' acts of violence. It is instead 'the ultimate resort of every specifically human violence' (Žižek 2008: 57). Žižek explains this apparently counter-intuitive point by drawing on the example of anti-Semitic pogroms. What perpetrators of such acts find unbearable is not the real Jew in front of them, but the phantasmatic figure of the Jew circulating in their tradition. 'Reality itself in its stupid existence is never intolerable,' he comments, 'it is language, its symbolisation, which makes it such' (Žižek 2008: 57). Through its capacity to name things and to create their apparent essence, language exercises a primordial violence stitched into the taken-for-granted fabric of our world (Žižek 2008: 55).

It is because violence needs to be understood in terms of the interaction of its subjective, systemic and symbolic variants that we should not allow ourselves to be dazzled by the subjective alone. To the extent that we accept systemic and symbolic violences as the normal state of affairs, we will associate transgression with subjective violence alone and fail to perceive the much larger transgression that is intrinsic to the normal itself. As Žižek explains,

> when we perceive something as an act of violence, we measure it by a presupposed standard of what the 'normal' non-violent situation is – and the highest form of violence is the imposition of this standard with reference to which some events appear as 'violent'. (Žižek 2008: 55)

As he moves towards the end of his book, drawing on Walter Benjamin, Žižek brings a new category, divine violence, into his discussion. Despite its name, this is not a punitive intervention from an angry deity but something that arises spontaneously in the absence of a protective God, state or other higher instance which would ensure justice is done. It occurs, Žižek explains, 'when those outside the structured social field strike "blindly," demanding and enacting immediate justice / vengeance' (Žižek 2008: 171). Without any guarantees from above, neither based in the law nor seeking to enact a new legality, this violence has no overarching frame to bestow it with meaning. 'It is just the sign', Žižek comments, 'of the injustice of the world, of the world being ethically "out of joint"' (Žižek 2008: 169).

Žižek's general discussion of violence lends itself to two interlinked criticisms: one, that he over-extends the concept of violence and thus blurs different forms of domination; the other that, because of this very blurring, he effectively legitimises the excesses of insurrectional or revolutionary violence (van der Linden 2012). Indeed, rather than seeing the exercise of power as a form of violence, Hannah Arendt, the celebrated philosopher and political theorist, argued that power and violence should be kept analytically separate. Power, she suggested, relates to the collective influence of groups achieved through argument and negotiation. It is only when people withdraw their consent from the existing order that power is lost and violence must be deployed to keep them in line (Arendt 1970). In Žižek's defence, it should initially be noted that, in their different ways, Marxist, anarchist, feminist, anti-racist and anti-colonial thinkers have all pointed to the violence inherent in the apparently tranquil functioning of the status quo. This violence has been seen either as an implicitly threatened repressive response to any radical challenge, a weaker claim, or as intrinsic to the dominant order itself, a stronger claim of the kind made by Žižek himself. We might also note that, precisely because he extends the concept of violence beyond the physical, Žižek cannot simply be accused of being an apologist for physical violence. In any case, his tripartite typology of violences clearly has considerable analytical power because of how it allows localised acts to be connected in meaningful ways to broader contexts.

Because it is an apparently isolated act, a killing of the self by the self, suicide might seem to be an archetypally subjective form of violence. However, since the father of French sociology, Émile Durkheim, produced his classic *Le Suicide* (1897), a whole sociological tradition has sought to connect it to social structures and their evolution. Durkheim himself famously associated suicide with either the social anomie that left individuals excessively isolated or the social regulation that gave them too little space to breath. Inserting Durkheim into Žižek's tripartite framework, we might say that he laboured on the symbolic level to link the apparently subjective violence of suicide to the systemic violences that explained it. A not dissimilar articulation of violences can be found, as we will shortly see, in the Brizé films we have been examining. Before we do that, we need to discuss the theorisation of worker suicide more closely, initially calling again on Žižek but then turning to Cederström and Fleming.

## Working men dead and dead men working

In *The Fragile Absolute*, Žižek (2000) draws on the Lacanian division between the real, the imaginary and the symbolic to differentiate between three types of suicide. Suicide in the real, a violently impulsive *passage à l'acte*, occurs when a subject in denial of its own incompleteness identifies directly with the object of its desire, thus suppressing itself as a necessarily empty frame. Suicide in the imaginary occurs when the subject seeks to send a message about political, erotic and other disappointments to the Other. The subject derives a narcissistic satisfaction from the imagined effect that her or his death will have on those chosen as witnesses of the act. Suicide in the symbolic, the third variation, is not simply a symbolic self-elimination in the sense of not really dying but equates to a radical severing from the symbolic network that defines the subject's identity (Žižek 2000: 27–30).

Cederström and Fleming take this general framework and use it to develop a tripartite typology of worker suicides. To explain what suicide in the real might mean in this context, they take the example of the banker who ends his life when the economy slumps, thus conveying 'a complete identification with the market and the failing firm'. They note that this act 'signifies only itself' and explain that 'there is no distance between the suicide's identity and the failed object that has slowly become their life (work, the stock market, the bank account)' (Cederström and Fleming 2012: 65). Coming to suicide in the imaginary, they cite the suicides at France Télécom to which we have already referred and explain that, 'in this type of suicide the Other is addressed directly, usually with texts or methods of termination that are horrendously graphic' (Cederström and Fleming 2012: 65). They add, however, that such suicides need one to imagine one is present at one's own funeral and address 'an undeserving Other [i.e. the employer] who in the end doesn't even care' (Cederström and Fleming 2012: 66). Suicide in the symbolic is potentially more politically productive in that, although profoundly painful, it has a liberatory potential. Involving a rethinking of life 'from the perspective of death', it acknowledges that 'it is only by killing ourselves, as we know it [sic], that we could start anew'. Because we have internalised the norms of the corporation, 'it is not enough for us to kill the boss or set the corporation on fire [. . .] ultimately, we are the boss; we are the embodiment of the corporation. To kill ourselves, symbolically, is to kill the boss function' (Cederström and Fleming 2012: 66). Because we have built our sense of self around enslavement to capitalist labour, we must unlearn life, killing the worker-in-the-self, to open a genuinely emancipated future. Alternatively, retreating from such a painful process, we can surrender those parts of life not already colonised by capitalist labour and become dead men or women working.

Brizé's two films align productively with two of Cederström and Fleming's three kinds of worker suicide. When the older woman worker kills herself in *La Loi du marché*, she leaves no explanation. A purely impulsive gesture that sends no message, her act approximates most closely to suicide in the real. Unlike the banker who over-identifies with his job, however, she over-identifies with her own disposability as a subaltern worker. The film works to transform the suicide from one in the real to one in the imaginary: that is, it uses the suicide to send a message not so much to an Other who is not listening as to a cinema audience that hopefully is. By giving the suicide a back-story that firmly connects it to workplace surveillance and callous managerial practices and the cynical pursuit of profit, the film gives it an eloquence that it lacks in the diegetic world. It invites us to connect the suicide's subjective violence to the systemic violence that lies behind it and, in the process, to ponder the specific and more general symbolic violence that is being enacted. Specifically, the company management categorises a work-related suicide as a purely private tragedy. More generally, systemic violences and the suffering and humiliations they generate are relegated to the unspoken. The hero's taciturn character comes into play here. We know that he has sought to move on from a defeated collective struggle. It is as if, leaving that struggle behind, becoming isolated, he has also lost access to a shared oppositional language that would allow him to name the oppressions to which he is exposed. As a result, he either witnesses events without comment or uses, with a clear lack of relish, the instrumental language that the situation requires. The film signals his growing disquiet in its later stages not by any dialogue but by shots that focus first on his pensive stillness and then on his mute departure from the workplace. Because he is so overwhelmingly the central character and our point of identification, we are in turn invited to bear witness and reflect with him and to approve of his final refusal of complicity. By this use of gesture and bodily movement to speak of how resistances have been deprived of a voice and to oppose their silencing, the film plays its own part in symbolic struggles.

The suicide in *En guerre* corresponds closely to Cederström and Fleming's suicide in the imaginary. By killing himself so spectacularly in front of the head office of the company, the hero is very clearly sending a message at whose reception he will not be present. His gesture, as we saw, might appear to have some success in that it persuades the company to return to talks about compensation for the factory closure. But, beyond this brief and limited listening, we know the Other is indeed not listening as, in the way indicated by the film, and noted by Lordon, the radical imbalance of the forces in play is hard-wired into the status quo. Locating his suicide at the end of a long causal chain, the film's narrative structure works determinedly to connect the subjective violence of the suicide to the systemic violences inflicted upon the workforce. This focus on a deeper, underlying causality develops an implicit critique of news media reports of the sort that, in fictionalised form, are brought into the film for their non-engagement with the systemic and their framing of strikes and protests as disruptions to the status quo. More broadly, the way in which the workers in the film are told that their demands are 'unrealistic' speaks to a shutting down of the field of possibilities that is of great symbolic as well as systemic violence. In its own embodied symbolism, and even as the workers' collective voice is rendered inaudible, the closing suicide, an act of mutely eloquent protest, speaks loudly of this collective silencing.

The moment in *En guerre* when the strikers overturn the car of the CEO of the parent company equates to what Žižek calls divine violence. A blind striking out, it occurs in the face of the inability of any superior instance, in this case the French state, to guarantee justice. It is not part of any overarching struggle for worker emancipation and thus has no intrinsic meaning within the diegetic world. A sign, in Žižek's words, of the times being out of joint, it is partly redeemed for signification by being made to speak of the structural violence that precedes it.

Brizé's two films speak compellingly of the contemporary shutting down of political alternatives. If we were to take them as the two bifurcating halves of the same *Sliding Doors* (Howitt, 1998) style film with Vincent Lindon playing the same charismatically ordinary worker in each, we would note that neither is able to move to a positive outcome, one (*En guerre*) leaving us with a sense of indignation at the violences done to a group of workers and the other (*La Loi du marché*) ending with a satisfying refusal of complicity but no prospect of anything beyond it. The two films work effectively to make subjective violences speak of systemic and symbolic ones, but their inability to open up alternatives points at best to the crying need for them and, at worst, takes us towards the kind of left moralism analysed by Brown (2001) that gains satisfaction from a sense of righteousness even while implicitly accepting the shutting down of historical horizons.

## The death of the trader

Barratier's *L'Outsider* recreates, in the form of a thriller, the still disputed story of Jérôme Kerviel, the unknown stock-market trader who, in 2007 and 2008, made such large, risky, and hidden trades that he almost bankrupted the Société Générale, the major bank for which he worked. The film's pre-title sequence shows an anonymous figure being fired and escorted off the premises of the bank's Paris headquarters carrying only a laptop case and two of the cardboard boxes which we have come to associate with the downfall of financial high-flyers, especially in the aftermath of the financial crisis. The film carefully chooses to block our view of his face and shows us only the back or top of his head or his torso. He is all the more anonymous because he wears the standard, dark-coloured suit that is the stereotypical attire of the financial and business elite. After he exits the bank, he climbs to the roof of an abandoned multi-storey car park, ascends a pile of rubble and pauses to look up at the massive bank building before jumping off the roof. At this stage, we are witnessing something very close to Cederström and Fleming's suicide in the real, an over-identification to the point of self-annihilation with the firm or the job. The camera positioning, framing, costumes and props all deprive the trader of any more individualised identity. This sense of someone subsumed by his job is confirmed by the final shot of the sequence, the moment of the fatal leap, which is lined up in such a way as to locate the man's body entirely within the massive outline of the bank building (Figure 3.3). The thing from which he has been ejected is also that beyond which he has no existence. Because an inter-title then tells us that what we are about to see is happening eight years before the suicide, we assume it may be an anticipation of the hero's fate, something whose genesis the rest of the film will explain. However, even if we are not already aware that the real-life Kerviel is very much still alive, we learn about halfway through the film, after we move back from the initial flash forward, that it is not in fact Kerviel but someone who works on the next trading table to him who has jumped. On this, his second appearance, the victim, whose story is probably inspired by the suicide of another real-life Société Générale trader in 2007, is individualised by shots that bring his face into view, dialogue which names him and a funeral sequence in which his photograph is displayed on a coffin.

The traders are present as a dark-suited block at the funeral ceremony. As the service proceeds, all of their phones begin to ring. They rush out of the ceremony en masse and the film quickly cuts to their trading room as they try to deal with the emerging consequences of the 2008 stock-market collapse. The timing here is contrived, the film perhaps too obviously ramming home their callous disregard for the dead man despite their performance of respect. As in the other films discussed, the Other, in this case finance or the bank, is clearly not really listening nor accepting any responsibility for the death. Within the film's own economy, however, the suicide resonates, not least because of its narrative repetition. In its

**Figure 3.3** The trader subsumed by his job (*L'Outsider*, Christophe Barratier, 2016)

first iteration, the anonymised dead man stands in for all the other traders who risk killing, albeit more slowly, those parts of themselves superfluous to their job. In its second, more personalised iteration, with the mass departure of the besuited men, it underscores the disposability of the traders as individuals. Even if the hero avoids the suicide which we might think awaits him, he is similarly poised between subsumption by work and disposability if he fails to deliver the required rate of return.

Working out these possibilities over the course of the film, the hero progresses from being a naive new recruit to a hardened, high-performing trader, before his eventual fall from grace. A key early scene sees him lamenting what seems a large trading loss of 100,000 euros, the price that his own apartment is worth. A senior trader takes him to the window of the glass-and-steel tower block in which they work and shows him how, viewed from their Olympian height, anything on the ground can be caught in the tiny gap between a barely separated finger and thumb. He is thus invited to align his vision with the viewpoint of financial capital from which normal human concerns seem infinitely small. As he becomes subsumed into a culture of financial risk-taking and speculation, his affects are increasingly plugged into the movements of the market. Much of the action of the film takes place in the trading room with its array of clocks, each representing the time in a different global trading centre. The screens in front of the traders tie their attention to global market fluctuations. They thus exist in an accelerated and globalised space-time seemingly detached from the slower and more restricted spatio-temporality of life on the ground. In service to a market increasingly wedded to speculative gain rather than more traditional sources of profit, the traders' aggressive, risk-taking subjectivities are a personalised embodiment of the market's own impersonal characteristics. The hero's closing expulsion from the bank when the scale of the losses he has caused is discovered is a killing not of him as an embodied individual, as the film's opening might have led us to expect, but a symbolic elimination of that version of himself defined by his role as high-flying trader.

If all the films discussed in this chapter use the subjective violence of worker suicide to force systemic and symbolic violences into view, the focus in *L'Outsider* is largely limited to the effect of these violences on the individual traders on whom the story is centred and the truncation of their humanity, especially that of the central character, rather than on the very real consequences of the rise of finance and speculation for the broader economy and society. In many ways, the film is rather clichéd.

The vision of a high-octane trader sub-culture with a cynical disregard for anything other than money and a cult of macho risk-taking is one we find in other films set in the financial world, from *Wall Street* (Stone, 1987) through to *The Wolf of Wall Street* (Scorsese, 2013). The iconography, from the men's smart suits to the arrays of computer screens with stock indices to the ultramodern building looking down on the city, is also eminently familiar. This does not mean that the film can teach us nothing. As we might expect, given the research that went into the production, it is well informed about high-risk trading, its language and practices. But, like other films, it struggles to move beyond the localised individual consequences of systemic violences and leads us to a conclusion – the unhappiness and failure of the trader – that is moralistic rather than more radically political. The one time in the film, apart from the 2008 crash, when outside events really break through is after the 7 July 2005 London bomb attacks which cause a dip in share prices that saves the hero, who has been betting against a rising market, from a sizeable loss and probable dismissal. Rather than connecting external violences to the behaviour inside the bank, this sequence of events rather confirms the violent disconnection between inside and outside and the distorted value system of those within. It would seem that, once it moves beyond questions of individual morality, the film can only figure the articulation between systemic violences and events in the broader world as a radical disjuncture that finds its most condensed expression in the share prices that continue to scroll across the bottom of the trading room television screen as it shows images from the London attacks.

## The murderous violence of the corporation

Like *L'Outsider*, Silhol's *Corporate* feeds off familiar media stories and supplements them with academic and other analyses of work-related bullying and suicide, notably the Catala report on the France Télécom suicides and Christophe Dejours' influential study of workplace suffering (Châtelet 2017; Dejours 1998). In its first post-title sequence, we witness, through the glass side of her office, Émilie Tesson-Hansen (Céline Sallette), an ambitious human resources manager, as she persuades a woman employee from the company's accounts department that, given the constant flux of the world, she should embrace mobility and seek a transfer. Another employee from the same section, Didier Dalmat (Xavier de Guillebon) demands to know what the company wants from him. Like the woman employee, he is being pushed to make transfer requests which are turned down. Émilie blurts out that they want him to resign. Soon after, as she sits at her desk, a bang is heard. He has thrown himself from a window into the company courtyard, another spectacular workplace suicide (Figure 3.4). The company's reaction is to produce a statement attributing the act to personal reasons. Émilie suggests that they should instead attribute the suicide to 'personal events', a more specific and therefore more convincing explanation that she expands upon by explaining that Dalmat has recently split from his wife. She is tasked with managing the presentational crisis by Stéphane Froncart (Lambert Wilson), the charismatic but ruthless head of human resources. A countervailing account of the death is put forward by representatives of the workers at the meeting of the company's health and safety committee. They link the death to a change in management practice.

What follows is a struggle over the meaning of the act between management and a particularly determined labour inspector, Marie Borrel (Violaine Fumeau), who decides to investigate practices at the company. Encouraged by Froncart, Émilie's initial reaction is to remove evidence of the pressure placed by the company on employees like Dalmat. Later, as she learns that she might be held personally liable for the death and the company seems ready to sacrifice her to save itself, she starts to work with Marie to bring the company's practices to light. In her very telling initial interview with the latter, she explains the company's 'battle plan', which

**Figure 3.4** An inert body soon to become an object of symbolic struggle (*Corporate*, Nicolas Silhol, 2017)

was to push individuals to seek transfers and proceed to 'trench warfare', an attritional campaign that would persuade them to resign, the idea being to shed 10 per cent of the workforce without the need for redundancies. Émilie struggles to provide proof of this strategy but, when the company sacks her, she tricks Froncart into acknowledging his responsibility for it. Having recorded his unwitting confession, she has her personal assistant put it out over the company's intranet. As the film ends, accompanied by Marie, she goes to the police to be interviewed. She may still face prosecution but, as she notes, she has made it possible for people to speak up about oppressive management practices.

Largely conventional in its *mise-en-scène* and filming and broadly predictable in its narrative trajectory, the film is nonetheless interesting for its treatment of the suicide and its articulation of violences. The death, as we noted, is an object of symbolic struggle. When it occurs, it clearly aligns with Cederström and Fleming's suicide in the imaginary: that is, because it happens at the workplace during the working day, it sends a message to the unlistening Other. Seizing on the lack of a note, however, the company presents it as a purely personal act, a gesture signifying nothing beyond itself. Others work to restore public eloquence to the gesture and, in the process, to connect systemic and symbolic violences to the subjective violence of the suicide. Tellingly, Émilie describes the company's treatment of its workers as a form of war, her linguistic choices underscoring the film's self-conscious intervention at the symbolic level to connect visible violences to the hidden systemic ones that underlie them. The symbolic violences that the film foregrounds relate not simply to struggles over the meaning of worker suicide but to the culture of silence within companies that shuts down space for discussion of oppressive managerial practices, leaving individuals to deal with them alone. In this context, Émilie's struggle to 'liberate the word', as she puts it, and to drive management's disavowed practices into the public domain, are emblematic of the film's broader attempt to enable public discussion of hitherto silenced experiences. Reflecting on the debates in which he took part after screenings around the country, the director commented, 'it's as if the liberation of the word that happens in the film spilled out into the auditorium . . . it was good to make this film because it liberates the word and encourages people to share experiences' (Immelen 2017, my translation).

Like *L'Outsider* and the other films discussed here, *Corporate* evidences a faith in cinema's capacity to transform the borders of the visible and sayable. Like the other films, although it demonstrates clear awareness that the issues it raises are structural, it works above all at the level of the individual. The satisfaction we are offered at the end is to witness the moral redemption of the heroine as she sacrifices her career and the triumph of her alliance with the labour inspector over the ruthless manager. This humanistic faith is accompanied by a perhaps nostalgic trust in the ordinary agents of the French Republic, in this case the labour inspector, to limit the excesses of neoliberal capitalism rather than challenge the foundations of its power.

## The Dardennes' ethical exits

The Dardennes' films may be better placed to find an exit from the violences of neoliberal labour. Avoiding the left moralism of the Brizé films and the conventionally humanist approach of films like *Corporate* and *L'Outsider*, they seek new and rigorously ethical grounds on which to build a non-violent approach to the Other. As we saw when we looked at *Le Silence de Lorna*, their films confront the brutality of the contemporary order with single-minded intensity. Their characters find themselves faced with a context in which productive places are rationed, people are expendable, and all are pitted against all. Murder haunts them in one form or another. Suicide often accompanies it, notably when socio-economic violence is turned inwards rather than directed outwards or when a character refuses to participate in the ambient violence and risks becoming its target. It is latently present in *Le Silence de Lorna*. When Lorna decides to break with Fabio's murderous gang, she not only effectively kills the ruthlessly calculating Lorna we have seen for much of the film, but also potentially signs her death warrant in a more obviously physical way, as if suicides, even by the same person, did not always come singly. Suicide is more explicitly present in two of the other Dardenne brothers' works, *Rosetta* (1999) and *Deux jours, une nuit* (*Two Days, One Night*, 2014) to which we will now turn.

The eponymous central character of *Rosetta* (Émilie Dequenne) is relegated to the social edges in a way made manifest by the caravan site where she lives with her alcoholic mother. Like a warrior, she lays siege to the inclusion that comes with salaried labour. When the film opens, and in typical Dardennes style, the handheld camera seems to be struggling to keep up with her as she hurtles down a corridor to confront the person she blames for her sacking. She is unceremoniously told that, as the last one in, she will be first out. She lays siege to another job, this time making waffles, but is only hired when someone else, a woman who has been late because of a sick child, is fired. When the owner of the business sacks her in turn to hire his son, she is on the outside again. Riquet (Fabrizio Rongione), who operates the waffle stand, befriends her. When he falls into the pond where she fishes illicitly on her caravan site, she pauses agonisingly before helping him out, the murderous temptation to let him drown and take his job playing out over her gestures and movements. Murders also coming in pairs, she finds a less physical way to eliminate him by denouncing him for selling his own waffles from the stand. His sacking frees a job up for her. He pursues her to confront her with what she has done to another person not as an abstract idea but as an embodied presence. She cracks and resigns, effectively erasing her social existence, given its dependence on employment. She then moves towards a more physical self-elimination as, with her mother passed out on her bed, she turns on the gas in the caravan. In what is a typical Dardennes reprieve, the gas runs out and, while she struggles back towards the caravan with another canister, Riquet arrives again. Rosetta, the warrior, finally breaks down, cries and accepts help. The film thus ends in neither murder nor suicide but in an ethical recognition of mutual exposure and vulnerability.

Like *Rosetta*, *Deux jours, une nuit* follows a driven woman, but the dynamics are different. It has a greater social density. Sandra (Marion Cotillard), the heroine, is not isolated but has support from her husband and a friend. While Rosetta fights for an isolated toehold in society, Sandra is part of a small workplace from which she faces exclusion. More obviously vulnerable than Rosetta, she has been off work with depression. Having decided that it can maintain productivity levels without her, management has offered her fellow workers the choice between retaining her and a bonus of one thousand euros. Pressured by an unscrupulous foreman, the workers have voted for their bonuses. Sandra persuades the boss to rerun the ballot and, when he agrees, visits each co-worker in turn, trying to persuade them to change their mind. A father and son, both co-workers, come to blows when one decides to support her and the other doesn't. A woman splits from her partner because he wants her to vote for the bonus and not Sandra. As always with the Dardennes, the systemic and symbolic violences implicit in human disposability and the preference for the thing over the person are driven to the surface as they play out in the embodied interactions between people. This is one essential part of the films' own symbolic labour. Another equally vital part is the way in which they seek to open an alternative where none seems to exist. As Sandra circulates, and in what is a virtuoso set of variations on essentially the same face-to-face encounter, she forces people to confront the effects of their actions, not on an abstract other, but on another human being exposed to them in their vulnerability. At the same time, she asks them, as they ask her, to see the world not from their own point of view but from the position of the Other, the often repeated 'mettez-vous à ma place' ('put yourself in my shoes') being a beautifully condensed ethical challenge to a world centred on the self and something I return to in Chapter 5.

Midway through the film, discouraged by some failed attempts to convince people, Sandra takes an overdose (Figure 3.5). She is saved when her friend arrives with good news about another colleague supporting her and goes to hospital to be treated. She returns to her labour of convincing her colleagues. As the film moves towards its conclusion, the ballot is rerun. The workers split evenly. The boss offers to keep her and shed another worker, a migrant on a temporary contract. Sandra refuses to accept this and walks away, a smile on her face as the film ends.

The film has a far more upbeat conclusion than *Rosetta*. Where the two works converge, however, is in the interplay of murder and suicide that they enact. Both point to how, in an economy of ruthless competition and rationed places, people seem faced with the choice between eliminating

**Figure 3.5** The worker's over-identification with her disposability (*Deux jours, une nuit*, Jean-Pierre and Luc Dardenne, 2014)

others (murder) or refusing to kill, literally or metaphorically, but accepting their own superfluity (suicide). They also converge in the way they seek to break out of this lethal alternative by providing an ethical opening based in a refusal to eliminate the Other. The suicide attempts initially tend towards suicide in the real whereby, sending no message, Rosetta and Sandra over-identify with their expendability. When they withdraw from workplaces, they move towards a suicide in the symbolic: that is, they begin to cut the symbolic ties that define them above all as workers. Yet, occurring as the films conclude, this symbolic suicide remains frustratingly undeveloped. There is no attempt, not least because of the films' deliberate refusal to probe their characters' interiority, to work through either all that ties the characters to capitalist labour or what a more fully developed exit might look like. Similarly, although *Deux jours, une nuit* painstakingly works to rebuild a vision of social connectivity by assembling ethical face-to-face encounters, it refuses to move beyond an individual ethics to engage with new forms that a collective action able to challenge systemic wrongs might take. It is perhaps significant that, like *La Loi du marché*, it ends with someone walking away from the workplace. It is as if it has come to the same limit imposed by the search for some form of individual solution to systemic ills and had to freeze at the moment beyond which it was unable to go.

## Finally, the exit? Kervern and Delépine's anarchic departures

The anarchic and sometimes dark comedies of Kervern and Delépine might not seem the obvious place to look for films that seriously engage with exit from the neoliberal workplace. Escape and eviction from labour has nonetheless been at the heart of their filmmaking project. *Mammuth* (2010), for example, recounts how, in order to collect a pension, a worker has to travel round France to assemble documentary proof of the ten or so different jobs he's had over the course of his career. *Louise-Michel* (2008) figures a group of workers who are made redundant and decide to use their pay-off to hire a hitman to kill the boss, only to find that, under neoliberal capitalism, identifying who exactly the boss is can be a major challenge. The more recent *I Feel Good* (2018) focuses on a sister and brother, the former who runs a charitable Emmaüs centre that accommodates the homeless and gives them work cultivating the land and restoring second-hand furniture, the latter who is convinced that poor people are too ugly to succeed and that selling them budget cosmetic surgery will both turn their lives around and make him rich. Across the films more broadly, we find bodies, ages, attitudes and chaotic or meandering trajectories that are counter-models to neoliberal definitions of success and the calculated career portfolios, disciplined ambition and well-groomed self-presentation that typically accompany them.

The pattern is continued in *Near Death Experience* (2014). Paul, the protagonist, played by celebrated author Michel Houellebecq, is a fifty-six-year-old call centre worker for France Télécom, an enterprise at the heart of one of France's most notorious workplace suicide waves (Waters 2020: 139–69). For most of the film's length, he wanders around on the slopes of Mont Saint-Victoire, his scrawniness accentuated by his cyclist's lycra, delivering a long monologue, as he tries to pluck up the courage to kill himself. It is not so much that he hates his job, we learn, it is that, in a society where the desired norm is to have and surpass goals, dress like a young person, be virile, sporty and creative, he no longer fits. Ageing men once waited quietly for retirement. Now, they have become obsolete. As the film concludes and we think he won't finally kill himself, he is picked up by a young woman in her car who talks to him patronisingly. He opens the door and throws himself, presumably to his death, from the moving vehicle in a radical identification with his own superfluity.

*Le Grand Soir* (2012), the other part of Kervern and Delépine's worker-suicide diptych, is more upbeat. It centres on two middle-aged brothers, the self-styled Not, a punk, and the more conventional Jean-Pierre. Not's name, which is tattooed on his forehead, is a proclamation of refusal, a self-engineered symbolic suicide. He loiters in a shopping centre on the edge of town, begging aggressively, trolley-surfing, showering naked in a fountain by a busy road and sleeping in a Wendy House in the children's play area. With his Mohican haircut, his mongrel dog, his loud, non-conformist behaviour, and lack of goals, he screams unemployability. His brother, in contrast, is an unhappy conformist who is beginning to unravel. He dresses in a suit and has a conventional haircut. He is separated from his wife and struggles to do his share of the childcare and his work selling mattresses in the shopping centre where his brother hangs out. His behaviour reaches a frantic pitch when his boss tells him that, in the context of the crisis, not everyone will keep their job and he is not meeting his targets. He is sacked after he is caught on CCTV bouncing manically on mattresses. He goes to the hypermarket in the shopping centre, pours petrol over his head, and sets light to himself while screaming for justice. None of the shoppers pay any attention and, when the sprinkler system is triggered, he is left singed but alive. With its spectacular self-staging, the gesture clearly equates to an attempted suicide in the imaginary. But no-one is listening. The gesture is a damp squib. What follows is more productive. He is taken in hand by Not who converts him into a punk. His initiation begins when Not shaves the sides of his head and tattoos 'dead' on his forehead. This is a symbolic death rather than a physical one. When the brothers stand side-by-side, the message across their foreheads reads 'not dead', an affirmation of living in negation, of another life not yet found (Figure 3.6). Not removes his brother's tie, his leash, teaches him to walk upright, open himself to the world and enjoy aimless wandering.

We can use Foucault's discussion of parrhesia (2011) to make sense of Not's behaviour. Foucault distinguishes between parrhesia and other forms of truth-telling such as wisdom or teaching. Wisdom is withdrawn and restrained. Teaching transmits acquired knowledge about the world in an institutional frame. In contrast, parrhesia is an ethical commitment to truth that exposes its practitioner to danger. For Foucault, it was most fully developed in the Greek Cynics and cynical thinkers such as Diogenes. The Cynics served as scouts for the rest of society, seeking out the contours not of an otherworldly life, but of another life in this world (Foucault 2011: 159–67, 244–5). Because of this, they had to travel light,

Figure 3.6 Not Dead: living in negation (*Le Grand Soir*, Gustave Kervern and Benoît Delépine, 2012)

detaching themselves from family or country, stripping away obstacles to clear-sightedness. They taught a disruptive truth not merely by proclaiming it, but by bearing witness to it in their appearance and behaviour, deliberately challenging convention (Foucault 2011: 170–4). This scandalous transgression exposed Cynics like Diogenes to comparison to animals, notably dogs, an insult that Diogenes welcomed as an indication of his indifference to human respect (Foucault 2011: 242–3).

The obvious resemblances between Not and the Cynics, including his affinity with his canine companion, are unsurprising given the filmmakers' desire to create a contemporary Diogenes (Delépine and Kervern 2012: 192). A scandalous Cynic teacher, Not does not simply teach his brother about another life, he embodies it scandalously for him and others. Showing him how to live another life in this life, he teaches him that he can kill his existing self, cutting the symbolic ties that bind him to the existing order, without dying. Yet Not is also aware of the limits of the transformative labour they are undertaking. As the film nears its conclusion, he goes to the hypermarket and, grabbing the public address microphone, calls upon the shoppers to rise up, explaining how hard it is for him to carry the fight on alone. He and his brother summon people to a revolutionary gathering in a disused car park, but no-one comes. This is the point of the film's title, *Le Grand Soir*, with its evocation of the naive popular mythology of the great uprising that would transform the world. Without some such revolutionary event or process, the political effectiveness of the Cynic's rejection of existing life is inevitably limited. As Foucault put it,

> the Cynic addresses all men. He [sic] shows all men that they are leading a life other than the one they should be leading. And thereby it is a whole other world which has to emerge, or at any rate be on the horizon, be the objective of this Cynic practice. (Foucault 2011: 315)

This is what makes *Le Grand Soir* such an interesting film politically. Despite its comic generic identity, it shows an acute awareness of the gap between ethical work on the self, an ethical commitment to teach the Other, and a more general transformation of life. It is also acutely conscious of the difficulty of sustaining work on the self in a hostile context. In this, it moves beyond what the other films discussed do.

## Conclusion

In his *Heroes*, Franco 'Bifo' Berardi suggests that the suicide waves and mass killing sprees seen in various countries are not simply isolated occurrences (subjective violences in Žižekian terms) but are privileged vantage points from which to consider the pathologies of financial capitalism and the violent identitarian reactions that it unleashes (Berardi 2015: 2–3). Along similar lines, I have argued here that worker-suicide films are not a mere subset of workplace cinema but offer important insights into the current moment and the kinds of stories we can tell ourselves about it. When I wrote *The New Face of Political Cinema*, one of the essential trends I noted was how, across a broad range of films, in the absence of a collectively articulated and institutionally grounded voice of leftist critique and in a situation where the violences of neoliberalism impacted in increasingly direct form on individuals, the struggling body had become a key locus of expression, able to speak silently of harms done to it and of refusals without words (O'Shaughnessy 2007: 139–40). The films discussed here do not necessarily privilege the body, although some do, notably those of the Dardenne brothers, but in their determination to use the subjective violence of worker suicide to bring out the underlying violences of an apparently peaceful status quo, they share some of the same thrust. In Chapter 2, we noted a coming-into-crisis of neoliberal subjectivity as the entrepreneurial subject mutated into the indebted one. Here, we have seen the radicalisation of this crisis and the foreclosure of the future that accompanied it as characters, and not simply proletarian ones, are increasingly confronted with their disposability but struggle to open any meaningful way forward. Capturing the oppressiveness of the current order and the removal or weakening of protective instances (unions, the Republican state) that mediate between individuals and structural violence, the films are increasingly haunted by variations of murder and suicide: murder as direct violence, complicity in the other's elimination or, more indirectly, preference for the thing over the person; suicide as self-erasing identification with increasingly toxic labour, over-identification with one's disposability or refusal of work in a world where it is a precondition of social existence.

Clear-sighted enough in their ability to connect subjective violences to the systemic and symbolic violences that condition them, the films have highlighted the difficulty that most mainstream cinema has in looking beyond individualising and moralising solutions to problems. A clear symptom of this is the way in which a number of them (*La Loi du marché, Corporate, Deux jours, une nuit* and *Rosetta*) end as characters walk away, their exits dispensing them and us from working through all that ties us to neoliberal labour and the pain and difficulty that any killing of the worker in the self entails. *Le Grand Soir* is more clear-sighted in this respect. Despite its comedic nature, it recognises both the demanding work on the self that exit requires and the impossibility of any durable individual exit in the absence of a broader collective project to remake society. Yet, even when they fail to provide an exit route, those other films highlight the need for one and reveal the depth of the crisis that increasingly haunts the neoliberal subject.

# 4

# The deconstructive materialism of Sciamma and Kechiche

Two of the most prominent contemporary French filmmakers are Céline Sciamma, director of the universally admired *Portrait de la jeune fille en feu* (*Portrait of a Lady on Fire*) (2019), and Abdellatif Kechiche, director of Cannes Palme d'Or winner *La Vie d'Adèle* (*Blue is the Warmest Colour*) (2013). In some ways, the two filmmakers are diametrically opposed. Sciamma's films typically feature girls and young women as they explore their gender identity and sexuality. They could be seen as systematic attempts to institute a female and often lesbian gaze. Kechiche's films give prominent roles to young women but could be cited as examples of an increasingly problematic male gaze. Yet, there are points of convergence between the two directors that are of particular interest to the current study with its focus on cinema's capacity to detect possibilities stirring in even the most hostile contexts. Put simply, both directors film characters who are driven to remake themselves, even though the social, economic or institutional contexts, or their own acquired dispositions, work to impede them. By so doing, they achieve two important and interconnected things. Firstly, they suggest that, beneath the apparent permanence of the socio-economic or institutional order, there is an instability constantly bubbling under, bodies whose capacities remain to be found and identities ripe for remaking or deconstructing. Secondly, through an attention to the very real constraints that limit these protean possibilities, they confront obstacles and refuse a politics based on the empty celebration of becoming. I use the term 'materialist deconstruction' to encapsulate this combination of qualities, its deconstructive component pointing to the films' refusal of fixity and essentialism, its materialist one underlining their attention to desiring bodies and the contexts that constrain them.

I will begin with an account of the chapter's theoretical grounding, drawing especially on a remarkable late essay by Louis Althusser, 'The underground current of the materialism of the encounter', and discussion of it by Catherine Malabou, the important contemporary thinker of 'plasticity', a concept which, in its mutable materiality, combines insights from materialism and deconstruction. I will then turn to the films. In Kechiche's case, I focus on three works, *La Graine et le mulet* (*Couscous*) (2007), *Vénus Noire* (*Black Venus*) (2010) and *La Vie d'Adèle*, that speak particularly eloquently to the concerns of this chapter. I will examine Sciamma's first four feature films, *Naissance des pieuvres* (*Water Lilies*) (2007), *Tomboy* (2011), *Bande de filles* (*Girlhood*) (2014) and *Portrait de la jeune fille en feu*. I will be particularly attentive to the contrasting ways in which the two directors confront the desiring, mutable body with limits to its becoming. But I will also discuss the films' reflexive engagement with the politics of the image and their blind spots. In Kechiche's case, the latter relate primarily to gendered power dynamics. In Sciamma's case, they are rooted in a neglect of class and, in the case of *Bande de filles*, a failure to probe stereotypes derived from a long history of racialised representation. These blind spots, if we accept them as such, will remind us of the importance, in any materialist analysis, of engaging with cinema's own production processes and contexts.

When I discussed Audiard in my first chapter, I noted how his films repeatedly figured characters remaking themselves to thrive in viciously competitive contexts. I suggested that, despite this mutability, the films were broadly conservative, the characters' flexibility, challenge to gendered norms and ability to form alliances making them ideal neoliberal subjects. If I am to argue that there is more political promise in the films discussed in this chapter, I will need to show how their deconstruction of established identities is not simply another version of the flexibility required of the neoliberal subject. I will come to this later.

## The materialism of the encounter

Louis Althusser had a profound influence on film and cultural studies with his accounts of ideology, interpellation and the subject being particularly important to the two disciplines. While this part of his work, with its pretention to scientific rigour, now seems dated, his late essay on the materialism of the encounter remains influential for important contemporary thinkers like Malabou, Rosi Braidotti (Dolphijn and van der Tuin 2012: 20–1) and others.

Althusser traces what he sees as an '*almost completely unknown materialist tradition in the history of philosophy: the 'materialism' ... of the rain, the swerve, the encounter, the take*' (Althusser 2006: 167 (emphasis in the original)), which goes from Epicurus, through Spinoza, Machiavelli, Hobbes, Darwin, Rousseau and some but not all of Marx, to Deleuze and Derrida. He opposes this non-teleological materialist tradition to another tradition, also including Marx, which, although materialist in name or intention, is 'a disguised form of idealism' (Althusser 2006: 168). He explains why Marx finds himself on both sides of the divide by discussing the contrasting accounts he gives of the emergence of the industrial proletariat, one more truly materialist, the other latently idealist. In the former, there is an encounter which takes hold between the owners of money and the proletarians expelled from the land and stripped of everything. The whole, the forms associated with it and its conceptualisation do not precede the encounter but follow it as its consequences. In the latter, the latently idealist, teleological account, the proletariat is produced by the industrial mode of production, with the structure preceding its elements. This, Althusser notes, is an account of the reproduction of a class, not its initial emergence. It grants explanatory priority to the conceptualised forms of a mode of production deemed historically necessary over the contingent encounters that preceded their taking hold (Althusser 2006: 197–202). He comments,

> *the specific histories no longer float in history*, like so many atoms in the void, at the mercy of an 'encounter' that might not take place. Everything is accomplished in advance; *the structure precedes its elements and reproduces them in order to reproduce the structure.* (Althusser 2006: 200 (emphasis in the original))

Althusser's critique can be applied more generally to other idealisms masquerading as materialism when they grant explanatory priority to necessity and to established forms and their conceptualisation. A genuinely materialist materialism starts from contingency and recognises that encounters precede the establishment of the forms to which they give rise with their associated properties. Crucially, they are always provisional. The reality of the accomplished fact, a form that endures following an encounter, is no guarantee of its permanence. There are no eternal laws outside of the flow of history (Althusser 2006: 173–4). Disorder therefore has priority with respect to order. Similarly, dissemination, the dispersal of meaning, has primacy over fixed meanings in a way which explains the later Althusser's perhaps surprising openness to Derrida's work (Althusser 2006: 189–90).

Malabou's debt to Derrida, her doctoral supervisor, is well known. Given her sustained exploration of plasticity (the mutability, 'explodability' and resistance of forms), the appeal of the later Althusser is also unsurprising. Commenting on his reference to Darwin, she notes that natural selection is ateleological and relies on the permanent selection and crystallisation of variations, with the latter, in their contingency assuming necessary explanatory primacy. She asks why social selection gives the feeling of being 'an expected or agreed-upon process, a simple logic of conformity and reproduction' (Malabou 2015: 52). She goes on to inquire, 'Can we not envision, in spite of everything, a plasticity of social condition and recover the wealth of variations and deviations of structure at the heart of culture?' (Malabou 2015: 53). She quotes Althusser's discussion of Machiavelli's Prince to underscore her more general point. The Prince emerges as, 'a man of nothing . . . starting out of an unassignable space,' one 'without qualities, without privilege, without legacies, without tradition'. She adds, '[f]rom there [this unassignable space] and there only can new forms emerge – singular, unseen, regenerating' (Malabou 2015: 57). She concludes: 'opening the unassignable place in a global world, where every place is assigned, has become the most urgent ethical and political task' (Malabou 2015: 58). In an interview that closes the same volume she declares her conviction of the usefulness of Marx's work providing it is balanced by recourse to a Heideggerian *Destruktion* and Derridean deconstruction that would probe the unanalysed, idealist concepts at its heart and the 'messianic' teleological horizon within which it positioned itself. Summing up, she comments that there should be no deconstruction without materialism nor Marxism without deconstruction (Bhandar and Goldberg-Hiller 2015: 288–9).

Althusser's essay and Malabou's response to it inform my analysis in this chapter. In their attention to the embodied subject's mutability and the material constraints upon it, the films of Kechiche and Sciamma resonate with a deconstructive materialism or materialism of the encounter.

The notion of the encounter speaks productively to meetings with situations or desired others within the films which prove *unpredictably* transformative and open a future not already contained in the present. The sense too that, because of material circumstances, not all encounters endure provides a way to make sense of the failures depicted. This contingency suggests how, without any empty celebration of becoming and in the absence of any grand narrative of transformation, we can identify what is politically hopeful in the films. By opening 'unassignable spaces' in which new forms could emerge, they reveal the provisional nature of existing arrangements and keep open the possibility of the new even where it seems precluded.

## Kechiche's vitalist materialism: *La Graine et le mulet*

In the space of a few years, Kechiche went from being one of France's most admired directors to one of its most controversial ones. He won the Golden Lion for best first work at the Venice Festival in 2000 for *La Faute à Voltaire* (*Poetical Refugee*, 2000). His next film, *L'Esquive* (*Games of Love and Chance*, 2003), and his *La Graine et le mulet* (*Couscous*, 2007) won no fewer than four Césars. *Cahiers du Cinéma* ranked the latter film in their top ten for the decade 2000–2010. The awards continued when his lesbian love story *La Vie d'Adèle* (*Blue is the Warmest Colour*, 2013) won the prestigious Palme d'Or at Cannes, an award exceptionally split between him and his two leads, Adèle Exarchopoulos and Léa Seydoux, in recognition of their outstanding contribution. The award, and Kechiche's reputation, were tarnished, however, when technicians launched a public complaint about working conditions on the film, the two stars commented on the director's exploitative practices and critics decried the film's quasi-pornographic treatment of women's bodies. Some of the same issues came back with a vengeance on the release of his *Mektoub, My Love: Intermezzo* (2019) which triggered walkouts at Cannes and loud complaints about the treatment of at least one of the female performers. These are issues to which we will return. We will begin, however, with *La Graine et le mulet*, a more universally admired work.

The film's lead, Slimane Beiji (Habib Boufares), is the father and grandfather of an extended multi-ethnic family living in the French Mediterranean port of Sète. His new partner, Latifa (Hatika Karaoui), runs the portside Hôtel de l'Orient helped by her daughter, Rym

(Hafsia Herzi). Slimane lodges there alongside a group of older Maghrebi-French men who get together to play North African music. Although married to Julia (Alice Houri), a young Russian immigrant, Slimane's elder son, Majid (Sami Zitouni), is having an affair with Mme Dorner (Violaine de Carné), the wife of the deputy mayor. He works as a guide on one of the port's pleasure boats. One of Slimane's daughters, Karima (Farida Benkhetache), is employed in a local cannery. Slimane himself works in a boatyard, alongside Jose, his son-in-law. Mario (Bruno Lochet), the husband of Lilia (Leila Dissernio), a close family friend or relative, is a fisherman who lands the *mulet* (mullet) of the film's title. This extended family, the rivalries, infidelities and sociability within it, and the mutual support it provides, are central to what follows.

We first encounter Slimane repairing an old boat. His ageing boss is castigating him for not keeping to the schedule. He is tired, no longer profitable, and needs to be flexible if he wants to stay on. Suspecting the boss wants to push him out, he evokes his thirty-five years of work. But, responds the boss, many of those years were for a previous employer and, as an immigrant worker, he was undeclared and did not accrue pensionable years. In his daughter's home, Jose, his son-in-law, tells him that employers don't want French workers like them anymore because migrants are cheaper to employ. Karima, his daughter, commandeers the conversation. Her bosses at the cannery have sought to take away their bonuses on the pretext that they have lost American markets. The workers have mobilised immediately, forcing a management retreat. Jose is more resigned: work is moving overseas; he has no permanent contract; soon tourism is all that will remain. Karima retorts that he needs to show more fight. Kechiche, as is his wont, captures her energy using long takes and tight close-ups. She stands while the two men are seated. The difference between her viewpoint and theirs is not simply to do with the words uttered, but also the forceful way in which they are spoken and the pugnacious bodily attitude that accompanies them. It would seem that, an ageing worker, Slimane may be not simply too old and inflexible for the neoliberal workplace, but too tired to fight back.

Prolonging this focus on the tired male body, we cut to his arrival at Latifa's hotel. There is an energy in the bar as the musicians play North African music and a blond belly dancer gyrates, watched by Rym and men in the room. Successive shots take in the dancer's behind, breasts and belly. Customers move with the music. Slimane, shoulders hunched, does not respond to the ambient energy. A sharp cut takes us to Latifa's bedroom and a close-up of his face as, gasping for air, he wipes his brow and coughs. Latifa lies back on the bed behind him. He has been unable to perform. Suggesting an exhaustion of energy and desire, the film uses failed sex to communicate the broader crisis of the older, male worker (Figure 4.1).

Matching the energy of Karima, Rym takes up the slack, her vitality conveyed by the same verbal eloquence and energy and her appetite for food. The camera observes, in typically tight close-up and at length, the sensuous gusto with which she consumes couscous, chews noisily and licks her lips, watched with obvious fascination by Slimane's younger son, Riadh (Mohamed Benabdeslem). Slimane's sons suggest that, now he is being made redundant, he should return to the *bled* (homeland). Unwilling to abandon his breadwinner role, he decides to restore an old boat and turn it into a restaurant. Mutating from hotel worker to aspiring entrepreneur, he is helped by Rym to seek a bank loan and the permissions he needs to moor the boat and run a restaurant. She arrives for the related appointments wearing tracksuit bottoms but pulls them down to reveal the lower half of her smart business suit underneath. Costume changes accompanying shifting roles; Slimane presents himself in a suit instead of his worker's overalls but lacks the dynamism required. Rym sells their business case with her usual energy.

When the administrative procedures get bogged down and Slimane cannot moor his boat in the prime location on the Quai de la République,

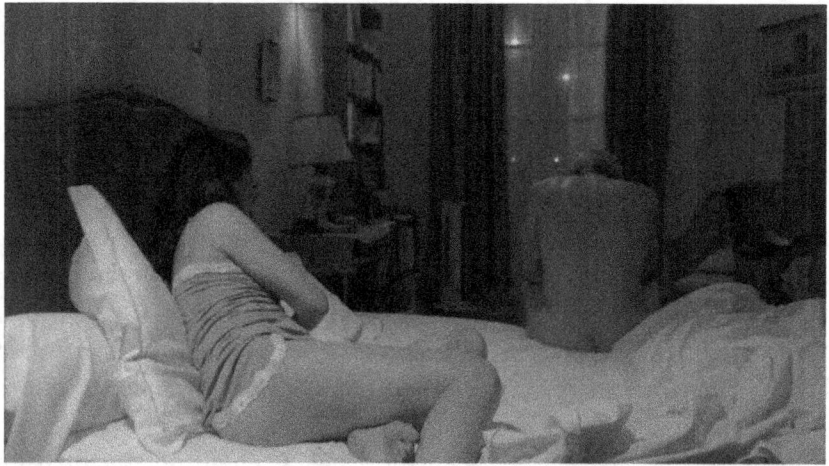

**Figure 4.1** The crisis of the older worker and the failure of desire (*La Graine et le mulet*, Abdellatif Kechiche, 2007)

he perseveres and arranges a grand opening to which he invites the different people whose permission or financial support he needs. His ex-wife cooks the food while his children act as kitchen assistants and waiters. The old musicians from the hotel provide the entertainment. All goes wrong, however, when the unreliable Majid takes off in his car with the couscous still in the boot. Slimane goes in search of him but his moped is stolen by three Maghrebi-French teenagers who, by driving around near him, make him run in pursuit. Now wearing a bright-red two-piece costume, Rym performs a belly dance to distract the hungry guests. For what seems an interminable period, the film intercuts between shots of her gyrating body – some in tight close-up, as it glistens with sweat – and Slimane's panting, exhausted body, until the latter finally falls over and lies still.

There are a number of things to unpick here. We might begin by noting how, until Slimane's final collapse, he and Rym repeatedly remake themselves but not in conditions of their choosing. Rym mutates from hotel worker to businesswoman to belly dancer, changing costume, gestures and appearance in each case. Slimane has more numerous avatars, some evoked in the film's back-story. He has been an undeclared immigrant worker, becomes a legal worker with pension rights, then one of a growing number of disposable French workers, before being thrown back on his immigrant status, but remaking himself as a restaurateur, hoping to marketise a version of his cultural identity, a process of self-commodification also expressed in Rym's belly dancing and the provision of 'ethnic' music. Far from indulging in an essentialising identity politics, the film frames identities as contingent productions arising in specific material contexts and with no guarantee of durability.

Although the film refuses to define Slimane by his origins, it foregrounds how racist attitudes and structures shape his trajectory. We know he has been denied rights accorded to other workers. We witness the patronising attitude of the authorities towards him and reluctance to allow him to moor his boat on the symbolically named Quai de la République, an attitude that suggests that France still hesitates to include its immigrant populations in its self-definition. One official repeatedly insists on the strictness of *French* hygiene regulations, as if Slimane, as part of a somehow unintegrated minority, were likely to open a dirty kitchen.

The film acknowledges this racism and the material obstacles it erects but refuses to counter it simply by presenting a positive image of Slimane as ethnic minority representative. Instead, it opens his history onto the broader history of the French working class. French cinema often uses the figure of the older male, broken or in crisis, to emblematise the decline of traditional industries and the stable, Fordist employment they provided. We might think of figures like the hero's father (Jean-Claude Vallod) in Cantet's *Ressources humaines* (*Human Resources*, 1999) or the protagonists of Brizé's *La Loi du marché* or *En guerre*, both played by Vincent Lindon. But because Kechiche figures his lead as an immigrant *and* a French worker, refusing to enclose him in any narrowly defined identity, he shows the mutual imbrication of the histories of the working class and immigration, setting both in motion in the process. Similarly, Slimane's extended family refuses any communitarian self-enclosure. With sons-in-law called Mario and Jose and a Russian daughter-in-law, the family's identity is defined more by class than ethnicity. The couscous cooked by Souad evokes a North African heritage but brings everyone together in a material communion that transcends ethnic belonging.

It could be argued that there is some resemblance between Slimane's extended family and Audiard's flexible, non-biological and entrepreneurial families. After all, Slimane's family, including Rym and, eventually, Latifa, rally round the restaurant business. But there is an openness, generosity and multi-ethnic solidarity around Slimane, his family and friends (the musicians who gift their labour, Souad's giving away of food) that is not matched in Audiard and which gestures towards something different to and in excess of the capitalist economy. Besides, and this is something we will return to, Slimane ultimately fails.

The originality of Kechiche's cinema is intrinsically connected to its vitalism, its aspiration to capture the energy generated by characters as they eat, socialise or engage in creative or sexual activity. As *Cahiers du Cinéma* critic Stéphane Delorme notes, Kechiche does not share mainstream cinema's concern with the psychological development of characters. He seeks to capture, in their detail and duration, the experience and energy of the characters. This explains why scenes often last much longer than required for efficient storytelling in a way enabled by digital cameras and the extended periods of continuous filming that they allow. It also helps explain why Kechiche will often film scenes an astonishing number of times until he has captured the life that he is determined to record, even to the point of exhaustion (Delorme 2007: 11–12).

The interplay between vitality and exhaustion condenses around the contrast between Slimane and Rym. The latter's strength, combativeness and confident self-expression are surely welcome for how, along with the portrayal of Karime, they challenge stereotypes of subjugated

French-Maghrebi women. Yet, the manner in which Rym becomes a privileged object for the film's scrutiny of sensual pleasure and bodily energy is problematic. Commenting on the closing sequence (Figure 4.2), for example, Ginette Vincendeau writes, 'Rym's belly dance [. . .] degenerates into crude worship of female fecundity with endless close-ups of her undulating tummy' (Vincendeau 2008). Kechiche himself acknowledged that he asked Hafsia Herzi to gain weight for the role: 'I thought it would suit her to have a rounder belly, for people to be able to believe there was life in that belly, something vibrant. I found that more sensual' (Fevret and Lalanne 2007, my translation). It is ironic that a film so focused on mutability should retreat to this biological essentialism.

Overall, there are two dimensions to Kechiche's deconstructive materialism. On the one hand, he scrutinises the socio-economic and institutional contexts that shape people's lives and constrain their possibilities. On the other, he shows a sustained attention to the sensuous materiality of embodied experience rivalled by few contemporary filmmakers. The socialised human body lies at the interface of these two dimensions. It is shaped and marked by contextual forces. Yet, in its desires, energy and mutability, it is the source of potential resistance and renewal and, through its fatigue or exhaustion, a marker of limits to the endless flexibility demanded of the neoliberal subject. Problems arise, however, if, in denial of the body's own historicity, it is fetishised along gendered lines.

**Figure 4.2** Rym's closely scrutinised body (*La Graine et le mulet*, Abdellatif Kechiche, 2007)

## The mobile body of the Black Venus

There is the same sustained attention to a resistant body as it mutates across a series of encounters in Kechiche's *Vénus Noire*. To that extent, the film confirms patterns observed in *La Graine et le mulet*. What it adds is a much greater level of reflexivity than in the earlier film. It follows, with reasonable fidelity to the historical record, the story of Saartjie Bartmaan, a Khoekhoe woman, from the East Cape (South Africa). Saartjie was brought to Britain in 1810 by Hendrik Caezar, who is usually thought of as Afrikaans but may have been 'free black' in the racist classifications of the time, and Alexander Dunlop, a British naval surgeon. She was put on display in London as the 'Hottentot Venus' and sold to a public hungry for freak shows and ethnographic displays as a marvel of nature, notably because of her prominent posterior, a feature then considered to be typical of 'Hottentot' women, the term Hottentot being a settler-colonial term for the Khoekhoe. A group called the Africa Institution sought but failed to prosecute Dunlop and Caezar for their treatment of her (Scully and Crais 2008). Later, she was hired or sold on to an animal trainer called Réaux who put her on display in Paris and may have forced her into prostitution. She was examined in 1815 by celebrated animal morphologist, Georges Cuvier, and, after her death later the same year, dissected by him. He presented his findings on her to the French National Academy of Medicine drawing attention to morphological markers of claimed racial inferiority. Her skeleton was displayed in French state museums until the 1970s but was returned to South Africa in 2002, after an official request by Nelson Mandela, and given a ceremonial reburial. She would become, as Magubane notes, an iconic figure for post-colonial and feminist scholars, one which encapsulated how the sexualised body of the Black African woman underpinned discourses of white superiority. Magubane argues that this well-intentioned critical discourse reproduced the same kind of ahistorical generalisation it sought to counter. Instead, she underscores the need to pay due attention to the shifting social, historical and discursive contexts in which meanings are ascribed to bodies (Magubane 2001). Kechiche's film could be seen as responding to this injunction.

Like *La Graine et le mulet*, the film tracks repeated, contingent productions of self, with their requisite changes of costume and gesture, in contexts over which the heroine has little control but in which she displays her recalcitrant agency. Its flashback structure begins with Cuvier's presentation of his post-mortem findings about Saartjie to the Academy of Medicine before cutting to the fairground-style freak show she found herself part of when she arrived in London. After showing her in and out of role as savage in London, it picks up on the court case before moving to her time in Paris, her encounter with Cuvier and her prostitution and death. Apparently closing the narrative circle, it shows Cuvier dissecting her corpse and preparing for his talk at the Academy. However, a documentary-style coda shows the ceremony that marked the return of her remains to contemporary South Africa. What emerges therefore is a sense not of an essential Saartjie of the sort Cuvier had sought to pin down but of multiple contingent Saartjies, each produced in response to different socio-economic and institutional contexts. On-screen artefacts and cultural forms (posters, statuettes, portraits, songs, scientific drawings) contribute to this proliferation of representations. While almost none of these Saartjies are enacted in conditions of her choosing, the film insists on her agency as expressed in gestures of refusal or physical or mental withdrawal. Despite its stylistic difference, the documentary coda ensures that this capacity for mobility and resignification continues after her death. The coda is a reminder that the values that lay behind her treatment are not simple historical traces but connect to contemporary struggles for justice and recognition.

If the film's opening shows Saartjie as objectified specimen, the rest of it foregrounds her embodied resistances. Her refusal is sometimes explicit: she challenges Caezar about the nature of their show, refuses to strip for Cuvier and his colleagues and flees from ethnographic observation while eating. Other resistances relate to her physical and emotional limits: she coughs periodically and dies after a coughing fit; she cries increasingly as her treatment becomes more humiliating; she drinks between performances; she catches venereal disease when prostituted. While the film brings out her capacity to remake herself, it also suggests, as with Slimane in *La Graine et le mulet*, that there are bodily and affective limits to her capacity to do so. This is part of its deconstructive materialism.

Sophisticated in its reflexivity, *Vénus* foregrounds how the conditions under which representations are received by audiences shape their production. We see this right from the opening scene, Cuvier's presentation to the Academy, which is the first of the film's many extended set pieces. For this learned and duly attentive white male audience, Saartjie is present only as body parts in specimen jars, drawings of her vulva, a cast of her body and a series of measurements and morphological observations with which Cuvier demonstrates, in learned tones, her proximity to the apes. The audience for the next set piece is mixed, rowdy and more popular in its class make-up. Saartjie is in a cage on a fairground stage. Caezar presents himself as an animal tamer, whip in hand. She performs wildness in a tight, flesh-coloured bodysuit that gives the appearance of nudity. A masquerade within the masquerade, Caezar has her 'promenade' in an exaggeratedly dainty manner, showing the grotesquery of her attempts to walk like a European lady. She does a 'savage' dance that emphasises her posterior. The crowd paw her. Her third audience, again a socially mixed one, is encountered in the court. Here, smartly dressed, she testifies that she is a freely contracted performer. Some of her audience clearly want to construct her as a melodramatic victim of cruel exploiters although the public is also quick to turn against her when she lays claim to the status of actress. When the case is dismissed, the prosecuting lawyer proclaims it demonstrates, to Britain's honour, that even a 'Hottentot' can find people to protect her interests. Across the different set pieces, a different Saartjie is produced for different audiences and purposes. Similar racist attitudes may underpin the exoticism of the fair, the patronising humanitarianism of the court and the coldly dispassionate scientific analysis of the Academy, but each requires a different Saartjie.

In its focus on the increasingly objectifying and sexualised exploitation of Saartjie, the film risks complicity in the very processes it depicts, not least because of the director's continued commitment to prolonged scenes and sustained tracking of bodily reactions. Three interconnected things redeem it. Firstly, although it dwells at length on Saartjie's body and the horrible duress inflicted upon it, it is above all committed to scrutiny of her face. During her performances, her features are often serious, as if reflecting concentration rather than any enjoyment. At other times, they are impassive, as if she were withdrawing into herself, pained, as when she cries, or tired. The film thus works to sustain a sense of her as a working, suffering and resistant subject. Secondly, in its probing of the different contexts in which she is framed, it draws our attention to the exploitative and racist processes which deny her subjecthood and agency. Thirdly, reversing the gaze as Mattoscio argues, it brings her white audiences unflatteringly within the frame, showing them to be prurient, frivolous, smugly humanitarian or callously analytical (Mattoscio 2017: 61–3). Evoking the troubling history of white European spectatorship, it makes disturbing viewing for contemporary audiences (Mattoscio 2017: 75).

## *La Vie d'Adèle* and its troubling encounters

As we shall see, *La Vie d'Adèle* would not avoid accusations of voyeurism so successfully and brought to the fore some underlying issues with Kechiche's filmmaking practices which the continued reflexivity of his work failed to guarantee against. It would also underscore his impressive ability to track the collision between desiring, mutable bodies and restrictive frames. The film is a relatively straightforward love story. Adèle is a sixth-form student (*lycéenne*) from a modest background with a passion for literature. Egged on by female friends, she has an abortive relationship with a young man. She encounters Emma, an art-school student from a more middle-class background embarking on a painting career. The two decide to live together, but, feeling neglected, Adèle has a fling with a male colleague. Emma finds out and, after a blazing row, throws her out and sets up home with a woman artist, Lise (Mona Walravens). She meets up with Adèle twice more; first, in a bar, when it becomes clear their mutual attraction is undiminished, second, when her first exhibition launches. The narrative closes as Adèle leaves the launch party and walks away down a side street. The love story is refreshingly original in having two female leads but otherwise relatively unremarkable. What makes the film stand out, and would arouse the controversy, is the sustained intensity with which the director tracks the embodied experiences of the two lovers, especially Adèle, including during love-making scenes.

We track Adèle's movements as she runs for the bus, crosses the road or brushes aside her unruly hair. The camera watches her when she sleeps. We hear her breathe deeply after an erotic dream. We see her flush when embarrassed. We see the muscle in her cheek twitch when pressured by her classmates over her sexuality. When she is upset, we see her face covered in snot and tears rather than a more decorous reaction. We watch her eating spaghetti bolognaise, her mouth half open, and see her lick her fingers, lips and knife. Her emotions and sensuous appetites for sex or food are present to us, not through dialogue, but in all their messy fleshiness as they play over her body.

When she first encounters Emma, her head is turned, not simply in the figural sense, but literally too (Figure 4.3). Although crossing a busy road, she pauses in her movement and looks back, not once but repeatedly, even as she walks to meet a boy, her body pulled in two directions at the same time. This is a material encounter in the sense that Althusser

**Figure 4.3** Adèle's head is turned by the encounter with Emma (*La Vie d'Adèle*, Abdellatif Kechiche, 2013)

gives to the expression. Emma has no words to define what is happening to her. She is horrified when her schoolmates call her a lesbian, an identity she does not associate herself with. All that we see, as it plays out across her gestures, is the sense of a potentially different Adèle emerging as yet undomesticated by any concept of who she may be. Something similar might be said of her burgeoning relationship with Emma. We witness two bodies drawn together to form a couple whose contours have yet to be defined and which may or may not take.

When the couple fails, the immediate trigger is Adèle's infidelity, but the deeper cause seems to lie in class-related divergences in attitude and taste. The parallel scenes that run through the film bring this out. There are dinner scenes with the two sets of parents and party scenes involving friends and / or family. The dinners bring out contrasting relationships to food: Adèle's father cooks his speciality, spaghetti bolognaise; Emma's mother and stepfather produce a meal based on sea food from a local supplier and a carefully selected white wine. Adèle's parents are concerned that Emma, as an artist, does not have a trade that will provide for her. Emma's parents suggest that Adèle is worried about financial insecurity when she talks of her planned career as a primary teacher. Emma and Adèle hide their relationship from Adèle's parents. Emma's are relaxed and toast 'love' with the two young women. These perhaps predictable class-related contrasts continue into the two parties. Adèle's mother organises a surprise birthday party in their modest garden where Adèle's multicultural friendship group dance spontaneously together. Emma's party is more formal and less fusional. It has footage from G. W. Pabst's

1929 classic, *Pandora's Box*, projected onto a screen behind the guests and includes a discussion about the relative merits of two Viennese artists, Klimt and Schiele. Some of the guests seem unimpressed by Adèle's lack of ambition. The fault-lines are clear: Adèle's more humble parents serve unimaginative food, are socially conservative and prioritise job security. Emma's mother and stepfather have more refined tastes, are socially liberal and prioritise self-development and creativity. The same is true for Emma, for whom Adèle's lack of ambition is an embarrassment. Emma's new partner, Lise, an artist, fits far better into what her social circle expects even though she is not stirred in the same way by her.

In an early conversation with Adèle, and in one of the many literary references one finds in Kechiche, Emma talks of the inspiration she takes from existentialist philosopher Jean-Paul Sartre and his anti-essentialist account of how we define ourselves by our actions and can therefore shape our lives with reference to no higher authority. Following a socially predictable path, Emma's trajectory fails to live up to this model of heroic self-definition. By the end of the film, she has shed her non-conformist blue hair as her career takes off. Rather than fully embracing the challenge to redefine herself or pursue an egalitarian, cross-class alliance with Adèle, she seeks to mould the latter to the expectations of her milieu and places Adèle in conventional subordinated roles. This comes across at her party when, working as a cook and waitress, Adèle finds herself in the role of a traditional housewife. It is also apparent in how Emma uses her as a model or muse, a role traditionally associated with lower-class women.

The presence of Emma as an artist, a producer of representations, is the most obvious indicator of the film's reflexivity. But repeated references to literature and art ensure that reflexivity runs through the film in general. In an early scene, we witness a classroom discussion of Pierre de Marivaux's *La Vie de Marianne* (1731–1742), which presents itself as a woman's own memoir, but is in fact the work of a male author. Later, at Emma's party, there is a discussion, around the mythological figure of Tiresias, about the knowability of a woman's sexual pleasure. At the same party, as we noted, the artists Klimt and Schiele are discussed, the former being associated with a deeply romantic depiction of the body, the latter with tortured bodily forms, both together paralleling the film's attention to ecstatic and suffering bodies. Through these different references, the film poses the question of the capacity of representations to capture the hurt, pleasure and evolution of embodied beings. When Adèle attends Emma's exhibition launch, there are two versions of her on view: the one immobilised in Emma's art, contained within frames, put to work for someone else's career and the living, moving Adèle whom the film shows walking away, her back to camera, her future still open. It is as if, claiming the mantle of Marivaux, Kechiche were asserting his ability to capture Adèle's ongoing life in a way beyond the reach of the film's on-screen female artist. This might seem problematic enough without the broader public outcry that surrounded the film on its release.

As Clarisse Fabre reported in *Le Monde* (2013), the glow of the film's Palme d'Or was tarnished almost immediately when the technicians' union accused the director of behaviour during production that would be seen as workplace harassment in other industrial sectors: sixteen-hour days declared as eight and paid 100 euros gross when the same figure net had been promised; an unpredictable work schedule with workers called in on rest days or phoned at night. This arose, as Fabre noted, in a tense industrial relations context where smaller producers had declared how much pressure the new sectoral contractual agreement, signed in 2012, would put them under. But, even given this, and in an industry where bending of the rules is routine practice, it suggested Kechiche was especially demanding.

This impression was confirmed when, in an interview with *The Daily Beast*, the film's two stars confessed how hard they had found the shooting and how uncomfortable aspects of it, especially the protracted nude love-making scene, had made them. Seydoux explained how, in France, the director is all powerful and the actors 'trapped'. She noted the tremendous over-run of the shoot and commented on how many takes Kechiche demanded, citing the more than one hundred required for the couple's first encounter. She added that the film's break-up fight scene had been shot in a gruelling one-hour continuous take. Her co-star, Exarchopoulos, was less critical but agreed about how demanding Kechiche had been, even in the sex scenes. Although she accepted the commitment demanded, there was a manipulation that was hard to handle (Stern 2013).

The film was also attacked by Julie Maroh, the creator of the work on which it was based, who described the long love-making sequence as 'a brutal, surgical, demonstrative and cold account of lesbian sex, leaning towards pornography' (my translation) (Gallard 2013). Linda Williams identified similar accusations among American responses to the film. She explained them by a tendency to condemn as pornographic any sex scene perceived as overlong, too explicit or more 'deviant' than Hollywood allows. She also suggested that criticisms of the film's apparently fetishistic focus on women's bodies and sadistic punishment of the heroines (the unhappy outcome) relied on a 'keen-jerk' application of Laura Mulvey's famous account of the male gaze (Williams 2017: 467–8). She herself defended the film's worth as an art film, a sex film and a lesbian sex film, and suggested that the love affair fails for classic reasons of age and class (Williams 2017: 466–8).

Other academic critics defended the film for its contribution to a cinema of the body. Tim Palmer, for example, situates Kechiche and his film within the French *cinéma du corps* or corporeal cinema as practised by directors such as Dumont, Denis, Breillat or Noé (Palmer 2017: 6–7). Like other examples of such cinema, *La Vie d'Adèle* is not simply concerned with 'stark sex' but 'with bodily discourse in all its messy abasing idyllic glory' (Palmer 2017: 8). Kechiche's camera, Palmer notes, undertakes a three-hour scrutiny of Adèle's body (Palmer 2017: 9), appraises Adèle's 'capacity for physical transfiguration and oscillation', and tracks the ebb and flow of her energy as it writes itself on her face, body and gestures (Palmer 2017: 15). Cezar Gheoghe's phenomenological reading takes a similar direction. He notes cinema's unique capacity to capture embodied human experience as 'the substance of its own expression' (Gheoghe 2014: 163). 'The real story of [Kechiche's] film', he suggests, 'is the history of what it means to live inside Adèle's body; it is a catalogue of sensory data, the report of the awareness of skin touching skin.' Viewed in this way, neither the prolonged sex scene nor the frequent close-ups of body parts are gratuitous or exploitative (Gheoghe 2014: 160).

These defences carry undoubted weight but do not engage with the important question of on-set power relations. Kechiche's work is admirably reflexive when framing class and minority ethnic bodies. He has an unfortunate blind spot, however, when it comes to the exercise of his directorial power over technicians and actors, especially female ones. This is exacerbated by the way his commitment to tracking bodies to the point of exhaustion intersects with his essentialising association of vitality and sensuality with young women. These blind spots, as we will see, are not shared by Sciamma. This does not mean she is without blind spots of her own.

## Sciamma's embodied becoming

In his discussion of the materialism of the encounter, Althusser locates Spinoza as a key figure. Spinoza is a philosopher of immanence. His God equates to nature, outside of which nothing exists. A vitalist God, he is associated, not with a single moment of creation, but with the ongoing capacity of nature to generate aleatory forms of life. Unpredictable encounters occur and things that we cannot know may or may not come into being (Althusser 2006: 176–7). Applying this more general vitalism, to the human, Althusser explains, 'we do not know all the powers of the body, just as, when it comes to thought, we do not know the unthought power of desire' (Althusser 2006: 177). The body and thought are not therefore unknowable because of some intrinsic limit to our understanding. They escape our grasp because of their capacity to form connections and openness to transformative encounters. This is something also emphasised by Deleuze when discussing Spinoza. In the latter's thought, he comments, 'what a body can do corresponds to the nature and limits of its capacity to be affected' (Deleuze 1990: 218). Given that the capacity to be affected by other bodies is necessarily dependent on encounters and connections, the body is defined by an open-ended becoming rather than a fixed being.

How does this help us to make sense of Sciamma's work? Put simply, Sciamma, like Kechiche, is a filmmaker of the body, its desiring encounters and capacity to become and form new connections. As Emma Wilson eloquently explains, Sciamma's films develop, 'a way of doing politics through sensuous cinema' (Wilson 2017: 12).

## *Tomboy*, or what a body can do

Sciamma's *Tomboy* begins with a series of long-take, tracking shots. We see a short-haired child's head as it moves against an out-of-focus background of green leaves dappled by bright sunlight. We cut to a low angle point-of-view shot of the trees which pans to frame the child's hand as the air moves through its finger. Another cut moves us in front of the child's face, captured in close-up, as he or she enjoys the movement through the air. There is a clear sensuous quality to this opening and a utopian sense of freedom as an unconstrained body savours its environment. Subsequent shots introduce the child's father to the sequence. Despite his presence, the sense of empowerment continues as the child sits on his knee and steers the car. The pair carry boxes into their new apartment. A long tracking shot follows the child's movement as they explore the space, moving from a living room to a blue-painted bedroom and then to a girly pink one where a younger sister, Jeanne (Malonn Lévana), with long, curly locks, waits, feigning sleep. Subsequent shots introduce the pregnant mother, resting on a couch. A shot framing the family group through two door-frames suggests both tight togetherness and the constraining nature of the nuclear family, the gender roles associated with it and their inscription in the space of the apartment. Two brief scenes of game-playing and reading underscore the sweet closeness of the siblings.

We pick up the child as they move into the space outside the apartment. A voice is heard, that of a girl sitting on the steps of a neighbouring block. 'T'es nouveau?' ('are you new?'), she inquires, using the masculine form of the adjective. She introduces herself as Lisa (Jeanne Disson) and asks the newcomer's name. After a pause, the latter says Mickaël, self-presenting as a boy. Lisa introduces Mickaël to the local children playing in the nearby woods. The next sequence moves us back inside the apartment. The two children are in the bath together. The mother gets the younger sister out and then says, 'Laure, sors du bain' ('Laura, get out of the bath'), just before the older child (Zoé Héran) stands, confirming her female biological gender.

The film's tension-filled drama is now in motion. Inside the apartment, the child is Laure, but outside, in the woods and play areas, Mickaël. The film's opening has suggested a utopian pre-social freedom for the body to encounter the world on its own terms, a situation which finds its ludic prolongation in the exterior spaces where the children play, away from adult control, where the androgynous, pre-pubescent Laure can be Mickaël. The initial meeting with Lisa has played a crucial role. An aleatory encounter, it has opened the possibility of Laure/Mickaël discovering what their body can do and feel when social and institutional constraints to a biologically female body's becomings are suspended.

Mickaël pushes the journey of discovery to the limits. Initially, they watch the boys play football. Then they join the game and show themselves to be a good player. The boys take their shirts off when they get too hot. Back in the apartment, Laure checks herself in the mirror: her breasts not yet showing, she can also go shirtless. She practises spitting in the sink so that she can spit on the pitch, as the boys do. When the children go swimming, she is hesitant but, cutting the upper part off her girl's swimming costume, fashions some swimming briefs and tries them on in front of the mirror with an improvised playdough penis inserted in them. She passes muster, goes swimming and wrestles successfully with one of the boys (Figure 4.4). Lisa is drawn to Mickaël. She blindfolds him

**118** Looking Beyond Neoliberalism

**Figure 4.4** Laure/Mickaël discovering what their body can do (*Tomboy,* Céline Sciamma, 2011)

and kisses him on the lips. Mickaël can also kiss girls. Allowed to accompany Mickaël in return for her complicity, Jeanne is pushed over by one of the boys. Mickaël jumps to her defence and fights the boy. Freed of the restrictive gender norms that govern girls' behaviour, Laure/Mickaël has been able to explore their bodily powers.

The fight puts an end to Mickaël's discovery of new abilities. A mother comes to the apartment looking for the boy who has hurt her son. Mickaël is outed as a girl. Her mother slaps her face. She tells her that school is to restart – Mickaël is Laure on the school roll. She forces her into a dress and takes her to the boy's home and Lisa's apartment to apologise. Laure sheds the dress in the woods but is caught by the boys. Lisa is made to confirm Laure's biological gender in a cruel gesture which, in a way typical of Sciamma's restrained style, remains out of frame. Laure retreats indoors. However, in a closing sequence that mirrors the opening, she goes outside and reintroduces herself to Lisa as Laure. As the film ends, conveying a sense that she has been temporarily halted but not definitively arrested, an ending repeated with variations across Sciamma's films, a smile plays across her face. We do not yet know what the relationship will become.

Monaghan (2019) suggests that contemporary films about queer girlhood fall into two main categories which, drawing on Beirne, she labels as *queer phase* and *coming out as coming of age*. Within the former, shutting down the radical potential of queer narratives, 'queerness has been associated with a passing phase of girls' adolescent development, through which queer sexualities, identities, and experiences are written off as temporary deviations from a linear path toward heteronormative adulthood'. Within the latter, despite its apparently more positive framing of the issues, 'complex negotiations of sexuality are rendered as simple rites of passage'. Monaghan notes that the more interesting recent American Indie films she is analysing do not fit neatly into either category because they 'shift the queer girl's narrative focus from questioning and articulating sexuality to negotiating belonging, sexual consent, familial relationships, and the complex intimacies of girlhood friendships'. Through this kind of polycentric narrative, the films refuse to represent queerness as a phase and use queer girl characters 'to challenge linear models of girlhood development and emphasize[s] the queerness of queer girlhood' (Monaghan 2019: 99).

*Tomboy* resonates with Monaghan's account of these other films. Although sexuality is undoubtedly an issue within it, it is about far more than that. The course of its narrative is shaped by its close tracking of the protagonist's desiring gaze and embodied actions as they navigate their way through a world in which established gender norms are hard-wired into bodily appearances, permitted behaviours, physical spaces (the pink and blue bedrooms in the home, for example) and institutional practices. There can be no smooth progression towards alignment with any pre-existing concept of self because the character does not have such a thing. All that we can say is that, through encounters, experiments and negotiations with obstacles, the character discovers how they can behave at specific times.

Similar patterns underlie Sciamma's other films up to and including *Portrait de la jeune fille en feu*. The lead characters of the other works may be older but are similarly tracked in encounters with material environments and people as they probe what their bodies can do and what desiring (and not necessarily sexual) connections they can make. Social and institutional constraints direct them towards similarly pre-determined roles and locations. Yet there is also a radical contingency in these other films. Like Laure/Mickaël, their characters do not proceed towards the realisation of some essential or already conceptualised self but plot an open-ended path between their desires and obstacles to them. And, even if the obstacles seem to win, as they do in different ways, a fundamental contingency has been revealed beneath the surface of the social.

## Women on fire and under water: what cinema can do

With *Portrait de la jeune fille en feu*, Sciamma moved from the contemporary world of her other films to eighteenth-century France but continued to pose similar questions. The film centres on a lesbian love story between Héloïse (Adèle Haenel), a young convent-educated woman from the lower nobility destined for marriage, and Marianne (Noémie Merlant), the artist commissioned to produce a portrait for her potential husband. The presence of a woman painter allows questions around the gendering of artistic production and the gaze to be raised. The story is expanded by the presence of a third major character, Sophie (Luàna Bajrami), a servant, who opens the romance onto a history of cross-class solidarity between women. The film goes even further than Sciamma's other films in creating a utopian space of female autonomy. The only authority figure on the Breton island where the story plays out is Héloïse's mother, the Countess (Valeria Golino), who is present at the start and finish. For most of the film, the young women have effective freedom to suspend the gendered norms of their time and probe their individual and collective powers.

The opening sets the tone. We are in an artist's studio. We see a series of close-ups of young women gazing intently and hear a woman's voice telling them how to look at her. We then see Marianne, the woman the young women are sketching. As she looks back at them, she asks who has got out a painting behind them, the one that gives the film its title, of a woman with flames lapping at her dress in a nocturnal landscape. The camera tracks forward to frame the painting. A reverse shot then tracks similarly forward to frame Marianne gazing pensively into space. The sound of the sea fades in, motivating the cut to an earlier time which will explain the painting's production. Marianne is sitting in a boat looking towards an island. The boat is rowed by four men while a fifth steers. A rectangular wooden crate that she has been holding goes into the water. The men look on. Removing her coat but still in a long dress and underskirt, Marianne jumps into the waves and swims to retrieve the box. We then see her on the island's beach, one man behind her carrying her bag and the crate. He leaves both on the beach. We cut immediately to a shot of Marianne carrying both objects up the steep climb away from the sea.

The painting scene is broadly static. The boat sequence is full of movement. But both probe the limits of what gendered bodies can do. The painting class, like the main body of the film, takes place between women.

By removing men from the situation, the film allows women to occupy all the roles and thereby destabilise habitual gender norms and the hierarchies that govern their distribution. The women are teacher and taught, painter and model, subject and object. The travel sequence has only one woman, Marianne, among a group of men. Initially, as she sits and they row, it seems to condemn her to decorous passivity. When she jumps unhesitatingly into the water, despite the constraint of the long dress, as the men look on, the roles are reversed. The same occurs on the beach when the man drops his burden and she assumes it, with, the edit implies, no hesitation. Similar dynamics will continue throughout the film. Given a temporary period of freedom and isolated by the island location from broader norms, women explore their bodily capacities, especially in exterior sequences. At the same time, through the exercise of art, they subvert gendered norms about who is allowed to paint and what subjects are deemed worthy of representation.

Unlike Marianne who, as the daughter of a painter, has learned a profession and achieved a degree of independence, Héloïse has never known freedom. A younger sister, she has been sent to a convent from which she only emerges, as a substitute bride, when her elder sister throws herself from the cliffs to avoid an arranged marriage. On her first walk with Marianne, and despite her long dress, she breaks into a headlong run towards the same cliff only to come to a halt right at the edge. She turns and says she has been dreaming of doing that for years. What, inquires Marianne, dying? No, replies Héloïse, running. Later, when the two women are together on the beach, Héloïse walks into the sea in her petticoat to see if she can swim. The experiment is inconclusive. She can float but does not know if she can swim. We do not know yet what her body can do.

The painting story is more complex in its unfolding. Marianne is passed off as a paid companion for Héloïse so that she can observe her reluctant subject unawares. When she confesses the truth and shows Héloïse the portrait, the latter is unimpressed by it. Marianne says there are rules and conventions. There is no life or presence in the painting, retorts Héloïse. She can accept that it does not resemble her, but it is sad that it does not reflect the artist. 'I didn't know you were a critic', replies Marianne. Marianne deliberately spoils the painting and begins the face again. This time, painting becomes a collaborative process informed by the burgeoning desire between the two women. Reaffirming her claim to an active gaze, Héloïse reminds Marianne that, even as she is being observed, she also observes and decodes her portraitist's expressions.

As conventions and the separation of roles break down, the number of paintings proliferates in a liberation of creativity. Sophie, the young servant, is pregnant but does not wish to have the child. Accompanied by the other two women, she has an abortion performed by another woman on the island. Héloïse decides that there should be a painting showing the operation and poses with Sophie as Marianne paints. Meanwhile, Marianne completes the official portrait in which both women now recognise themselves. Immediately afterwards, as they lie in bed together, Marianne paints a miniature of Héloïse as a keepsake. The latter also wants a picture, this time of the naked painter. Marianne takes Ovid's *Metamorphosis*, the book Héloïse is reading, and, observing herself in a mirror cradled in the latter's groin, paints her self-portrait on one of its pages. Years later, when attending an art salon, she comes across a picture of Héloïse with a child. Although the painting suggests that the latter has been recaptured by her social destiny, Marianne sees that she has the Ovid on her lap, her fingers holding back the corner of the page on which the portrait was painted (Figure 4.5). Under her father's name, Marianne herself is exhibiting a painting depicting the myth of Orpheus and Eurydice from the same book. Earlier in the film, the women had discussed why Orpheus looks back at Eurydice, condemning her to be taken

**Figure 4.5** Resisting social destiny: Héloïse signals her attachment to Marianne (*Portrait de la jeune fille en feu*, Céline Sciamma, 2019)

back into the underworld. In Marianne's painting, as an older man at the salon remarks, it is as if the two lovers were saluting each other at their moment of separation. When Marianne stands in front of the painting, her blue dress echoing Orpheus's blue robe, it as if she were aligned with the poet, saluting her own lost lesbian lover.

With its destabilisation of the socially and institutionally gendered dynamics of painting, Sciamma's film is obviously if implicitly challenging the gendering of the cinematic gaze and, more broadly, of cinema as institution. The production of a portrait of Héloïse for her future husband's inspection underscores women's objectification. The difficulty Marianne has exhibiting her work and being allowed to paint the 'noble' subjects open to male artists confirms women's marginalisation in the sphere of visual production. But the opening lesson and the painting done on the island reveal a radical potential for destabilisation beneath the surface: women's capacity to paint, judge, and define the gendered field of acceptable themes (the abortion painting) is brought to the fore even as the roles of artist, model or critic begin to blur. This potential collides with social and institutional frames and is driven underground. But the film underscores a capacity for individual and collective reinvention bubbling under even though the weight of existing conditions has not allowed it to take durable form. The painting of Héloïse and the one by Marianne in the salon underscore their enduring if forbidden love. They also affirm women's capacity for voice and artistic agency even in apparently impossible circumstances.

*Naissance des pieuvres*, Sciamma's first feature film, is less obviously reflexive but nonetheless probes questions about performance, the *mise-en-scène* of femininity and spectatorship. The story of three adolescent girls, Marie (Pauline Acquart), Floriane (Adèle Haenel) and Anne (Louise Blachère), it takes place in the new town of Cergy-Pontoise around the activities of a synchronised swimming team. Adults are largely absent from the film. There is a boy's water polo team in the background and one of its members, François (Warren Jacquin), is dating Floriane and is the love object of Anne. But the boys are peripheral to the story. The film revolves around the young women.

The film's opening stages the crucial encounter between Floriane and Marie. Marie enters the spectator area of the pool when the synchronised swimmers are performing. She shows no particular interest in the younger girls and is leaving when the older girls, with Floriane at their centre, begin to perform to dramatic music. Marie watches spellbound.

As the performance reaches its finale, Floriane rises, as if effortlessly, from the water, the only girl in view. Afterwards, Marie waits at the door to the girls' changing room, drawn by Floriane, we presume, but also waiting for Anne, her friend. Later, Floriane helps her join the synchronised swimmers and in return asks her to provide cover for her meetings with François.

Marie witnesses the performances but also the work that goes into them. In one sequence, Floriane tells her to watch the training from under the water. Instead of the graceful movements seen from above the surface, Marie can see lower bodies, thighs splayed, legs working furiously. Behind the scenes, in the changing rooms, she witnesses all the preparation, the work on hair and make-up, that goes into producing the elegance of the performance. In one sequence, a coach inspects the girls' armpits to ensure they are smooth. One hasn't shaved. The coach asks if she would present herself to her husband that way. Floriane is under a more diffuse inspection by the other girls in the changing rooms. One girl pulls her up for how she eats a banana, saying that all the boys watch how girls eat bananas in the canteen. She adds that Floriane won't mind as she has been with many boys. Floriane says that is true, carries on eating the fruit and looks provocatively at the other girl. In the changing room or out partying, Floriane performs the persona of a girl desired by men. She is only able to confess her virginity and the pressure she feels under in the various scenes with Marie, away from prying eyes.

Rather than the truth of the pool spectacle simply being found behind the scenes, there is a complex, multi-directional dynamic. The synchronised swimming offers the most concentrated account of femininity as spectacle and women as fetishised objects of the gaze (Belot 2012: 173). It also contains its own star system, with Floriane at its centre, thrust into view, even as others support her. The changing room and spaces like parties or discotheques show femininity as an ongoing performance subject to more diffuse surveillance and constraint. The unseen (underwater or private) zones reveal the hidden physical and emotional efforts required to produce heterosexual femininity as spectacle and performance. The girls' movement between the spaces brings out the connections and tensions between them, the pain behind the smiles. In its reflexive probing of the spectacle, the film reveals its mechanisms and objectifying consequences. But, at the same time, through its formal choices, it claims the machinery of cinema for a female gaze and the exploration of women's experience. This is signalled clearly from the start when Marie's response is differentiated from that of the other spectators. She arrives late, is leaving early and then stands in front of the others and has to be asked to sit down. Her gaze is out of synch with the more general gaze and continues to be so. By watching her watching Floriane, and centring her as a desiring subject, the film decentres and disrupts the machinery that produces women as heterosexual objects to be desired and policed.

## *Bande de filles*: mutability and material limits

With its sustained attention to women's sensuality and solidarity, the mutability of their bodies and the material obstacles to their becoming, *Bande de filles* is very much part of Sciamma's broader cinematic project. But, with its story of a frustrated but defiant search for empowerment in the outer city *banlieue* (suburb) and its predominantly black cast it would take the director onto new and, as we will see, problematic ground.

Some of *Bande de filles*' core dynamics are encapsulated in its stunning opening sequence. The initial mood is set, as the titles roll, by the up-tempo synthesiser sound of Para One, Sciamma's habitual musical collaborators. Then, splitting left or right according to their colours, a line of red- and white-clad American football players run towards the camera. Slow-motion shots show individual plays and a huddle leading to a touch down sequence. The players' cheers blend with the music. The two teams mingle, high five each other and break into dance (Figure 4.6). A cut takes us into an extreme long shot of them in the middle of the pitch as they move and chant, euphoric, but suddenly more isolated in

**Figure 4.6** *Bande de filles'* utopian opening (Céline Sciamma, 2014)

the space. The lights are switched off, but the chant continues as we cut to the film's title. It gives way to a hubbub of voices as, back into their everyday clothes, the excited girls walk towards a backward tracking camera. A reverse angle shot then films them from a low angle as they climb some steps and the tower blocks of the *banlieue* loom over them. Their voices fall silent as male voices are heard. The group breaks up until one girl, Marieme (Karidja Touré), the main protagonist, is left. She lingers with a young man, Ismaël (Idrissa Diabaté). Then, up in her apartment, she takes charge of her two younger sisters. A comically tender scene between Marieme and her sister Bébé sees the former worry that the latter's breasts are beginning to show. She asks if their brother, Djibril (Cyril Mendy), has noticed yet, and advises Bébé to wear a baggy t-shirt. Marieme plays the FIFA videogame until Djibril arrives, demands the remote and slaps her hard round the head when she doesn't obey. We cut to another tender scene with Marieme and Bébé lying in the dark. Synthesiser music returns but is softer, slower and more meditative than in the opening. A cut takes us into a different time and space as Marieme, facing the camera, announces to an unseen figure that she does not want to do the C.A.P., the *Certificat d'Aptitude Professionnelle*, the vocational 16–18 qualification that young French people take when they are not accepted onto a more academic pathway.

The football game is one of the spatio-temporally circumscribed utopias that recur in *Bande de filles* and throughout Sciamma's cinema. In *Tomboy*, the utopian escape from adult surveillance takes place in exterior spaces during the school holiday, an islet of liberty. *Portrait* suspends gendered constraints on what its characters can do for the whole central part of the film. The football game in *Bande de filles* opens a narrower spacetime for its protagonists to test out capacities to run, tackle, compete and form alliances beyond those to which they are normally restricted. Their padded uniforms and helmets separate them from their routine selves and suggest the collective production of assertive bodies, their empowerment signalled both in the occupation of the space and the loud cries that close the game. From the moment the floodlights are doused and the whoops cease, the repressive normality of the girls' everyday lives reasserts its gendered grip. This is rendered on the soundtrack when male voices replace the female ones and visually by the way the girls' group loses its expansive gestures, fragments and is absorbed back into the *banlieue* under the watchful gaze of the males. Marieme finds herself recaptured by traditional roles: a nascent romance with Ismaël, a quasi-maternal role with her sisters and a subjugated role with her brother enforced through violence. The sense of social destiny closing in around her is underscored by the brusque cut to the school sequence: a working-class, black girl from the devalued *banlieue*, it would seem her fate is subaltern labour. The power of the film lies in the way it plays off the endless possibilities generated by embodied encounters against rigid social structures and hierarchies that seem to shut down possibilities as they arise. The rest of the film shows Marieme's inventive attempts, each one a contingent response to an evolving situation, to retain the sense of empowerment that was there at the start.

Her first chance encounter, the crucial one, is with a gang of three girls, Lady (Assa Sylla), Adiatou (Lindsay Karamoh) and Fily (Marietou Touré), who recruit her to replace a departed member. Led by Lady, the gang trouble conventional gender identifications. In their taste for fashionable clothes, the care they take with their hair and their celebration of their collective sensual beauty, they correspond to traditional definitions of femininity. In other ways, they behave as a boy gang might: extorting money, challenging other gangs, fighting, and ostentatiously laying claim to public space. Their status is threatened when, having challenged another girl, Lady is defeated and her top pulled off, her semi-nakedness making her appear suddenly vulnerable. The local boys immediately treat her with scorn. 'Tu n'es qu'une meuf' ('You're only a woman'), they tell her. Marieme temporarily retrieves the situation by challenging and defeating the other girl. She cuts off her bra as a trophy, leaving the girl covering her breasts with her hands. Marieme is now at her most empowered, having demonstrated her fighting prowess to the *banlieue*. Impressed, Djibril invites her to play FIFA with him, implicitly accepting her as one of the 'lads'. She visits Ismaël and initiates sex with him, telling him to remove his clothes and lie face down before running her hand over his naked body. What seems to be another sequence of utopian empowerment and togetherness follows when, in front of a crowd of mostly black girls, she dances with Lady in front of the Arche de la Défense, a sequence introduced by a long lateral tracking shot along the line of girls, with upbeat synthesiser music, reminding us of the film's joyful opening. The moment is quickly punctured, however, when Marieme sees Bébé with a group of girls mugging a young white girl and slaps her. Bébé tells her she is no better than her brother. They reconcile but, when they return home, Djibril assaults Marieme, calling her 'une pute' ('a whore') for sleeping with Ismaël.

Marieme has reached an impasse. The utopian opening sequence held a tantalising glimpse of how, amongst women, ludic enjoyment could be combined with a sense of empowerment and a liberation of bodily capacities. What we have now seen is that, taken back into a world of patriarchal domination, the girl gang only achieves recognition and empowerment through a willingness to exercise violence against other women and remains exposed to humiliation if a battle is lost and to male violence if they seek to achieve genuine sexual agency.

Marieme's escape route is to join another gang, a criminal one, led by Abou, a drug dealer and pimp. She becomes a dealer, dresses 'as a diva to pass in Parisian gatherings', but, with the gang, 'dresses as a boy, muting her gender' (Wilson 2017: 17). Visiting her in her room, Ismaël is horrified to discover, as he begins to caress her, that her breasts are tightly bound in white bandages. This deliberate ungendering of her body does not save her from Abou's attentions at his party. When she dances with her beautiful prostitute friend, their faces close together, as if about to kiss, Abou tries to force his attention on her. She pushes him angrily away, burning her bridges with the gang. Ismaël offers to marry her and restore her 'good girl' status, but a future as housewife and mother is not what she wants. As the film ends, we see her alone, looking from the *banlieue* towards Paris. The upbeat synthesiser music comes in one last time but her crying undercuts any euphoria it might convey. The camera tracks forward and past her, leaving us with just a very out-of-focus Paris, its blurring suggesting the unattainability of escape. Just as we feel that everything is over, however, Marieme walks back into view, pauses, swallows, and walks determinedly out of shot, her refusal to accept defeat now aligning with the mood of the music.

Marieme is a model of resistant mutability. Each mutation is signalled by a shift in appearance: the androgynous football uniforms at the start; the purple hoodie and long cornrows of her 'good girl' phase; the black jacket and straightened hair she adopts with the gang; the elegant purple dress she wears when the gang lip-synchs to Rhianna's song 'Diamonds' in a hotel room, and so on. These shifts are not simply superficial modifications: each signals a more profound self-adaptation as Marieme adjusts to contexts and seeks empowerment in a patriarchal world. Her most utopian moments come at times, like the lip-synching sequence, when there are only women present, exulting in their power and beauty. But these moments are exceptions. For most of the film, she and the other girls are forced to navigate male-dominated terrain. With the girl gang, the young women achieve visibility and respect by behaving like a boy gang but still remaining proudly feminine. With Abou's gang, Marieme preserves a level of autonomy by creating two figures, the diva and the androgynous woman, that allow her to blend into different milieux, no longer attempting to remake the broader terrain but reconfiguring herself to fit it. In both cases, there is a queering of gender boundaries that underscores the capacity of the young women to remake themselves and probe the limits of what a body can do. But, in the end, their battles for self-definition collide with social forces that they cannot defeat. The film signals the contingency of the social order and the capacity for change bubbling beneath it but also underscores its grip.

## *Bande de filles* and the limits we do not see

The outcry following the release of Kechiche's *La Vie d'Adèle* was highly publicised. Expressions of disquiet from Black French women following the release of *Bande de filles* had less media resonance but were nonetheless important. They are discussed by Mame-Fatou Niang who, adding her own insights to the criticism, locates them in the broader context of the representation of post-colonial minorities and their access to cultural production in France. The core of the problem for Niang is how Sciamma treats the story of the girls as a universal story without processing the whole history of negative stereotypes of France's post-colonial minorities and the *banlieue*. This history blocks access to a universalism which is neutral in name only (Niang 2019: 207–12). By failing to address it, the film condemns itself to recycle a series of familiar stereotypes about black families with their repressed daughters, violent brothers, single, silent mothers and absent fathers. Lacking any sociological depth, its *banlieue* is reduced to the clichéd images of dealers, gang fights or defeated mothers familiar from other films or the evening news (Niang 2019: 212–34). In recent years, cultural producers from the *banlieue* have posed a vibrant cultural challenge to this kind of mainstream stereotyping but have struggled for audibility and access to resources. Rather than responding to their voices, Sciamma has helped perpetuate their marginalisation (Niang 2019: 245–50).

Can the blind spots that Niang discusses be found in the other films? To the extent that none of them engage with ethnicity, no. But there is a broader reluctance to deal with class as a meaningful influence on characters' trajectories. The stories of *Naissance des pieuvres* and *Tomboy* are set in relatively generic, middle-class suburbs. Class is effectively evacuated from them as something that might limit characters' ability to explore their potential to reshape themselves. *Portrait* seems more class-centred: the female trio at its heart comprises a representative of the minor nobility, a self-employed professional and a servant. Yet, in its utopian drive, its urge to explore what these characters can do, individually and collectively, it seems happy to suspend the grasp of class on them. The women's burgeoning solidarity is too effortless. Class differences are discounted rather than worked through, in the same way as *Bande de filles* brackets a whole history of stereotyping and marginalisation.

## Conclusion

When we seek to identify what characterises a political cinema, we are probably often drawn to one which already seems to know the answers to the questions it poses or which has a model of the world's functioning that precedes its investigation of a particular context or case. Yet, there is also considerable value in a cinema, like that of Kechiche or Sciamma, which exposes the contingency of the current order and the unknown and unconceptualised possibilities that lurk beneath its surface, constantly being repressed by reified identities and existing socio-economic and institutional arrangements, yet constantly bubbling away. Through its exploration of unpredictable encounters between mutable, desiring bodies, others and the world around them, such a cinema helps keep open what, following Althusser, Malabou labels the 'unassignable space', the void in which something as yet undefined may arise. Of course, there is a danger of, at best, a naive utopianism in such a cinema and, at worst, a conformist celebration of the type of flexibility that neoliberalism routinely demands masquerading as something progressive. But, in their attention to the frictions of encounters, the pain and exhaustion of bodies and the failures of blocked becomings, Kechiche and Sciamma remind us of the durability of existing forms, a durability that must be held in tension, as their films do, in their deconstructive materialism, with its contingency.

In the period after 1968, it was assumed that a truly radical cinema would shatter the illusionism of mainstream narrative cinema by drawing attention to its own production practices. It was also assumed that such a cinema would foreground the essentially collective nature of cinematic production by refusing to fetishise the creativity of the individual *auteur*. Although undoubtedly part of the commerce of auteurism, Kechiche and Sciamma highlight the existence of a space for questioning within the mainstream. While neither rejects cinematic illusionism within their films or draws explicit attention to their working practices, both develop a broader, recurrent reflexivity around the production of images, stereotypes and identities and the power relations that surround them. But both, I have argued, have blind spots that relate closely but very differently to their privileged positions as star auteurs. If the kind of deconstructive materialist approach that I have been discussing here is particularly drawn to the tension between the radical potential of local embodied encounters and the socio-economic and institutional frames that constrain them, a materialist analysis worthy of the name must also pay close attention to how such frames, and the power aysmmetries embedded within them, operate within cinema itself.

# 5

# The Dardennes' unwitting gifts

Cinema, André Malraux famously reflected, is an art that is also an industry. Film, he might have added, is a gift that is also a commercial product. Filmmakers, individually and collectively, draw hungrily on a rich cultural heritage. Digesting it and working on it, they develop their own vision and style. They give back to cinematic tradition through implicit and explicit acknowledgement of their influences. But they also give forwards, as others respond to their work and enrich it through interpretations and responses that accrete to it and make it something more than what it might originally have been. Yet, as we know all too well, cinema is also thoroughly commercialised. An aggressive machinery of copyright works to ensure that films circulate only in approved ways and that the profits that accrue from their distribution and exhibition, through cinemas, DVDs or online streaming, return to those considered legitimate beneficiaries. At the same time, whenever films are successful, symbolic capital accrues to names associated with them, making future projects easier to finance and films and DVDs easier to sell. The unpaid labour of cinema spectators is an essential part of this reputational labour. Films give but they also take back.

The Dardenne brothers are not outside this broader pattern. Explicitly, in their writings and interviews, and implicitly, through the stylistic and other choices deployed in their films, they acknowledge their debt to those that have influenced them, whether it be film directors such as Roberto Rossellini, Ken Loach, Robert Bresson and Maurice Pialat or thinkers such as Emmanuel Levinas (Dardenne 2005: 10, 27, 33, 106, 145). At the same time, their films offer a clear affective and intellectual gift to their audience in their capacity to move us and to make us think about non-destructive ways to live under a neoliberal order. Yet, the Dardennes are clearly also part of the business of cinema: leading European arthouse directors, their names attract money to films, promote festivals, fill cinemas and sell DVDS and video on demand. While they undeniably give something to us that defies reduction to monetary value, they participate in the commerce of authorship and of cinema more broadly. Should we therefore conclude that the gift given to us by their films and those of others is an entirely counterfeit one, any form of gift economy inevitably being instrumentalised by the market in the age of neoliberal capital? Or should we retain some hope in cinema's capacity to produce something in excess of and irreducible to its commodity value that we might call a gift? The latter, I would suggest, while adding that films may often give their most valuable gifts despite or unbeknownst to themselves. This is what I will argue in relation to the Dardennes: I will suggest that their principal *knowing* gift to us relates to their unstinting search for an ethical alternative to the violences of neoliberalism. However, I will also argue, that, as they flesh out the relations between their characters and root them in a social and material world from which the stability of the old Fordist bargain between capital and labour has been withdrawn, alternative economic practices and forms of exchange seem to proliferate in them. Amongst these, a perhaps unwitting gift of the films to us, different forms of gift-giving are of most interest for the purposes of this book. All conditional in one way or another, these gifts lack the apparent purity of the films' explicit ethics. They are ultimately of more political interest, however, because of their capacity to offer us, not a fully-fledged account of some alternative way of co-existing, but a glimpse of less destructive, more generous and potentially collective forms of human interaction. While a glimpse might seem a meagre gift, I will suggest that it is more bounteous than it appears. By underscoring the mutability – the plasticity – of human relations, bodies and objects, and even of gifts themselves, it opens a space for us to imagine other less oppressive forms of life. *La Promesse* (*The Promise*, 1996), the film that introduced the Dardennes' mature style and thematic universe, is a good place to start as we begin to flesh out this argument.

## *La Promesse*: Finding a way to live in a new world

*La Promesse* was far from the Dardenne brothers' first film, even if it was the one that first brought them serious international recognition. Before it, they had made a cluster of documentaries recording a tradition of collective resistances, as well as several more or less successful fiction films. But, as the last of the earlier fictions, *Je pense à vous* (*I'm Thinking of You*, 1992), a film about the closure of a steelworks, underscored, the militant tradition that the brothers had tracked was running into the ground, its socio-economic foundations undone, its institutional bases crumbling, its oppositional language no longer available to make sense of the world or to give direction to struggle. Something new needed to be built in the ruins of the old politics. *La Promesse* was the brothers' response to this challenge and set the pattern for their subsequent films. In the absence of an elaborated political language and of collective solidarities, it worked through an ethical dilemma in the raw, embodied encounter of individuals, an encounter tracked in close proximity by the restlessly mobile camera that would become so strongly associated with their work.

The film's core dynamics are established in its early moments. Set in a service station, the first sequence finds Igor (Jérémie Renier), an apprentice mechanic, fixing an old lady's car for no charge but opportunistically stealing her purse before emptying it of its cash and burying it in the yard. He is then summoned by the garage owner to practise the art of soldering (Figure 5.1). The lesson is aborted when his father Roger (Olivier Gourmet) commandeers him to help collect a consignment of

**Figure 5.1** The garage owner passing on skills to Igor in *La Promesse* (Jean-Pierre and Luc Dardenne, 1996)

illegal immigrants. As he departs, he takes the exhaust pipe that the garage owner has given him for the go-kart he is building with two young friends. This takes us to the sequence in which the migrants are collected. An illicit human supplement to the licit circulations of a globalising economy, they arrive hidden in cars on a transporter lorry before being transferred to a van driven by Roger. They are promised that there is plentiful work and money in Belgium. Igor is quick to offer cigarettes to everyone. When they disembark, money quickly changes hands for accommodation in the slum housing that Roger operates. A discount is promised for illegal labour on a house that Roger is buying for him and Igor to live in. Although we see most of what happens in close proximity to the small group of characters involved, extreme long shots of the moving van draw our attention to a monumental industrial landscape whose inert background presence reminds us of what came before the narrative and serves as an implicit context for the much smaller story that is now unfolding. The film's compelling ethical drama is already in motion, but gifts of things and skills are also already in circulation around its edges in ways I will come to. Let us look first at the ethical drama staged by the film.

Igor is torn between helping people and harming them. By stealing and burying the old lady's purse, he provides an initial insight into the ethical consequences of the preference for material wealth over the person. The human element, the purse, has to be discarded for the money inside to enter into free circulation. Igor avoids confronting the consequences of his act by sending the old lady in vain pursuit of the lost object. The film will not let him off so easily. It continues to confront him with the same essential dilemma but in increasingly radical form. The first reiteration comes when Roger responds to the town mayor's need to demonstrate his toughness by rounding up some illegal migrants. Roger fulfils his quota by taking some of his recent arrivals to a bar, apparently to start their journey to America, while actually betraying them to the authorities. Igor hides away in the toilet only to be grabbed by one of the migrants before he is hauled away. Directly embodied in such importunate form, the ethical consequences of treating people as disposable have become harder to evade. Their summons becomes even more urgent in the next iteration. Immigration officers raid the house that Roger has the migrants labouring on. One of the men, Hamidou (Rasmane Ouedraogo), falls from the scaffolding and badly hurts his leg. Seeing that he is bleeding to death, Igor applies a tourniquet. Fearing discovery as a trafficker or illegal employer, Olivier removes it, lets Hamidou die and makes Igor help him bury the body in the house in which they intend to live. Igor is now effectively an accomplice to murder. The consequences of the choice of material gain over human well-being first expressed in the theft and discarding of the woman's purse has been taken to its ultimate conclusion, a home for some being built over the body of another. Igor seems to have damned himself. However, the Dardennes always open an ethical escape route to their characters. Before Hamidou dies, he makes the young man promise to protect his wife, Assita (Assita Ouedraogo), and child who had arrived with the latest consignment of migrants. Reacting in a way typical of the Dardennes' heroes, Igor tries to contain the logical consequences of this ethical commitment by helping Assita without betraying Roger. The film again pushes him to an ethical decision. Roger decides to get rid of the awkward, questioning Assita by trafficking her into prostitution in Germany. Igor must now take the plunge. Stealing his father's van, he drives Assita away and hides her temporarily in the garage. With her help, he immobilises Roger who has tracked the pair down. Finally, as he takes her to catch a train to safety, he confesses to her what has happened. The film ends as he follows her and her baby, carrying her bag, having broken decisively with his previous existence and arrived at an open-ended commitment to the vulnerable Other.

Alongside this compelling ethical drama, from the film's first sequence onwards, gifts circulate and seem to call forth more gifts. The garage proprietor gives two gifts to Igor, one an object (the exhaust pipe), the other a skill (the art of soldering). The former is intended for the go-kart that Igor is assembling with his friends: never simply an inert thing, it helps the boys build something together and play at adulthood while remaining children. Its giving points towards the capacity of one generation to help the next find its way. Later, Igor passes the go-kart on to his two young friends, a giving away that suggests a broader renunciation of his childhood even as he encourages his friends to continue to play. The soldering likewise establishes bonds that are not simply metallic. The transmission of a skill that the garage proprietor himself learned, another sign of intergenerational solidarity, should help Igor establish himself in the material and social world through the exercise of a trade. In its modest way, it opens a future but demands commitment in return. Although Igor cannot yet respect the required discipline because of his father's demands for help in his illicit activities, he does later put his acquired mechanical skills to good if unforeseen use. He uses the garage's drill to fix a statue that Assita carries and which had been broken in a racist attack. He also draws on his know-how with the garage hoist when he needs to immobilise his threatening father. He gives other things to Assita after her husband's death: he has money passed to her although this leads to a beating from his father; he sells the gold signet ring that Roger had given him, so that he can buy her a rail ticket to Italy; he gives the radio that Hamidou had been listening to when the accident occurred. Roger, perhaps against expectations, is also a giver of gifts, although not beneficial ones; he buys migrants drinks to gain their confidence; he gives Igor money and the gold ring identical to his own; he helps Igor learn to drive, a skill that will be turned against him when Igor steals his van to rescue Assita; he tattoos the young man, literally leaving his mark on his flesh. More broadly, he inducts him into people trafficking and has him fake signatures on ID cards, another skill that will be put to indirect good use when Igor persuades Assita she can travel to Italy on an ID card borrowed from another African woman.

The complex web of obligations and interconnections at play here already gives a sense of how much the film's social, temporal and material economy depends on forms of gift-giving. It nonetheless requires some analytical unpicking to draw out its main fault-lines and to ask whether it gives something more than is strictly required by the staging of the film's ethical drama. It is worth noting initially that, within this gift economy, things are never simply things or mere commodities. They all take on their meaning through their embeddedness in relationships and histories. Hamidou's radio, for example, bears his mark, in the shape of an improvised repair to the carrying strap, and the memory of his death in which it played no small part. Assita's statue bears a wealth of cultural and religious signification but also carries the traces of the racist attack and, after Igor's repair, the emergent bond between the two characters (Mai 2010: 58–60). Roger's gift of the ring condenses the character's broader attempt to remake Igor in his own monstrous likeness. The gold it is made from embodies a commitment to material wealth while the blood it becomes stained with suggests the human consequences such an attitude leads to. When Igor sells it to generate cash for the railway ticket, he underscores his rejection of what his father represents and his commitment to Assita. Because things are embedded in histories and shifting interpersonal relationships, far from being inert objects, they can mutate in significance and function. A similar capacity for mutation seems to characterise the skills passed between characters. Although the mechanical skills taught to Igor by the garage owner seem to call for a predictable giving back, which is already a giving forward, through the learning and exercise of a trade, Igor, as we have seen, puts his skills to a very different use, just as he did with the driving skills transferred to him by his father. While similarly mutable, skills have a particular quality denied to objects. Their giving does not deprive their giver of them. Nor did the giver really own them in the way that we can own things. The fruit of a collective and typically inter-generational know-how, they demand to be transmitted, put to work and passed on again if they are not to shrivel.

We typically associate gifts with generosity and often with unconditionality. Many of the gifts in *La Promesse* are conditional and some anything but generous, even if they might initially appear to be so. They do vary, however. We might initially identify three broad categories of gift. Firstly, there are generous but conditional gifts. With the demand for discipline in the present and productive use in the future, the garage owner's transmission of skills exemplifies these. Secondly, there are toxic gifts, like those given by Roger to Igor in his attempt to remake his son in his image. In some ways, these toxic gifts could all be considered to follow the pattern set by Igor's theft from the old woman at the start of the film. By fixing her car, he gained her trust even whilst he stole her purse. Toxic gifts are inevitably deceptive in this way. They take more than they give and are typically not what they seem. Finally, there are gifts given in a vain attempt to repay what might be considered an infinite debt. Igor's inevitably failed attempt to atone for his part in the killing of Hamidou by providing objects and services to Assita falls into this category. Tentatively, adding a fourth category, we could suggest that, through their very vulnerability, the dying Hamidou, his widow and their child make a priceless gift to Igor by rescuing him from a murderous world centred on the self and its calculations. But these categories themselves tend to break down as we repeatedly see gifts, like the ring, or mechanical skills, being reworked for new purposes.

The Dardenne brothers have repeatedly made their debt to ethical philosopher Emmanuel Levinas clear (Dardenne 2005: 35, 42, 56). When their characters are placed in a struggle of all against all and in a context in which the thing is often preferred to the person, they are driven towards murder, real or symbolic. Repeatedly confronting them with vulnerable others, the films push them towards an ethics based in a commitment to the Other, and thus open the possibility of alternative forms of relationship where none seemed to exist. At least some of the diverse forms of gift-giving we have identified in *La Promesse* could be seen as building on this ethical core. Bernasconi (1997) explains how the Levinasian exposure to the Other puts into question my possessions and commands me to give so that I no longer have the right to keep anything. This giving away is not simply a gift of material things: rather, the imperative to give to the Other interrupts a world of exchange, circulation and rationality centred on the self and its calculations, thereby opening another world to me (Bernasconi 1997: 258–9). There is a command to give here but there is more. The Levinasian encounter with the Other, Diprose notes, forces me to rethink my existing sense of the world: 'the other's alterity is also a teaching', she explains, 'because it opens me to think beyond myself and therefore beyond what I already know (Diprose 2002: 137). She adds, 'it is the other's alterity that makes me think, rather than ideas I live from and that seem to make me what I am' (Diprose 2002: 141). Some of the circulation of gifts in *La Promesse* clearly aligns with this Levinasian giving as described by Bernasconi and Diprose. Igor initially tries to maintain a compromise between an ethical and an instrumental economy by giving Assita a series of gifts (a stove, money) that are somehow meant to compensate for the effective murder of her husband. Finally, recognising that the debt cannot be repaid, he moves to an unconditional commitment that means the gifting, or sacrifice, of his old life with his father. At the same time, the way in which Hamidou and then Assita and their child open a world to him centred on the Other's needs could be seen as a precious pedagogic gift along the lines described by Diprose. Yet these Levinasian gifts cannot account for all of the film's complex gift economy, the circulation of skills, services and things that it sets in motion, and their capacity to sustain social connections and open potentially different futures. A more rounded discussion of the gift is required.

## Theorising the gift

Back in 1925, Marcel Mauss, Émile Durkheim's nephew, published his most famous work, *Le Don* (*The Gift*). The book might have seemed primarily anthropological in its thrust but Mauss, a socialist, was driven by an urgent search for a contemporary alternative to both the inhumanity of the capitalist market economy and revolutionary communism with its state-driven command economy. Writing in the aftermath of the slaughter of the Great War (1914–1918), he was also spurred on by a conviction that a punitive attitude to German war reparation payments would only lead to renewed conflict and that some sort of debt forgiveness, or gift, was a much better way to build relations of peaceful cooperation between the ex-belligerents (Mallard 2011). The book brought together a wide-ranging set of gift-giving practices from pre-modern societies and sought to identify patterns connecting them. Going against dominant accounts that framed pre-modern exchange as forms of barter that anticipated modern market exchange, Mauss asserted the centrality of gift exchange to pre-modern social relationships. He famously framed gifts as 'total social facts' that were inextricably juridical, cultural, religious and moral in a way that challenged the narrow, instrumental calculus of modern economics (Mauss 2012: 64). Also sitting ill with idealised modern accounts of gift-giving as something purely generous, his gifts were governed by three rules: the obligation to give, to receive and to reciprocate (Mauss 2012: 142–53), to which were added the requirement to give, or sacrifice, to the gods as givers of all (Mauss 2012: 86). Why, Mauss asked, did people feel obliged to reciprocate gifts? His simple answer, as summarised by David Graeber, was that a gift was never simply the thing or service given but always bore some mark of the spirit or identity of the giver and thus exerted a pull on the receiver (Graeber 2001: 33–4, 154–5).

This sense that objects had, to some extent, a life of their own might suggest that Mauss was seduced by something like commodity fetishism, as famously described by Marx, whereby social relationships between people were misperceived as relationships between things in a way that obscured the exploitative nature of capitalist production. Graeber reads Mauss more positively. By giving a life and history to things, he suggests, Mauss invited us to see how the creation of objects and their meanings does not end when they leave the factory but is continually open to reinvention in a way that exceeds their insertion into any narrowly utilitarian calculus (Graeber 2001: 162–3). More broadly, Mauss's account of the gift challenged classical accounts of market exchange as something which occurred between two individuals and was ended by the transfer of goods or services for a fixed sum of money. Although they varied enormously from one pre-modern society to the next, the exchanges described by Mauss typically involved groups not individuals, sustained lasting or open-ended connections and, resisting any easy separation of people, services and things, defied instrumental calculation.

Mauss did not simply associate gift-giving with pre-modern societies. He considered it an abiding social impulse that resisted the capitalist market's drive to marginalise or instrumentalise it. He noted the existence around himself of numerous gift-giving practices: the joy of public giving, festive hospitality and generous artistic expenditure. He welcomed an emergent social security regime but also praised more autonomous institutions such as mutuals and cooperatives which connected people together in a relationship of giving and receiving. He wrote of the need to limit the accumulation of capital through speculation and suggested that the rich needed to rediscover practices of generous expenditure and debt forgiveness in a way which acknowledged that they were simply custodians of collectively generated wealth (Mauss 2012: 213–22). Despite his conviction of the importance of generous giving and its capacity to bind people together in peace, he knew gifts could be poisonous. They could generate overwhelming obligations if from the powerful and could be involved in potentially ruinous relationships such as seen with the competitively destructive potlach rites of some North American tribes (Mauss 2012: 148–53).

Possibly the most famous critique of Mauss came from Jacques Derrida. Derrida accused Mauss of gathering a heterogeneous collection of social practices under the flattening label of the gift (Derrida 1992: 26). He also suggested, as summarised in discussion with Jean-Luc Marion, that the inherent conditionality of Maussian giving disqualified it qua gift:

> As soon as a gift is identified as a gift, with the meaning of a gift, then it is cancelled as a gift. It is reintroduced into the circle of an exchange and destroyed as a gift. As soon as the donee knows it is a gift, he already thanks the donator, and cancels the gift. As soon as the donator is conscious of giving, he himself thanks himself and again cancels the gift by re-inscribing it into a circle, an economic circle. (Kearney 1999: 59)

What complicates matters is that Derrida is not simply referring here to material gifts or conventional economics. He is concerned more broadly with how giving of any sort works to create obligations and generate recognition, thus always ensuring a material or symbolic return to the giver and confirming existing identities, understanding and power relations (Derrida 1992: 10–15). To escape from this economy of the proper, whereby gifts always pay back the giver, gifts have to be the object of such a radical forgetting as not to leave even an unconscious trace or obligation. The (true) gift then becomes not so much impossible, as *the* impossible, a desire for a generous giving that negates itself as soon as it is willed but which nonetheless persists (Derrida 1992: 7). Marion opens a potential way out of this aporia by suggesting that, freed from any individual act of donation, escaping from an economy of the proper, the gift could be equated with the *given,* or that which is given to our consciousness by experience in a way that echoes Heidegger's description of Being as *es gibt* or it (Being) gives. Derrida responds that the notion of the *given* describes that which has already been incorporated into our existing conceptual framework and is thus not a true gift which would have to arrive in excess of it. He thus moves us towards a sense of the gift as an event, as something which creates an opening to the new within our experience prior to any understanding we may have of it (Kearney 1999: 63–7).

Predictably, Pierre Bourdieu takes a very different position. It is only because the capitalist market has become so dominant, he argues, that thinkers like Derrida analyse the gift in relation to calculating, self-conscious actors. Starting from such a position, gifts are inevitably seen as deferred loans demanding repayment or as investments generating symbolic capital and 'true' gifts must indeed appear as (the) impossible (Bourdieu 1997, 233–4). For Bourdieu, however, individual actions and attitudes always result from the internalisation of the habits and practices associated with specific social fields. As such, they resist positioning as either selfish or disinterested, individual or collective, free or constrained, willed or unwilled so that the polarities which underpin Derrida's aporia seem to dissolve. While Bourdieu very usefully underscores the collective dimension of gift-giving, something that was there from the start in Mauss, he is not necessarily able to escape his own blind spots, notably a tendency to see all human behaviours as instrumental. He suggests that it is only the delay between giving and reciprocating that allows the gift to be subjectively perceived as disinterested while objectively it transforms financial wealth into the symbolic capital of recognition through what he calls 'the alchemy of symbolic exchanges' (Bourdieu 1997: 235). He thus risks returning to a narrowly transactional understanding of the gift. He does, however, point to the unequal distribution of the (socially acquired) disposition to be generous and the way in which some are clearly better placed to give than others, an aspect of gift-giving which Mauss and Derrida rather ignore (Bourdieu 1997: 235). Yet, gift-giving has clearly always relied on the invisible labour of some while turning others, often women, into objects of exchange. For example, Claude Lévi-Strauss, the great structuralist anthropologist, analysed how the exchange of women was used to cement relationships between different tribes (Lévi-Strauss 1967). Feminist scholars have also examined how the interchange of women was used to consolidate the male homosocial bond (Irigaray 1997; Rubin 1975).

What can we take forward from this? Derrida is right, of course, about the heterogeneity of the gift-giving practices described by Mauss. But, from the point of view of my argument here, this heterogeneity and the fact that gifts can range from the generous to the toxic, is precisely what is of interest. What Mauss brings to the fore is not simply how gifts offer something exceeding capitalist exchange relations but the plasticity of gift-giving as a practice, its capacity to be more or less productive or destructive according to the context into which it is inserted. Bourdieu similarly notes the historical variability and context dependence of gift-giving practices and crucially points to their social dimension. While, under current conditions of neoliberal capitalism and the acquisitive individualism that goes with it, it may indeed be difficult to see beyond the gift as either calculating or impossibly idealistic, its historical embedding in a wide range of more collective practices suggests that it retains the (Maussian) capacity to point beyond the market and to offer a glimpse of a different, more generous future. This same variability of the gift speaks productively to the diversity of gift-giving in *La Promesse* and the Dardenne brothers' other films and helps us to see how, beyond their core ethical dramas, these films bring into view potentially more generous ways of relating which could blossom in alternative contexts.

A similar analysis might be developed around the conditionality and therefore the impurity of the gift: while conditionality would disqualify it as a gift it in the eyes of Derrida or Levinas, from a Maussian point of view, it is precisely what endows it with the capacity to open and sustain social connectivity. A Levinasian reading of *La Promesse* might speak productively to gift relations which either clearly instrumentalise the Other or which open a new life no longer centred on the self and its goals. But such a reading is too fundamentally dichotomous to help us distinguish between the different kinds of conditional or impure gift which proliferate in the film. These need a more nuanced approach of the sort which recourse to Mauss can offer. Both Roger and the garage owner transmit skills to Igor. In both cases, these gifts carry implicit or explicit conditions and, passed from an older to a younger male, could be connected to what Derrida might call an economy of the proper which confirms existing identities and hierarchies. But, in one case, the skills are destructive and exploitative and separate Igor from those outside his family circle, while in the other, they call for productive use and re-transmission, a giving forward as much as a giving back. And, in any case, as we have noted, Igor is adept at putting skills learned from both older men to new uses, for example, turning his father's driving lessons against him, when he helps Assita escape.

As Graeber noted, Mauss is particularly attentive to how objects refuse reduction to mere commodity status as they are gifted from one person to another, shift in function and meaning, and become intertwined with human histories. We saw this in *La Promesse* with objects like Assita's statue as it is used ceremonially, defiled by racists and then, in a gifting of skills, repaired by Igor. We also saw how Roger's gifted gold ring played shifting roles and became intertwined in interpersonal histories as it became coated in Hamidou's blood before being sold on to help Assita. This mutability and historicity of the object world in the film responds to and underpins the plasticity of human relationality within its shifting gift economy.

*La Promesse* introduces us to the richness of the gift economy that runs through the Dardenne brothers' films. I will now explore how that richness expresses itself in the other films. In the process, I will revisit some films discussed in earlier chapters to show how discussion of the gift can bring out new dimensions in them.

## Finite gifts, infinite debts and mutable objects

When Igor tries to repay the infinite debt caused by Hamidou's death in *La Promesse* by giving material gifts, thereby seeking an impossible compromise between an ethical commitment to the Other and calculating instrumentalism, he begins a series that runs through the Dardenne brothers' later films. In *Le Silence de Lorna*, for example, when Lorna fails to prevent her husband, Claudy, from being murdered by the gang she is working with, she tries to give the money he has left behind to his family. They refuse to have anything to do with it. Similarly, Francis (Morgan Marinne), the young murderer of *Le Fils* (*The Son*, 2002), feels he has paid for his crime by spending a specific amount of time in prison. In both cases, characters misapply the measurable and material to the ethical and immaterial rather than genuinely confronting the human consequences of their actions. This pattern also runs through *L'Enfant*, a film within which gifts and their dark cousins, thefts, multiply and objects shift in significance just as do those in *La Promesse*.

As the film begins, Bruno, its deeply irresponsible hero, has rented out the flat of Sonia (Déborah François), his girlfriend, even as she is giving birth to their child, with the consequence that she is locked out, along with the newborn infant. In typical fashion, the hero has failed an ethical test which will be radicalised as the film proceeds. Will he take responsibility for Sonia and their baby or prioritise material gain? After his initial wrong choice, he quickly gains Sonia's forgiveness for the hurt caused, but the film will not let him off so lightly. He repeats his mistake in severely aggravated form. In the same way as consumer capitalism can manufacture endless numbers of identical objects, he judges that they can make another baby and that their existing child can be sold for gain, an act he duly carries out. Sonia is utterly devastated. He shows her the money the sale has brought but she cannot be bought off. He is forced to undo the sale and return the child to her. He seeks forgiveness a second time, but to no avail. He seems lost. The film, in characteristic Dardennes fashion, gives him another chance by pushing him to make a decisive ethical choice. The gang that were selling the child on for him do not simply expect the return of the money paid for the baby: they demand compensation for their 'costs' and tell him that he will have to put his little gang to work for them. Their next robbery leads to the capture of his young accomplice, not before the latter nearly drowns as the two hide in the water at the river's edge to evade their pursuers. Finally taking responsibility both for his acts and for his younger, more vulnerable companion in a way he failed to for his son, Bruno hands himself in to the police. In the final redemptive scene, Sonia visits him in prison and the pair hold hands and cry together.

Bruno, like Igor before him, has sought to navigate between two radically opposed economies: an ethical one in which one takes responsibility for vulnerable others and an instrumental one within which people are essentially used or valued for their monetary equivalence. The film's different gifts and thefts are woven into these two economies. The material gifts that Bruno gives bear the history of his passage between them. The thefts seem to condense the destructiveness of the instrumental economy but also connect to the gifts in two ways. On a more obvious level, they provide funds for their giving. More interestingly they reverse their underlying logic through a violent unweaving of the ties between people and things that gifts tie more peacefully.

The film's first theft occurs near the start. Bruno has his young accomplices steal from an old man. The money is easily shared out. A padlocked box resists them. Bruno eventually forces it open. To his disappointment, it contains only a will. Too intertwined in the personal to be commodified, it is quickly got rid of. One of the accomplices wants the CD player as a birthday present for his sister. Bruno makes him pay for it in cash. Later, he will sell the digital camera they have also stolen to a fence. As at the start of *La Promesse*, when Igor buries the old lady's purse after stealing her money, the theft tears things out of their embeddedness in a person's existence to turn them into objects of pure exchange. Something similar happens at the end of the film when a woman carrying a day's takings is mugged. As Bruno and his young accomplice make their escape on a motor scooter, the latter goes through the woman's bag, removing the money and inspecting and discarding the rest, including the bag itself. By treating anything personal as effectively rubbish, the young men's sifting makes manifest what happens when the thing is prioritised over the person, the former being fetishised, the latter becoming disposable. Their actions are therefore both outside the normal because of their illegality and a condensation of violence intrinsic to the normal itself. The selling of the child in the middle of the film, a theft of indescribable magnitude from Sonia, condenses this violence by turning the human itself into a commodity and discarding even its deepest attachments. The traditional Marxist critique of commodity fetishism focuses on how the fetishisation of the object obscures the relations of production so that relationships between people misleadingly present themselves as relations between things. Here, what we are seeing is how, later in their life cycle, objects which have been woven into lives can only be commodified again by being violently removed from their human context.

Funded by the proceeds of the thefts, Bruno's gifts attempt to restore human bonds torn apart by his cynical instrumentalism. The two principal amongst them are a child's pram and a jacket. He buys the pram as he seeks to win Sonia back after renting out her flat. Her acceptance of it signifies a reconciliation and implies a commitment to the child on his part. Later, out walking with her, he spots an expensive jacket in a shop window identical to the one he is wearing. When he buys it for her and she puts it on, it moves from its pristine status as mass-produced commodity to being a marker of their closeness (Figure 5.2). After he has sold and then recovered their child, his failed attempts to give the pram back to her underscore her refusal to accept him back as a partner and a parent for their child. He is forced to sell the pram, turning it back into a commodity, but at a drastically reduced price. Finding the jacket he bought for her inside the pram, he sells that too, but is given the derisory sum of one euro.

**Figure 5.2** The identical jackets that seem to seal Bruno's forgiveness in *L'Enfant* (Jean-Pierre and Luc Dardenne, 2005)

It is as if, since its first seductive shop window appearance, its precipitous drop in monetary value now speaks not simply of the jacket's worth but of the loss of appeal of the commodity more broadly in comparison to the value that the character comes to attach to human connections.

## Poisonous and ethical gifts

While the attempt to compensate for incalculable harms through finite gifts is indicative above all of self-deception or self-preservation, the poisonous gifts that run through the films have no such worthy but misguided intent. Hiding their instrumentality behind an apparent generosity, their deceptiveness is targeted towards others who will be won over all the better to be harmed. They typically bring returns to the giver of the gift while stealing from the receiver something far in excess of or incomparable to whatever is given. The gold ring given by Roger to Igor in *La Promesse* is emblematic of this kind of gift. A valuable although soon to be bloodied object, its apparently generous giving in fact helps strip Igor of his innocence by committing him to resemble his father and dedicate himself to the cult of material gain. Similar gifts recur with variations throughout the films, all of them bringing their own baggage of human harm.

Two of the more recent works provide telling and contrasting examples, one, *Le Gamin au vélo* (*The Kid with the Bike*, 2011), focuses on a directly interpersonal and obviously toxic gift, the other, *Deux jours, une nuit*, centres on a less personal and less obviously toxic one. In the former, a local drug dealer and petty criminal, Wes (Egon di Mateo), seems to befriend the hero, Cyril (Thomas Doret), much to the dismay of Samantha (Cécile de France), the hairdresser who has committed herself to looking after the young man. Wes first tests out Cyril's mettle by having another child steal his bicycle. When Cyril gives a demonstration of his fighting abilities, Wes invites him to his house, offers him drinks and invites him to play on his Play-Station. He also pays to have the puncture in Cyril's bike tyre, a result of the attempted theft, repaired. Finally, in what is a perverse pedagogic gift, he trains Cyril to carry out a mugging by striking his intended victim, a bookseller, with a baseball bat. The robbery predictably goes wrong when the bookseller's son appears and Cyril strikes him too. Neither Wes nor the father who has abandoned Cyril wants anything to do with the stolen money as it would implicate them in a crime. Toxic gifts seem to break social links rather than build them and halt circulation rather than promote it. With its accompaniment of gifts of things, skills and services, Wes's induction of Cyril into crime, a reproduction of his own criminality, seems very much in the same mould as Roger's perversion of Igor in *La Promesse*.

Involving no criminal intent and no obvious seduction of innocence, the toxic gift in *Deux jours, une nuit* is less obviously harmful than in the other films. The solar panel factory workers, we will remember, are balloted on whether they prefer to receive a bonus of one thousand euros each or keep their colleague, Sandra, the film's heroine, on the company's books. When they choose their bonus, the company's apparent gift in fact takes things away. In Sandra's case, the nature of the loss is obvious. She will lose her job. In the other workers' case, it is less clear what may be taken from them, although it is driven to the surface when Sandra visits them all individually and tells them of her situation even as they tell her of their motives. By voting for their bonus, they are effectively prioritising financial advantage over the person, a choice that, it could be argued, many of us routinely make but hold at an insulating distance when we choose our own material benefit or the consumer goods that seduce us over the lives of often distant others whom those choices affect. Some of those who vote against Sandra under pressure from the foreman, as the majority do, do so for their family or their relationship. Yet, rather than representing a real excuse, this suggests the narrowing of the scope of generosity to those one is close to, something which we already saw in *La Promesse* in which Olivier's gifts were focused on his son even as he treated others as disposable. What is therefore taken from the workers is their broader sense of social solidarity. In return for the poisonous gift of the euros, they are diminished as people and workers.

The way in which Sandra confronts them, not in abstract terms but as an embodied and importunate presence, constitutes its own paradoxical gift (Figure 5.3). Through her vulnerability and insistent bodily presence, she disrupts any self-centred or instrumental calculations they have made and re-opens them to an ethical commitment to the Other. This is her unwitting gift to them, one that aligns clearly with the Levinasian gift discussed above. In return, they invite her to put herself in their shoes and to understand what drove them to choose their bonus over her. This is their ethical gift to her, an opening of her world to theirs. Such ethical gifts, and the invitation they bear to see the world from the position of the Other, to acknowledge mutual exposure and, ultimately, to take responsibility for the Other, run through all the Dardenne brothers' films and constitute their ethical core. In some ways, they might seem to open the possibility of a radically different future. However, these gifts come with some intrinsic limitations. To begin with, they are grounded in the subject's embodied vulnerability rather than some other more creative capacity.

**Figure 5.3** Sandra's insistent bodily presence (*Deux jours, une nuit*, Jean-Pierre and Luc Dardenne, 2014)

It is no accident that the films are full of vulnerable characters, from the widowed mother and her infant in *La Promesse*, through the newly delivered mother and her infant in *L'Enfant*, the child murderer in *Le Fils*, the recovering junkie in *Le Silence de Lorna* and the abandoned child in *Le Gamin au vélo* to the recovering depressive in *Deux jours, une nuit*. The films need this vulnerability to stage their recurrent opposition between systemic murderous and human fragility as it plays out over two individualised bodies. But, as I have been suggesting here, they also always seem to need some more positive and socially connective capacity to open a future for their characters, even if they do not acknowledge it. It is here that the next group of gifts come into their own.

## Generous gifts

When we looked at *Rosetta* earlier, we said little about Riquet, the young man who helps Rosetta, whom she sees as a rival for scarce labour, and who refuses to disappear even when she has caused him to be sacked. But Riquet, a giver of gifts, merits our attention here. The first time he helps the heroine, she attacks him for coming to her caravan park home, knocks him to the ground, and wrestles with him in the mud before he manages to subdue her and tell her why he is there. It is as if, a warrior in a violently competitive labour market, her body only knows how to work or fight. Later, he invites her to the house where he lives and offers to ask the landlord if she can rent there too. He gives her food and beer and plays music by the amateur group he is in. He persuades her to dance although she has no idea how, the idea of co-ordinating her movements harmoniously with those of another human being lying outside her experience. Later, when she is once again excluded from work, he offers to let her take over his scam selling his own waffles on the stall. As we have seen, she betrays him to the boss. Thereafter, he will harass her, following her on his moped with its angry wasp-like sound, until she can take no more and resigns her job before attempting to kill herself. She is saved when her gas canister runs out. As she lugs a heavy replacement canister, Riquet is again there, at first still harassing her, but then helping her to her feet when she falls to the ground and cries.

A Levinasian reading might argue that Riquet is simply manifesting care for another person who is clearly in need and that his different gifts of food, hospitality or illicit business skills simply follow from this open-ended ethical commitment. Similarly, there is a clear Levinasian pedagogic gift from Riquet to Rosetta, when, through his very vulnerability, he forces her to confront the murderousness of her competitive and calculating individualism. When she faces him in the last moments of the film, defeated but also rescued, it is in implied recognition of their mutual exposure and vulnerability, an ending which recurs with variations across the Dardenne brothers' films. Yet something overflowing this ethical drama and its associated gifts also unfolds. A privileged way to approach it is to consider what transpires in and between bodies. The Rosetta who fights with Riquet is a warrior for whom another body is an enemy. The Rosetta at the end is a defeated figure who falls to the ground and has to be helped to her feet. These two bodies are those required for the film's central conflict between murderousness and vulnerability. But the Riquet who teaches Rosetta to dance and the Rosetta who rather clumsily receives the lesson are neither warlike nor vulnerable. Without losing a skill, dancing, which was given to him and which he uses rather than owns, Riquet transfers it to Rosetta. In the process, he offers her a body open to the transmission of skills and collaboration with another body. This is a different body, a social and sociable one, one that does not meet others in warlike or vulnerable separation, but which is productively open to others and to a generous sharing.

A similar transmission of gifts between sociable bodies can be found in *Le Fils*. The drama begins when Francis, the young murderer, arrives as a pupil in the offenders' school where Olivier, the murdered boy's father, works. From the point of view of my argument here, there is a particularly interesting scene around the middle of the film. Olivier is teaching Francis how to make a wooden box in which to carry tools and possessions, a box modelled exactly on his own. As the two work together, a camera that cleaves close to their embodied interaction throughout the film draws our attention to the contrast between the two bodies, the large, menacing body of Olivier, with its wide, weight-lifter style belt, and the slender body of Francis, with its much thinner arms. Two very different dynamics are being woven together in such a way that they might seem to merge but also leaves room for them to be teased apart. Condensing the film's ethical drama, two bodies are brought together in their separation and potential confrontation, the power of one a latent menace to the fragility of the other. Yet something else is also happening. A skill and the associated gestures that the first body does not own but which are in its possession are being transferred to another body that is empowered in the process (Figure 5.4). A gift is transmitted that can only be repaid by putting it to future use or through its undiminished retransmission to another body. There is a double connectivity here: the connectivity of two bodies sharing skills and collaborating and the connectivity between the past, whence the skill has come, to the future, where its as yet undetermined uses reside.

At the film's conclusion, the same two bodies are once again confronted as they are driven, in classic Dardennes style, to the moment of ethical decision. Olivier has driven Francis to his brother's isolated lumber yard to select some timber. After testing the young man on his newly acquired knowledge of different woods, Olivier finally tells him that he is the murdered boy's father. Francis unsurprisingly takes flight but is caught by Olivier and pinned to the ground. Olivier places his powerful hands around the helpless young man's throat but, faced with his vulnerability, draws back from murder and returns to loading the timber they have sawn into his trailer. Silently, Francis returns and helps the older man tie up the wood, their bodies once again joined in collaboration. In some ways, and as we have already seen, the interactions invite interpretation in terms of the essentially static and dichotomous opposition of two logics, an ethical command not to murder the vulnerable Other and a desire for revenge for a murder that was rooted in self-preservation and a preference for the

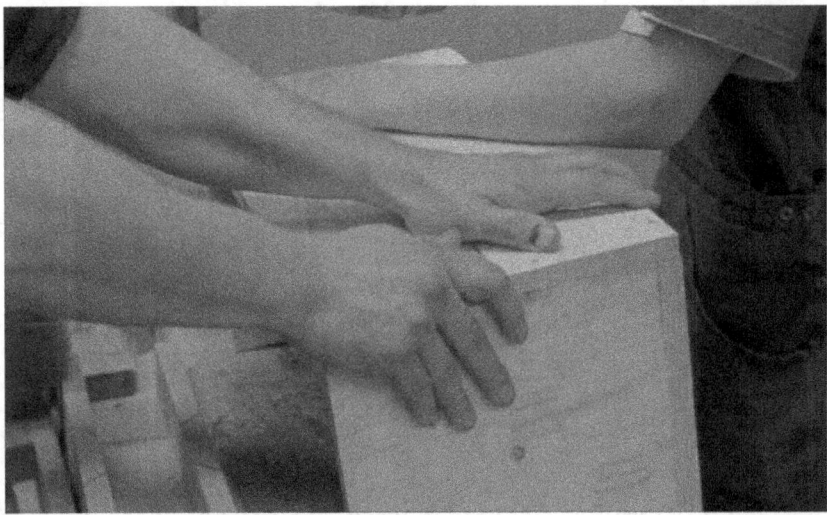

**Figure 5.4** Menace and collaboration: two dynamics in the same frame (*Le Fils*, Jean-Pierre and Luc Dardenne, 2002)

thing over the person. Yet, masked by this dramatic opposition, another quieter logic is at work whereby one person passes on knowledge and skills that he himself was given to another person. It is the latter interaction which, continuing quietly after the decision not to kill, opens a future for both characters.

In 1935, Mauss published another famous essay, 'Techniques of the body', which was independent of his work on the gift. In that essay, he analysed the social and historical dimension of how we use our bodies. His interest had initially been aroused by an encyclopaedia entry about swimming which led him to observe how movements and gestures taught to new swimmers had changed during his lifetime. This led him to the more general observation that bodily gestures, even ones as apparently natural and personal as walking, are techniques learned through imitative action and assembled, 'for the individual, not by himself [sic] alone but by all his education, by the whole society to which he belongs, in the place he occupies in it' (Mauss 1973: 76). He himself noted cinema's general capacity to record and transmit gestures when he observed how French women seemed to have acquired a new way of walking from Hollywood films (Mauss 1973: 72). But what makes the Dardennes particularly interesting in this respect is the way in which their recurrent interest in inter-generational relations and their close attention to embodied interactions converge to record the transmission of skills and gestures from one body to another. This giving of embodied capacities brings into view not simply the social nature of gestures but the plasticity of bodies themselves, their capacity to develop new behaviours and relate collaboratively to other bodies.

## The reconnective power of the gift

The gift-giving patterns analysed so far continue into some of the brothers' more recent films like *Le Gamin au vélo* and *La Fille inconnue* (*The Unknown Girl*, 2016). They have the familiar ethical struggles at their core but, like *Deux jours, une nuit* which comes between them, tend to emphasise social reconnection rather than acts of socio-economic violence. The films still need that violence, whether it be the abandonment of a child (*Le Gamin au vélo*), ejection from a workplace (*Deux jours, une nuit*), or a murder (*La Fille inconnue*), to ground their ethics. But it comes before or at the start of the action in a way which underscores the shift in emphasis towards reparation. In any case, pedagogic and other transformative gifts are still required to produce bodies that are neither murderous nor simply vulnerable and which, crucially, can learn, evolve and connect in ways which open potentially different futures.

As if to confirm the continued centrality of gifts, *Le Gamin au vélo* has a traditional gift from parent to child in its title. As it begins, Cyril, its young hero, escapes from his children's home to engage in a desperate hunt for Guy (Jérémie Renier), the father who has abandoned him. He is particularly concerned about the whereabouts of his bicycle, something he is convinced Guy would never have got rid of. He is caught by his carers in a clinic in the building where Guy used to live and grabs onto the body of Samantha (Cécile de France), a hairdresser, knocking her to the ground in the process, before being taken back to the home. She arrives there the next day with his bike, having brought it back from the man Cyril's father had sold it to. Cyril shows Samantha how confidently he can ride it. Thereafter, it will allow him to move fluently through the world and from person to person. After its theft, as we noted, Wes, the local criminal has it repaired, as he recruits Cyril to mug the bookseller. As the film nears its conclusion, Cyril is knocked off the bike by the bookseller's son who wants revenge for the mugging. Cornered by the latter, he escapes up a tree from which he falls and lies motionless on the ground as if dead. Awakened by Samantha's call to his mobile, he jumps back on his bike and pedals towards her and the barbecue they have arranged as the film ends.

As in *La Promesse* and *Le Fils*, gifted objects are always embedded in relationships and shift in meaning as those relationships evolve. In the process, the objects reveal their capacity to serve as vectors of human connectivity and memory. Perhaps unsurprisingly, given the film's title, the bicycle in *Le Gamin au vélo* carries probably the richest history of connections of any object in the Dardennes' films. Its gifting and ungifting, damage and repair, and use and abuse testify to the film's evolving interpersonal relationships as well as the bike's own ability, never a merely passive thing, to shift in meaning and function. When Guy sells it, putting it back into the anonymous world of commodity circulation, he is effectively signalling his abandonment of his son, his discarding of the personal attachments that the bike was woven into. By buying it back, and re-gifting it to the boy, Samantha restores its capacity for interpersonal connectivity, the same capacity that Wes seeks to hijack. The bike clearly helps Cyril feel connected to others. But, enabling and accelerating his movement through the world, it is also physically empowering. Its spatial and social powers of connection converge at moments when he uses it to move towards someone, as in the closing moments when he happily returns to Samantha.

If Samantha's gift of the bike signals her initial willingness to do what is necessary to renew the broken inter-generational bond, her subsequent behaviour, often at considerable financial, emotional and physical cost, confirms her total commitment to Cyril. To some extent, what she does can be seen as an ethical recognition of responsibility for a vulnerable Other. The way Cyril wraps himself around her in the clinic at the start expresses a pressing, embodied and almost infant-like demand for care of the sort we have identified across the Dardenne brothers' films. But caring for Cyril also means teaching him how to live non-destructively in the world alongside others: enjoying a shared cycle ride and a picnic (Figure 5.5); not pouring water down the drain as an expression of anger; organising a barbecue with neighbours. This is a less formal pedagogic gift than the apprenticeship in *La Promesse* and the joinery lessons in *Le Fils* but still implies the transfer of a set of skills and attitudes from one person to another and the production of bodies that are not simply vulnerable or murderous, but which are empowered, cooperative and giving. The film needs the vulnerable, clinging Cyril, and Cyril, the violent mugger, for its ethical narrative of care but it also requires a different boy with a less dichotomously divided body in order to open a future.

**Figure 5.5** The bike's connective powers in *Le Gamin au vélo* (Jean-Pierre and Luc Dardenne, 2011)

A similar analysis might be applied to *La Fille inconnue*. Its heroine, Jenny (Adèle Haenel), the doctor, is training Julien (Olivier Bonnaud), a medical student, as the pair deal with evening surgery. When a boy has a fit in the waiting room, Julien freezes, much to Jenny's frustration. We later learn that he reacts this way because the sight of the suffering child on the floor reminds him of his own vulnerability as a child beaten by his father. An hour after the surgery is due to close, Julien wants to open the door to a late caller, the young Black woman who later turns up dead. Again, Jenny chastises him for being too emotional and not establishing boundaries between reasonable and unreasonable demands. After she learns of the young woman's death, she seeks to make amends. Julien is convinced he does not have what it takes to be a doctor: she strives to teach him otherwise. At considerable risk to herself, she commits to identifying the dead woman and her killer. She also endeavours to make amends for not opening the door by paying for a better cemetery plot for the body to lie in. At the same time, she decides to take over her current surgery, with its clientele of poor families and elderly people, rather than further her career through a move to a larger, more upmarket practice.

The film has a degree of reflexivity absent in other Dardenne brothers' films. Its chief protagonist, a doctor who reads the signs of internal suffering as they manifest themselves in bodily symptoms, is a partial double of the filmmakers themselves, with their similar close attention to bodily signs. Yet its underlying dynamics otherwise resemble those of the other Dardenne films discussed. By introducing the fitting patient, Julien's memories of beatings and the murdered girl, the film quickly establishes an ethical core centred on vulnerability and how we respond to it. When Jenny fails to open the door to the girl, thereby circumscribing the limits of her responsibility, she effectively condenses the behaviour of the broader society which washes its hands of the fate of its more marginalised members. As she retrospectively seeks to make amends for her action, and triggers responses in others, she opens an alternative based on a taking of responsibility and a shared recognition of vulnerability. As in the other films, a rich web of gifts comes into existence as the necessary supplement to the ethical drama at the film's core. We might hesitate to see the job offer from the prosperous practice as a poisonous gift, although it does invite Jenny to place her career and personal security ahead of that of others. But we could not deny that, by offering to pay for the girl's grave, giving of time and energy to her under-privileged patients and Julien and pursuing the truth of the killing, she is seeking means to repay the infinite ethical debt she contracted when she failed to open the surgery door. We might also agree that, in her very vulnerability, the dead girl unknowingly gives an ethical gift to Jenny, forcing her to rethink her attitudes and priorities in a way that places the Other and not the self and its goals at the centre. But we might overlook the apparently trivial little gifts that seem less central to the film, a light-hearted leavening for the more general weightiness, but without which it could not create the sense of potential for social reconnection that it does.

One of these occurs when a teenage patient, Bryan (Louka Minnella), performs a song of thanks to Jenny after she has told him she will be leaving the practice, the decision which she later reverses. Another presents itself when Bryan's addict mother (Christelle Cornil), another patient, cooks some waffles which she gives to Jenny who will eat them in the little room where she stays above her surgery (Figure 5.6). Along similar lines, an old lady who has forgotten to give Jenny a present during a house call drops a box of panettone into her hands from an upstairs window. An elderly man invites her to have a coffee with him after she has helped him with social services. These little gifts seem marginal to the film's weightier concerns but are in fact essential. In their role as counter-gifts, they retrospectively confirm that Jenny's care for her patients is an act of giving and not the mere exercise of her professional duty. They also testify to the establishment of bonds of mutual obligation between doctor and patient,

**Figure 5.6** The connective gift of the waffles (*La Fille inconnue,* Jean-Pierre and Luc Dardenne, 2016)

something that is essential to the film's implicit project of social reconnection. Finally, they show how, perhaps despite themselves, Jenny's patients move away from the role of receivers of care into that of more active and productive shapers of relationships. The bodies making waffles, giving panettone, performing songs or making coffee are inventive and actively sociable rather than simply vulnerable. They are not the same bodies as those which Jenny or the Dardennes read for symptoms of suffering or guilt.

## Conclusion

Because films never know what their audience will make of them or what their precise influence will be, they always give more than they know, even as they take our time, our attention and perhaps our money. The Dardenne brothers' films are no exception. They make a knowing gift to their characters and us: plunging the characters into a world where instrumental behaviours prevail, they force them to see the world from the perspective of a vulnerable Other and thereby offer them an ethical alternative to systemic violence where none had appeared to exist. Placing us alongside the characters, and typically in tight proximity to them, they also confront us with a human vulnerability we might typically choose not to see. The limitation of these gifts is that they are framed in terms of one-to-one encounters, foreground vulnerability as opposed to other human qualities, and rely on the very systemic murderousness that they oppose to ground themselves and thus struggle to move meaningfully beyond it. Other gifts, more modest and conditional, point to more promising avenues in their capacity to forge social connections, tie people together productively and connect past to future. Amongst them, perhaps most worthy of note are the pedagogic gifts whereby people transmit skills and gestures they do not own in the expectation that the recipients will give them on in turn or put them to productive use. When they show gestures circulating in this way, the films underscore both their fundamental sociality and the plasticity of the bodies that they inhabit. At the same time, by showing how objects shift in meaning, and become vectors of memory and connectivity, the films give us glimpses of other ways of relating to the material world and to others in excess of any narrowly instrumental uses or straightforward commodification. And, this, ultimately is perhaps where the most vital gift of the films resides, not so much in any impossibly pure alternative to systemic violences, but in a more modest revelation of more generous but typically conditional ways of relating to each other and the material world which are always there waiting to be developed, given the right contexts. It could be argued that, if viewed in the right light, all films carry a similar sense of the plasticity of human gestures and the capacity of objects to refuse their reduction to commodities. But, with their tight focus on bodies and gestures in their shifting interactions with their material surroundings, the Dardennes are particularly adept at bringing this to the fore.

# 6

# Machinic enslavement and cinema's machinic powers

As Maurizio Lazzarato observes, contemporary subjection has two radically different but complementary dimensions: subjectivation and machinic enslavement. On the one hand, through a range of processes, we are constituted as individualised subjects with named roles, positions and rewards such as man, woman, boss, worker, creditor and debtor. On the other, we are torn apart and inserted as cogs into larger machineries which may involve technical machines but, given their necessary imbrication in a social context, are never simply reducible to them. In the past, machinic enslavement was above all associated with the factory: workers were 'hands' attached to machines or production lines and inserted into the factory's broader productive apparatus. Now, in the age of data and the digital, machinic enslavement is no longer contained by factory walls. Our information, affects, attention and labour are ripped apart and reassembled as elements of multiple larger machineries on a continuous basis. Machinic enslavement, Lazzarato comments acerbically, is everywhere except in critical theory which is too drawn to language and the subject to engage with the machinic and the non-linguistic forms of semiosis (the data, the graph, the code) at its core (Lazzarato 2014: 13). And what of cinema, that most machinic and semiotically diverse of cultural forms? Is it able to engage with machinic enslavement in a way that critical theory generally fails to do or does it simply put its own machineries and semiotic diversity to work to monetise our attention while narratively re-centring the bounded individual?

These are questions that I will explore as the chapter proceeds, in the process both radicalising my probing of the crisis of the individual subject and seeking to move beyond it. I begin by looking at two broadly social realist films which engage frontally with the crisis but where the machinic is effectively relegated to the margins and cinema's semiotic diversity is put in the service of the production of centred subjects. These are Brizé's *La Loi du marché*, a work already discussed from a different angle in Chapter 3, and Cédric Klapisch's *Ma part du gâteau* (*My Piece of the Pie*, 2011), a social realist comedy hybrid, a film not yet considered. I then explore Lazzarato's account of the machinic and its relationship to plural semiosis before discussing how it casts light on the films. I move on to discuss Luc Besson's blockbuster *Lucy* (2014). A far from self-evident choice, *Lucy* is notable for the way it allows analysis of how cinema's own digital resources can paradoxically be used both to render visible and erase machinic enslavement. I conclude with a discussion of experimental documentaries by Sylvain George which bring together young, male migrants as they move around Calais, Madrid or Paris and austerity-driven protest movements in the latter two cities, probing convergences and seeking the outlines of a politics adequate to the current time. If the other films discussed underscore how the machinic and cinema's plural semiosis are typically subordinated and marginalised by a subject, narrative and language-centred mainstream cinema, George's films will be used to probe how, when the individual subject and narrative are decentred, cinema's machinic powers might allow it to become the self-consciousness of a collective oppositional subject.

## Centred subjects, machinic margins and ex-centric looks

In *La Loi du marché*, as we saw, there is a highly individualised foreground story of how a man experiences a job loss and responds to oppressive workplace conditions that drive a woman to suicide. I would now like to pick up on something else that is happening around the edges of the film. It is there, for example, in the scene where the supermarket workers assemble in a staff room to say farewell to one of their colleagues. The narrative, staging and focus draw our eyes to the faces of the protagonists as they play their roles in the touching little retirement scene. However, on the wall behind them, out of focus, a mere realist background, there are tables, a multi-coloured pie chart and graphs. As the scene unfolds, and if we look carefully, we can pick out labels. The one with the largest lettering reads 'démarque totale', the name given to the total difference between the nominal amount of stock a company possesses and the real amount, which is lower due to known deductions (breakages and so on) and unknown ones such as thefts. The functionalist indifference of the charts speaks of a different reality to the emotionally charged personal events in the foreground, although we perhaps infer that, recoded as figures, put to work by an impersonal machinery, the workers' performance somehow finds its way into them. We see a similar pattern when the suicide of the checkout assistant is announced to her co-workers. Our attention is drawn by the staging, focus and dialogue to the faces in the foreground and the interaction between them. But in the background and out of focus, we see graphs and bar charts, their mute impassivity in sharp contrast to the foreground emotion (Figure 6.1). The underlying dynamic continues into the woman's funeral sequence and what follows it. The funeral is organised around individual faces and bodies: the dead woman's photograph on her coffin; the hero's grim expression during the service. Then, we cut to a montage of hands moving purchases in front of a barcode scanner at a cash-desk (Figure 6.2) and fingers typing a credit or debit card code into a card reader. Within the film's person-centred visual and narrative economy, this brief anonymous interlude signals the closing of the waters over the suicide and the return of routine commercial activity. Yet, despite its only fleeting engagement with them, the film seems to know that these interconnected flows of figures, data, money and goods are essential to the normal functioning of the depicted world.

Some of the film's difficulty engaging with workplace machineries and the place of human cogs within them become particularly apparent when

**Figure 6.1** Behind the human drama: the graphs and charts (*La Loi du marché*, Stéphane Brizé, 2015)

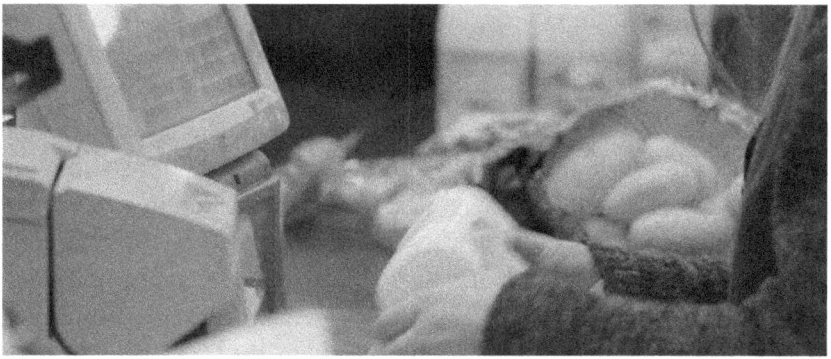

**Figure 6.2** Human hands harnessed to the barcode scanner (*La Loi du marché*, Stéphane Brizé, 2015)

we consider the hero's job. As a security guard, he is part of an apparatus of surveillance that involves both him and his colleagues and the CCTV cameras and monitors. Rather than probing the functioning of this complex apparatus or the hybrid human-machine vision that results from it, the film is above all interested in the hero's reactions. This dynamic comes to the fore in the decisive late sequence when a cashier who has been observed swiping uncollected customer loyalty points onto her own card is brought into a back room for questioning. The hero is left to guard her while a colleague fetches the card, itself part of another complex machinery of surveillance, to prove her guilt. Refusing to be complicit with an oppressive procedure, the hero leaves, his departure tracked by the camera. As a result, the complementary functioning of the two surveillance systems in play is touched upon but not properly explored. Firstly, there is the loyalty card with its capacity to record purchases, harvest customer data and stitch individuals into the machinery of marketing. Secondly, enforcing conformity to the first system, there is the security apparatus which flags up staff and customers who do not pay or scan correctly. Of the two systems, the latter, with its cameras, screens and capacity to render individual misdemeanours visible, is given more narrative prominence. But the film is still far more drawn to the hero, his actions and reactions.

The broader pattern is clear. Almost everything in the film takes us back to the interpersonal and individual. The staging and camera positioning repeatedly foreground human interactions and especially the reactions of the hero played by the charismatically ordinary Lindon. Along the lines described by the great theorist of cinematic sound, Michel Chion, the human voice is centred in the auditory field in the same way as the face and the look attached to it orientate the visual field (Chion 1999: 5–6). The narrative predictably recounts a personal trajectory and ends with an individual's ethico-moral decision. Being a work of social realism, the film accords considerable importance to financial considerations and workplace dynamics: the hero struggling to cater for his family's needs and keep ahead of his debts; the worker driven to suicide by the company's desire to drive up its profitability; the workforce rendered disposable and targeted by machineries of surveillance. Yet, even when it pays attention to figures or data and the apparatuses behind them, the film still approaches them in terms of how they affect discrete individuals and neglects the more banal insertion of human cogs into complex machineries.

*La Loi du marché* is not somehow atypical in this respect. If we consider another mainstream, socially oriented film, *Ma part du gâteau*, we also find that it only really engages with our cog-like insertion into complex machineries around its edges. A typical Klapisch social comedy, the film recounts the improbable encounter between France, a newly redundant worker who has retrained as a cleaner, and Stéphane (Gilles Lellouche), the investment banker who helped trigger the closure of her factory by shorting the stock of the company which owned it. Although the recourse to such a contrived plot to address the impact of finance on ordinary lives is worthy of comment, what interests me here is the title sequence and how, before the narrative proper gets under way, it brings cinema's machinic powers to the fore. It begins conventionally enough. We see, from the point of view of someone carrying a birthday cake, a series of shots of faces and hear the clamour of voices. Things become more interesting when, abandoning this human perspective, we cut to an overhead, fast-motion shot of the cake being divided up, the pie effectively turning into a pie chart and moving us away from the concrete relationships of family interactions towards the more abstract notions of shares referenced in the film's title. The ensuing montage sequence confirms this decentring of the human. It takes its rhythm from an up-tempo piece of music by Kraked Unit, a French group specialising in creating film music. It consists of the following: shots of computer screens displaying changing share prices, financial graphs and currency indices; lateral tracking shots from train windows of graffiti on concrete walls; views of a container port from a car window and a view of presumably the same car in the port; bird's-eye shots of colourful shipping containers from increasing heights; lateral tracking shots of posters for concerts or political groups;

overhead shots of a carnival parade; low-angle lateral tracking shots of high buildings; close-ups of hands working on keyboard or calculator keys; a fast-motion long shot of a busy trading room; lateral tracking shots of women crossing a bridge in what looks like Paris; shots from increasing distance of a woman smoking alone on a high balcony with the City of London behind her; fast-motion shots brought together through jump cuts of people on escalators; shots of hands holding a handrail, maybe on the metro, people dismounting a metro car, mainly besuited people going through metal doors and people at a bus stop as buses go by. As the montage nears an end, we have an over-the-shoulder shot of two girls looking out to sea before a cut to another overhead shot of the cake being cut into portions. This gives way to a series of medium close-ups of excited faces as the voices linked to them become increasingly alarmed: someone has swallowed an overdose of pills and the emergency services must be called. A story is beginning.

Because we are viewing a title sequence, we expect its openness, its simultaneous lack and excess of meaning, to be retrospectively tamed by the individual-centred narrative that will follow. Briefly, however, we are obliged to ponder the interconnection of the different elements that the montage assembles. The gaps in meaning suggest that the meaning may be in the gaps, in some relationship between the elements that is not already given and defies encapsulation in any unilinear cause–effect relationship. Certainly, the sequence seems to point to the power of finance as manifested both in the trading room shots and, more abstractly, in the repeated shots of share prices or currency indices. We are implicitly invited to connect these images to human activity on the ground (the movement of commuters, the shots of carnival) but it is not clear if we are to see the link in terms of disjunction (finance's disconnection from people's day-to-day concerns) or determination (finance's power to shape the fabric of everyday life). A bridge between the quasi-abstraction of the figures and charts and the concrete solidity of the material world is perhaps provided by the containers. As successive shots show them from an increasing height, they become rectangles, similar in their shape and diversity of colour to the rectangles on the computer screens (Figure 6.3). It is as if, when seen from sufficient distance, the circulation of goods reveals its own inherent abstraction, the pursuit of profit that lies behind the production and exchange of any specific commodity (Toscano and Kinkle 2015: 195–7). We may also note a becoming mechanical of the human elements as, no longer tied to recognisable individuals, repeatedly seen as

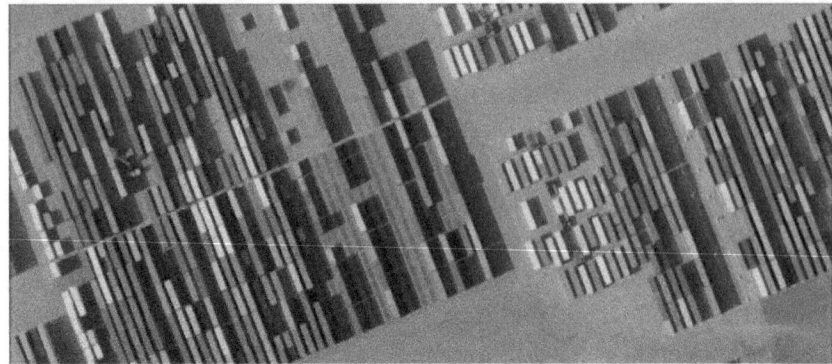

**Figure 6.3** The containers becoming abstract (*Ma part du gâteau*, Cédric Klapisch, 2011)

body parts rather than whole bodies, they take on a cog-like functionality, especially when associated with technologies of circulation, communication or calculation. This sense of humans becoming cogs is reinforced by the subsumption of individuals into groups or numbers either within shots (multiple bodies riding an escalator) or when similar shots (of, say, hands on keyboards) are assembled. Detached from specific biographies or defined identities by their multiplicity, the bodies are better able to embody the processes of which they are part, whether it be data entry or a circulation driven by the temporality of the working day. The prominence of multiplicity (number) in the shots of human activity further shrinks the gap between the apparently concrete (working and moving bodies) and the apparently abstract (financial data on screens) and makes it easier to ponder their interconnection. The film itself rehearsed this connection when the birthday cake effectively became a pie chart when viewed from above.

The sequence's capacity to evoke connections between financial data, the circulation of goods and human activity is tightly dependent on the initial absence of a person-centred narrative and a conventional anthropocentric perspective. We do not yet see facial close-ups and the kind of shot-reverse-shot set-ups that would implicitly tie the image to one or more individuals' point-of-view, a stylistic choice accentuated by the repeated preference of low angle or extreme high angle or overhead shots over more conventional eye-level ones. In a related way, although the human voice is present on the music track, the sequence breaks with the vococentrism of mainstream narrative by not yet privileging dialogue. Along with rhythmic use of camera movement (the many tracking shots), and repeated use of fast-motion filming that drives normally unnoticed patterns into view, the beat of the music also brings the machinic side of human activity to the fore. This temporary suspension of the normal audio-visual hierarchies also drives cinema's capacity for semiotic diversity into view: numbers, shapes, colours, rhythms and the written word achieve a more egalitarian presence when no longer subordinated to narrative, the individual, face and voice.

Considering *La Loi du marché* alongside *Ma part du gâteau*, we can come to an initial conclusion. It seems that cinema has the tools required to probe the imbrication of human cogs within larger machineries, including financial ones. It also appears that the medium is amply equipped to engage with the semiotic diversity that such machineries require. Yet, it is apparent that, within mainstream narrative cinema, these tools are typically marginalised or put in the service of the centred individual and interpersonal relations. As a result, if we wish to locate where mainstream films engage with the machinic, we need to look around the edges or excentrically: in the out-of-focus background of shots, in montage and title sequences, in those parts of films where the human point of view and voice are decentred or their reign temporarily suspended. Developing these initial insights, we now turn to Lazzarato's theorisation of the questions concerned.

## Lazzarato and machinic subjection

As we have noted elsewhere in this volume, Lazzarato's main influences are Foucault, Deleuze and Guattari. With respect to the former, Lazzarato has consistently sought to critique and develop his account of the production of subjectivity under neoliberalism. He has drawn repeatedly on Deleuze and Guattari to help him in that project but also builds on their discussion of machinic enslavement, a complementary but radically different component of our subjection. Guattari's unorthodox theory of semiotics is an essential reference in that latter venture.

As we noted, the concept of the machine refers to something wider in scope that the technical machine as a tool used by the human subject to extend and project its powers. Rather, it is a functional whole or assemblage (another key Deleuzo-Guattarian term), the functioning of which typically supposes the bringing together of material, semiotic and human elements (Lazzarato 2014: 81). Thus, rather than the factory simply being a building for housing machines, it is better seen as a machine itself, one that incorporates human elements ('hands') into a productive assemblage that mobilises technical machines, material flows and different forms of semiosis (accounts, inventories, diagrams, plans etc.). Because of this imbrication of the human, rather than being narrowly technical, machinic assemblages are necessarily social: that is, they depend intrinsically on a specific set of social arrangements with its distribution of roles and places. While, in Marx's day, it might have made sense to associate machinic enslavement with the factory, now, with the massive development of mass and social media, consumerism and information technology, it permeates all aspects of our lives, plugging us into larger mechanisms, putting us to work as cogs. It is this mobilisation of human cogs that differentiates machinic enslavement from subjectivation. The latter functions by producing discrete individuals (man, woman, boss, worker, creditor, debtor) to whom specific socio-economic roles, responsibilities, rewards and property rights are allocated. In contrast, machinic enslavement shatters the unity of the individual and inserts sub- and supra-individual elements as 'dividuals' into machinic assemblages. Lazzarato explains it thus:

> Not only is the dividual *of a piece with* the machinic assemblage but he [sic] is also *torn to pieces* by it: the component parts of subjectivity (intelligence, affects, sensations, cognition, memory, physical force) are no longer unified in an 'I,' they no longer have an individuated subject as referent. Intelligence, affects, sensations, cognition, memory, and physical force are now components whose synthesis no longer lies in the person but in the assemblage or process. (Lazzarato 2014: 27, original emphasis)

Subjectivation and machinic enslavement are equally necessary to the functioning of the capitalist socio-economic model. The latter is deterritorialising in the Deleuzian sense; that is, it shatters individuals so that they can be inserted into complex mechanisms and processes from which profit can be extracted. Providing a necessary counter-balance, stabilising the allocation of roles and rewards, subjectivation is re-territorialising. Thus, for example, we might consider how, in the run-up to the subprime crisis, the American mortgage system needed debts to be attached to named individuals who would be responsible for repayment to particular institutions and had to put up specific properties as collateral. At the same time, these individual subjects were torn apart as their debts were detached from particular locations and properties, packaged up with other debts, sold on, and speculated upon using complex derivatives. Without these complementary processes of subjectivation and machinic enslavement the system could not have worked (or malfunctioned!) as it did. Similarly, when we sign up to a social media platform like Facebook we are both constituted as centred subjects, with our friends, profiles and histories, and torn apart so that fragments of our attention, affects and tastes can be plugged into algorithms that measure the popularity of specific pages or themes, decide which content to target us with and monetise our data by selling it on to advertisers or political campaigns.

Because contemporary subjection systematically mobilises both subjectivation and machinic enslavement in this way, Lazzarato is highly critical of the work of some leading contemporary critical theorists, Alain Badiou, Jacques Rancière, Judith Butler or Slavoj Žižek, all of whom he considers too focused on subjectivity to the exclusion of the machinic and thus radically unable to develop a rounded account of contemporary subjection and how it might be opposed (2014: 13). In a related way, he is critical of a similar group of thinkers for the undue centrality they grant to language in the realms of politics (Rancière), production (Paolo Virno) or the constitution of the subject (Butler and Žižek) (Lazzarato 2014: 16–17). Because machinic subjection largely by-passes language and mobilises other forms of semiotics, any language-centric account of subjection is condemned to significant omissions.

This takes us to Guattari's account of semiosis and the use Lazzarato makes of it. Guattari establishes a four-part categorisation of semiotic forms. He begins with what he calls a-semiotic signs which include things like crystal structures or DNA and which, although they might seem to lie outside the traditional boundaries of semiosis, contain information and shape forms. His second category, symbolic semiotics, has its roots in early human societies and relates to art, music, dance and gesture, forms which, in their non-hierarchical co-existence and interaction were an integral part of the life of the group as opposed to something which sought to describe it from a privileged external location. The third category, signifying semiotics, relates principally to language with its capacity to fix identities and meanings and separate a represented world from the world of action. The fourth category, essential for our purposes here, is asignifying semiotics: it encapsulates diagrams, graphs, balance sheets, digital data, computer code and so on (Lazzarato 2014: 39–49, 55–94).

How do these forms of semiosis combine in the contemporary world? Language's signifying semiotics plays roles of subordination, separation and territorialisation essential to the functioning of capitalism. To begin with, the plural and egalitarian forms of symbolic semiosis must be subordinated to language to produce a defined reality (Lazzarato 2014: 72). Secondly, faced with capitalism's capacity to dissolve separate identities into its flows, language is needed to fix the individuated roles, rewards and property relations without which unequal social relationships could not be maintained (Lazzarato 2014: 94). However, precisely because of this territorialising capacity, language lacks the fluidity that capitalism requires for its functioning. It is here that asignifying semiotics is so important. Unencumbered by sedimented meanings, it can perform the vital roles of capture, evaluation and transfer without which capitalism could not function as it puts a range of radically divergent activities and resources to work and extracts value from them (Lazzarato 2014: 41). In contrast to linguistic representations which necessarily separate themselves from what they describe, asignifying signs 'act directly on the real, for example, in the way that the signs of computer language make a technical machine like the computer function, that monetary signs activate the economic machine, that a mathematical equation enters into the construction of a bridge or an apartment building, and so on' (Lazzarato 2014: 40–1). This reach and power explain why, in the era of the ascendancy of financial capital and the digital, asignifying semiotics has become the dominant form of semiosis.

Lazzarato's powerful account of the complementary machineries of subjectivation and signifying semiotics on the one hand and machinic enslavement and asignifying semiotics on the other might seem to leave little room for political optimism. We seem trapped: pinned to existing identities and hierarchies by one set of mechanisms and shattered and put to work as cogs by the other. Yet, Lazzarato leaves room for hope. Firstly, as we have noted, he considers neoliberal subjectivation to be in crisis. The previously dominant figure of the neoliberal entrepreneur of the self is no longer able to make any claim to general applicability in the age of austerity and debt (Lazzarato 2014: 9–11; Lazzarato 2015: 14). Secondly, precisely because of the differences between them, subjectivation and symbolic enslavement can work against each other, the deterritorialising power of one undermining the territorialisation of the other and allowing glimpses of new forms of identity. Thirdly, because he discusses machineries of subjectivation and enslavement as Deleuzo-Guattarian assemblages, with the contingent articulations that implies, he leaves room for progressive reassemblages to occur in a way that more rigid systems-based accounts would not.

## Cinema's semiotic pluralism

Unsurprisingly, Lazzarato calls on Guattari again when he analyses the combination of symbolic, signifying and asignifying semiotics involved in cinema. He identifies the following elements at work.

- The phonic fabric of expression that refers to spoken language (signifying semiology);
- The sonorous but non-phonic fabric that refers to instrumental music (asignifying semiotics);
- The visual fabric that refers to painting (both symbolic and asignifying semiotics);
- The gestures and movements of the human body, etc. (symbolic semiologies);
- The durations, movements, breaks in space and time, gaps, sequence, etc., that make up asignifying 'intensities' (Lazzarato 2014: 109)

He then comments in a way expressing clear disappointment,

> The cinema, whose effects derive above all from its use of asignifying symbolic semiotics . . . represented *for a brief moment* the possibility of moving beyond signifying semiologies, of bypassing personological individuations, and opening up possibilities that were not already inscribed in dominant subjectivations (Lazzarato 2014: 109 [my emphasis]).

Although it echoes his general account of the interplay of different forms of semiosis, this vision seems overly pessimistic and pays insufficient attention to the range of cinematic practices both contemporary and historical. Cinema's rich semiotic diversity, suggests Lazzarato, is subordinated to the signifying 'machine' in a way which enables the film industry to function as a form of collective psychoanalysis, 'powerfully aiding in the construction of the roles and functions and, especially, in the fabrication of the individuated subject and his [sic] unconscious' (Lazzarato 2014: 108). Yet, opening up some room for optimism, he observes how the medium's semiotic richness creates potential for interpretations that reintroduce 'ambiguity, uncertainty, and instability into denotation and signification' (Lazzarato 2014: 110). This is what I sought to show in my reading of the two films I used to open this chapter. Both contain elements which underscore how cinema's machinic powers and semiotic diversity can be used to bring machinic enslavement into view. But both also underline how, once cause-effect narrative, dialogue and the centred subject reassert their habitual grip, these elements are marginalised or instrumentalised. The films set up stories that seek to force normally unseen systemic violences into view, showing how they trigger self-destructive behaviours (successful or failed suicides) in individuals along the lines discussed in Chapter 4. But, by using psychologically rounded individuals as their sounding boards in this way, they largely fail to engage with the way human cogs are exploited through their insertion into larger machineries. We might see an inadvertent acknowledgement of this, for example, in the scene in *La Loi du marché* where the suicide is announced but the figures and charts on the wall remain out of focus. It is as if the film knew of the difficulty its own person-centred narrative would face when trying to deal with the conversion of human activity into the numbers and data that constantly monitor performances and trigger decisions. We might perceive a similar acknowledgement in the radical shift that occurs between *Ma part du gâteau*'s opening montage and the story proper. With its evocation of finance, the power of figures, a container port, commuting, work and the broader fabric of everyday life, it might simply be seen as providing the raw materials that will be given shape by the ensuing narrative. Yet, in its decentring of human perception and focus on human cogs in larger machineries and in the prominence given to figures and data, it invites us to ponder a multi-directional set of interconnections that will be shorn of its complexity by the linear person-centred narrative that follows.

Unsurprisingly, Lazzarato is a great admirer of Dziga Vertov's legendary *Man with a Movie Camera* (1929) for the simultaneous semiotic, technical, social and aesthetic revolution it represented. It took cinema away from its habitual fixed roles (director, actor), fictional scripts and closed locations (the studio) and opened it to the new world emerging around it, making it a mass, participatory medium. The film and the practices associated with it sought to generate a new post-human machinery for perception and thought. The camera provided the capacity for a new human-machine vision freed from the spatio-temporal limits that made normal human perception unable to apprehend the complexity of the new world. But, crucial to the power of the medium was montage, with its capacity to assemble movements and images from different locations and bring out relations between them. And the ultimate power of montage was not in the images assembled but in the intervals between them and the unseen relationships that lay behind them. It was these deterritorialised relationships that preceded and ultimately generated the spatially located activities whose image the camera captured. The power of cinema thus lay in its capacity to bring together new machineries of production, circulation and reception with new forms of machinic perception in which montage and its asignifiying semiotics (its invisible intervals) were key (Lazzarato 2019: 18–36).

Any claimed resemblance between Vertov's still unsurpassed masterwork and Klapisch's conventionally produced, distributed and narrated social comedy would clearly be absurd. But in its title sequence, a distant inheritor of Soviet montage as digested by mainstream film, there is nonetheless a reminder of cinema's still live machinic powers and especially the capacity of montage to point to the unseen relationships hidden by the immediately visible.

Central to Klapisch's *Ma part du gâteau* is the trader, Stéphane. Lazzarato analyses the production of what he calls 'the trader's machinic subjectivity' in his *Signs and Machines*. He notes how components of the trader's subjectivity (memory, understanding, attention, perception) combine with the machinic proto-subjectivity expressed in financial curves and data to establish 'focal points of proto-enunciation', bidding prices up and down or anticipating profitability or its opposite. Far from the heroic image that is often presented, the human subjectivity involved is obliged to interact with technical machines, the asignifying semiotics of data and the information encoded by mathematical instruments in order to perform its role. Similarly, when the trader expresses the mood of interest groups, they can only do so by being connected to all the apparatuses of modern communication. Contrary to our habitual view of a psyche firmly lodged in the individual, the trader's feelings about the state of the market are never the simple expressions of human cognitions or affectivity but emerge from complex hybrid assemblages that mobilise multiple forms of semiosis. However, the discourses of economists, the media, experts or, when things go wrong, judges, make us believe that it is the individual who acts and deserves to be compensated or punished. Unsurprisingly, rather than probing the imbrication of the trader, or elements of them, in intersecting machineries, cinema also tends to focus on the trader as individual hero or villain, offering us a sense of moral superiority to them in place of any deeper understanding of trading, markets and the functioning of financial capital more broadly. *Ma part du gâteau* is no exception to this rule. Only in its opening and closing montages is there an invitation to locate trading at the intersection of different machineries and in interaction with multiple human cogs and different forms of semiosis.

## Besson's Lucy: a cog with superpowers

*Lucy*, Luc Besson's star and CGI-driven English-language, French-produced spectacular, might seem a strange film to turn to in any discussion of cinema and machinic enslavement, unless it were as an example of how our own spectatorial attention and affects are plugged into the cinematic machine. However, the particular interest of the film lies in the way it both engages with our radical cog-like disempowerment and seeks to conjure it magically away with its own variant on the fantasy of the enhanced-human. While broadly social realist films like *La Loi du marché* and *Ma part du gâteau* bring everything back to the level of individuals, as we saw, and thus marginalise or occlude machinic enslavement, *Lucy* is far less tied by realist conventions and therefore more able to engage with the machinic and even to use its digital effects to bring it into view.

The cartoon-like plot of the film will surprise no-one familiar with Besson's work. The action begins outside a luxury hotel in Taipei (Taiwan) where Lucy, the film's eponymous heroine played by Hollywood A-lister Scarlett Johansson, is studying. She is tricked by her good-for-nothing boyfriend, Richard (Pilou Asbæk), into delivering an attaché case to Mr Jang (Min-Sik Choi), a violent mob boss. The case contains four bags of synthetic CPH4, the hormone supposedly released in the mother's womb during pregnancy to trigger the foetus's development. Along with three minor characters, Lucy is made to act as a drugs mule when the gang has her abdomen cut open and one of the bags inserted. When she resists a sexual assault by one of her captors, she is kicked in the stomach. The bag is burst, the hormone released into her body and a transformation triggered. The product unlocks her unused brain capacity allowing her to process even usually inaccessible information at superhuman speeds and deploy telekinetic powers. Having rid herself of her captors, she uses a laptop to learn Mandarin in what seems like seconds and becomes a medical expert at similar speed. She gains access to her own bodily processes and natural flows such as the sap rising in trees. She reads Mr Jang's memories by pressing her fingers into his forehead. Realising her time is short, she flies to Paris to meet Professor Norman (Morgan Freeman), the leading global authority on the potential of the brain, while enlisting the support of a French detective, Pierre del Rio (Amr Waked), to capture the other mules and obtain the rest of the hormone. Her powers continue to develop. She can control radio and television signals. She can see, sort and listen in on a myriad of mobile phone conversations rendered as coloured lines in front of her through the CGI (Figure 6.4). She can alter bodily features at will, but also risks a complete loss of form, as when her face becomes misshapen or she starts to dissolve into a stream of molecules, both transformations again rendered through CGI. Once she has found Norman and his team of scientists, she absorbs the remaining hormone and overflows her body to connect to and incorporate the electronic devices that surround her in the laboratory. As a fast montage reveals, she becomes able to travel in time and finds another Lucy, this time the famous humanoid mother of humanity, and touches her finger in a way that suggests that she may somehow have retrospectively unleashed human evolution. In the meantime, Mr Jang, the gangster, is still hunting her. He fires his gun at the back of Lucy's head just as her body finally dissolves, having fused with the machines and networks of which they are part. The mobile dark, reddish-black substance she seems to have become forms a hand that passes what looks to be a memory stick to Professor Norman who concludes that it represents the next generation

**Figure 6.4** Lucy's semiotic superpowers (*Lucy*, Luc Besson, 2014)

of computers. When del Rio, who by now has shot Jang, asks where she is, she takes over the screen of his mobile phone to reassure him that she is everywhere.

The film's central conceit, a long-since discredited myth, is that humans only use 10 per cent of their brain and could have far greater capacities if the unused 90 per cent were activated, which is what happens, in Lucy's case, after the ingestion of the maternal hormone. While this improbable plot development feeds off a broader cultural and societal interest in human enhancement through technological implants or biotechnological interventions, it is more productive to read it in terms of the fundamental tension between the two contemporary forms of subjection, the production of humans as individuated subjects, on the one hand, and their shattering and insertion as cogs in complex machinic assemblages, on the other. With the aid of CGI, the tension comes forcibly into view in the aeroplane sequence when Lucy starts to dissolve into a stream of matter and energy and has to ingest more of the hormone to regain control of her body, literally pulling herself back together. It is also eminently visible in the final sequence when Lucy completely loses her human form, becomes one with the technical machines around her and dissolves into the network while remaining entirely herself, an apotheosis confirmed by her final, godlike statement, 'I am everywhere'. These two central moments highlight the threat of dissolution that the subject faces as it is inserted into multiple machineries. On its most banal level, this is expressed in the drugs plot within which Lucy is initially very much a cog, first put to work by her boyfriend as an unwitting courier, secondly becoming a bodily repository for the drugs, her role in the process defined not by any individual characteristics but by her functioning within a multinational criminal enterprise. Similarly, the other unwitting mules are only of interest to the gang, Lucy and the police for the product hidden inside their bodies. The drug plot thus allows the film to condense a broader sense of humans being unaware cogs while offering a compensatory narrative whereby one human cog takes the powers vested in machinic assemblages back into herself.

Lucy's re-empowerment tellingly relies on her becoming a semiotic superhero with access to codes normally unintelligible to the merely human. Apart from learning new languages, she accesses natural flows, bodily information and electronic signals. In the process, she acquires the ability to control networked processes of which humans are usually only terminals. Her apotheosis, when she becomes one with networked devices, achieves ubiquity with them and can speak through them, confirms this. The film therefore recognises our cog-like insertion into multiple assemblages whose semiotic flows typically by-pass our consciousness while offering us the fantasy of a re-centred and re-empowered individual. This re-centring is consolidated by the persistence of human language – Lucy's final 'I am everywhere', even when she becomes a disembodied, networked being – and by the continued dominance of the visual, as notably seen when normally unseen flows are apparently rendered visible by the CGI. This is the paradox of CGI use in the film: if it might seem to signal the ascendancy of the digital, it is in fact used to bring the normally invisible power of communication networks and asignifying semiotics within the sphere of visual representation and thereby to re-centre the human sensory apparatus. In the same way, Lucy's final subsumption into the networked, electronic world suggests a post-human future in which the human individual still remains central. This, in part, is the point of the montage sequence within which the modern Lucy touches fingers with her namesake, Lucy the hominid mother of humanity. If it suggests, as we saw, a retrospective acceleration of evolution, it also promises a passing of the baton to humanity's new cyborg but oh so human mother. In this regard, it is worth remembering that the growth hormone that triggers the whole improbable plot is a synthetic version of a hormone released in the mother's womb, another cyborg creation reassuringly rooted in a promised continuity of human corporeality.

When Lucy effectively becomes a cyborg, we might think we are moving beyond the traditional binary oppositions (man/woman, human/machine, subject/object) that define us and into a posthuman world of fluid identifications along the lines described by Donna Haraway in her celebrated *Cyborg Manifesto* (1991). However, in a film which re-centres the human individual, it is unsurprising to find familiar gender divisions reasserting themselves. When a drug-smuggling cog, Lucy occupies an apparently gender-neutral position. After all, her fellow cogs are male. However, it is worth remembering the maternal connotations of her role: the woman drug mule as a bodily receptacle for a male gangster's cargo; her association, through the albeit synthetic maternal growth hormone, with the mother's role; the female lineage from hominid Lucy to Lucy as originary mothers of new human forms. Tellingly, the three authority figures Lucy engages with are male: Professor Norman, the scientist; Inspector del Rio as bearer of state legal power; Mr Jang, the gangster. Given that Jang is driven by a murderous appetite for financial gain, we can consider him to embody, not capitalism per se, but its viciously excessive side. His eventual elimination signals the triumph of the alliance between Lucy and the two legitimate forms of male authority. What the film thereby gives us, in familiar fashion, is an imaginary resolution of real contradictions. Capitalism's excess is quarantined in the figure of the gangster and removed. Traditional authorities, gender roles and a human-centred world are left in place. There is no attempt to engage with the social relationships, identities and hierarchies that inevitably condition the form taken by human imbrication in different machineries. Rather, the space of the collective is completely evacuated as the human potential for reinvention is corralled within the boundaries of the biologically and technologically enhanced individual or dissolved into a depoliticised technosphere. This is entirely consonant with the way in which the film's own techno-euphoric celebration of its digital possibilities (the obligatory deployment of CGI in the contemporary blockbuster) is subordinated to its individualistic and ultimately conservative narrative. For a more productive convergence of cinema's machinic powers with the collective human capacity for reinvention, we will perhaps need to look at a different kind of cinema.

## Sylvain George and the power of montage

Sylvain George is one of the most interesting directors working in France today. A maker of experimental poetic documentaries, he came to public notice with a series of interconnected works focused on young, male migrants in and around the Calais camps or elsewhere, notably *Qu'ils reposent en révolte (des figures de guerre I)* (2010) and *Les Eclats (The Fragments*, 2012). Shot almost exclusively in black and white, refusing the objectification of migrants typical of mainstream representations, these films tracked their young protagonists as, resistant agents, they struggled to survive, occupied spaces, confronted obstacles and faced police repression. They were complemented by a triptych of films (*L'Impossible, pages arrachées* (2009), *Vers Madrid, the burning bright* (2011–2014) and *Paris est une fête, un film en 18 vagues (Paris is a Moveable Feast: a Film in 18 Waves*, 2017) which, while still focused on migrants, expanded their frames in two directions. On the one hand, they engaged with large-scale political mobilisations against repressive policing in the aftermath of terror attacks and austerity measures in the wake of the crisis. On the other hand, they broadened the chronological frame of reference by connecting the present to a history of struggle. They are interesting in the broader context of this book for the way they probe the possibilities and limits of a politics of resistance to precarity in a national frame. In the specific context of this chapter, they are significant for the way in which, by evacuating narrative and disrupting traditional representational forms, they allow cinema's machinic powers and plural semiotics to come to the surface, especially in their encounter with an emergent collective subject. I will concentrate on *Vers Madrid* and *Paris est une fête* here.

*Vers Madrid* gives a degree of centrality, in its cinematic construction, to the Spanish 'Toma la plaza' (Occupy the Square) movement which sprang from anti-austerity protests in Spain in 2011. It shows the movement in both its politically creative phase, as it works to develop new, non-hierarchical ways to organise and think the political, and in its defensive phase, as it seeks to prolong its existence in the face of police repression. At the same time, the film locates the occupation in a broader context. This is signalled from the start by shots of the Acropolis which invite us to see contemporary events in a longer history of European democracy. It is confirmed by subsequent cross-cutting between the demonstration and other types of footage. On the one hand, the film follows the existence and the peregrinations around Madrid of Bader, an undocumented Tunisian migrant. His memory of arriving in the southern port of Algeciras cues the introduction of images of the country's southern coast and shoreline. On the other, the film develops a broader Spanish socio-economic and historical context by showing shots of homeless people, buildings and statues in the capital, the Valle de los Caídos (the Valley of the Fallen), the Francoist monument to those who fell in the Civil War, and Seseña, a municipality south of Madrid which, with its ghostly spaces and empty apartment blocks, embodies the runaway wave of property speculation that so characterised Spain's housing market in the run-up to the 2008 crash.

While this interweaving of elements through montage suggests that no shot or sequence can find its meaning entirely within itself, we might also note how many of the shots already resist being put to work for any obvious narrative purpose or, reaching out beyond their immediate material context, invite allegorical interpretation. This is most obviously the case in the brief sequence in a field of sunflowers which bears no obvious connection to what precedes or follows it but may possess, as we will see, some allegorical charge. But it also applies to the many shots of natural objects (running water, trees, flowers and plants) or man-made artefacts (statues, signs, graffiti) which either resist narrative incorporation in their brute materiality or suggest some intertextual or allegorical connection to what lies around them. Thus, for example, in the sequence filmed in the south of Spain and around Gibraltar, we see a series of locations and things with no simple link between them: an RAF trainer plane; barbed wire around the British base; broken down motorbikes; religious statues in a (shop?) window; a vinyl record with hymns on it; broken metal rods on the beach; a jet ski pirouetting in the water; a yacht; a cargo ship; waves; seagulls flying; a group of boys on the beach; a rock (or perhaps more than one rock) in the water hollowed out in such a way as to evoke a human face with wide eyes and open mouth; crabs climbing a rock; a discarded t-shirt on the beach; a lifeboat being pulled onto the beach amidst leisure users of the space. To the extent that the shots are summoned up by Bader's memories, they seem connected to his migration journey and its difficulty. But the connection is loose or allegorical. Thus, the presence of frontiers and a machinery of repression, different forms and speeds of movement, the sea as site of leisure but also of potential danger (the rescue boat) provide a general context in which to situate the journey rather than relating to it more precisely. Similarly, the face-like rock in the water, the abandoned t-shirt and the twisted metal could be connected to threats and affects linked to Bader's experience but not with absolute certainty. Equally ambiguous, the Christian statues and hymns might evoke either the Christ-like suffering of the migrants or a Europe which, in its failure to welcome migrants, is betraying the Christian values it professes. The ambiguity of individual shots is directly linked to their potential for multi-directional reverberation through montage.

*Paris est une fête* follows similar lines with overarching strands and specific shots reverberating with each other in a way that refuses their self-enclosure or their instrumentalisation for any straightforward narrative purpose. The film's main strands involve migrants and refugees, on the one hand, and protest movements in Paris against the state of emergency, austerity and precarity, on the other. The former consists of reportage footage of groups of migrants or refugees being moved on from places in the city, including the iconic Place de la République, where they have set up camp. It also involves footage of Mohamad, a paperless migrant, as, like Bader in *Vers Madrid*, he re-enacts his movements in the city, cobbles together open-air beds for himself, tells his story, and beatboxes or recites a Michaux poem, 'Liberté d'action' ('Freedom of action').

The latter strand also accords a prominent place to the Place de la République and revolves around major Paris protests: the first, on 29 November 2015, against the state of emergency in the aftermath of the Bataclan terrorist attack; the second, on 9 April 2016, and involving large numbers of young people, against the El Khomri employment 'reforms', named after Miriam El Khomri the Labour Minister of the time; the third, the impromptu 'Apéro chez Valls' ('an aperitif at Valls' place') action, an improvised march by protesters on the residence of Manuel Valls, the right-wing Socialist prime minister who had been determined to drive through the El Khomri legislation even if it meant by-passing parliamentary processes. Interspersed with these strands are other elements that react with them: a nocturnal sequence, with melancholy musical accompaniment, around the very modest memorial to Zyed Benna and Bouna Traoré, two teenagers who were electrocuted when, seeking to escape from police pursuing them, they attempted to hide in an electricity substation; a sequence in a field of sunflowers echoing that in *Vers Madrid* and with a similar lack of apparent connection to other sequences; a sequence in New York, seemingly triggered by the Michaux poem read by Mohamed, ending with a shot of the famous Wall Street bull statue.

The film's overarching dependence on montage and determination to destabilise taken-for-granted meanings through unsettling juxtapositions is clear from its opening minutes. It takes its title from Hemingway's posthumously published *Paris is a Moveable Feast* (1964), a work which was read on air by a retired lawyer, Danielle Mérian, after the Islamist terror attacks of 13 November, then sold in large numbers before inspiring an official campaign by the Paris authorities to promote the city's spirit and cultural resilience as Christmas approached. The film initially seems to respond to this official messaging. It begins with a montage of flashing lights on display screens and shots of festive activities, some Christmas related. There is a quick-fire montage of fast-motion shots of skates moving on ice followed by several slow-motion shots of a young boy skating. There is a shot of the iconic 'Your Empire Needs You' Darth Vader poster with its evocation of the Star Wars film franchise but also its capacity for darker connections. There is a brief montage of three rearing horses' heads – or perhaps one head from three angles – which fits badly with any festive image and evokes the startled horse from Picasso's painting, *Guernica*. There are shots of the obelisk in the Place de la Concorde which give way to a succession of shots of water and statues of human figures which, in their mute impassivity, disrupt any sense of festivity. There is another group of slow-motion shots, this time of an armed soldier with, behind him, a Ferris wheel. We see a homeless woman, a migrant perhaps, with a child who has settled down, presumably for the night, in front of the display window of Kenzo, the luxury fashion brand. The sequence moves on to shots of the French flag and the facade of the neo-classical Church of the Madeleine, including a close-up of its pediment with its scene of the last judgement. Breaking with the prevailing black and white, there is a single colour shot showing the colours of the French flag presumably projected against a brick surface. The shot fades to black.

A prelude to the film, the sequence lays bare some of the strategies it will deploy. A more consensual work might have sought a harmonious montage of similar elements to confirm an upbeat view of the City of Light for difficult times. George's film moves us in a different direction. By putting festive elements alongside disquieting or ambiguous ones, it makes any consensual synthesis impossible even as it unsettles the conventional connotations of what any given shot contains by opening it to new connections. Some of this broader process is condensed in the shot of the woman and her child bedding down in front of the Kenzo window: a found montage of luxury and consumption, poverty and marginalisation, it shows how dissonant elements within a shot can be combined to create a higher meaning not contained in any element taken separately. Although the meaning of this particular shot – the inequalities it evokes – might be considered over-obvious, it should be remembered that the broader privileging of montage invites us to place its resonance or, rather, dissonance in the context of the French flag and national colours, the Christmas story and the consensual post-Bataclan image of Paris in a way which complicates the associations of each. The film's dissonant montage is also evident in the soundtrack of this opening sequence with its uneasy mixture of ambient noise (the traffic, the unpleasant clanking of the Ferris wheel), electronic sounds and moments of silence.

## George's Benjaminian machinery

Anyone familiar with Walter Benjamin's work will be unsurprised to learn that he is a key reference for George and an inspiration for his practice of montage and allegory (Débordements 2014). Benjamin is particularly known for his non-linear, Messianic view of history, whereby, particularly in moments of danger, moments of the past flash up, their unrealised aspirations aligning with the present, ripping it out of its embeddedness in the flow of history and revealing new possibilities. He encapsulated this in the concepts of the dialectical image or the constellation as famously deployed in his *Theses on the Philosophy of History* and *Arcades Project*. The sense that the past must cut itself free from dominant historical narratives and align with the present to generate new meaning has an obvious affinity with cinematic montage (Rutsky 2007: 20–1).

Montage was also key to Benjamin's treatment of discarded consumer objects and cultural artefacts in the *Arcades Project*. Max Pensky's account of Benjamin's 'materialist' approach is helpful here. 'The materialist critic', Pensky notes, 'scavenges the detritus of history for those objects that resist incorporation into a triumphant story of capitalism as endless progress and that therefore express (in their very quality as trash) the frustrated utopian fantasies of a particular generation' (Pensky 2006: 187). It is only when such objects are 'blasted out of' capitalism's history of endless newness and placed in alternative contexts through a process of montage that they can speak not only of the hopes that they embodied but their inevitable disappointment. Ripped free from the flow of narrative in this way, they appear as images which freeze the flow of apparent progress and reveal the stillness, the essentially unchanging compulsion to repeat in pursuit of endlessly deferred satisfaction, at the heart of the story of apparently endless capitalist progress (Buck-Morss 1991: 218–20; Pensky 2006: 187–8).

This sense that objects can be made to speak when taken out of their original context and especially as they decay moves us towards Benjamin's account of allegory. He initially discusses it in his *The Origin of German Tragic Drama* (1928), a work in which he examined how allegory arose in the context of the waning of 'Christian hermeneutic hegemony' (Wilkens 2006: 292). He noted that, although a transcendental meaning was no longer self-evidently available in transient worldly things, they could still speak of the transcendental as they decayed, their mortality pointing, paradoxically and indirectly, to the permanence of the eternal (Caygill 2006; Cowan 1981: 116–9). In a similar vein, in the *Arcades Project*, objects became available for allegorical exploitation as their novelty wore off and they were located in new contexts. Only then could they express the overarching truth of capitalist commodity production, the genuine aspirations it disappoints and its turning of living processes into dead objects (Cowan 1981: 120–2).

We can now see how Benjamin helps us to make sense of George's particular use of cinema's machinic powers. To begin with, the main films discussed have consistent recourse to Benjaminian constellations either as they are generated by the ready-made montage that occurs within the shot when contemporary demonstrations organise themselves around historical buildings or monuments, awakening and reorienting their connotations, or when the film's own montage aligns historical events or the historical resonances of particular objects and places with contemporary occurrences, or through a combination of both things. We can see how this works in practice if we look, for example, at the shifting role of the Place de la République and of its famous statue of Marianne, the symbol of the French Republic, in *Paris est une fête*. We initially see the statue in the aftermath of the Bataclan massacre when it becomes the site of an improvised shrine to the victims of the terrorist attacks. The sequence follows directly on from the nocturnal sequence of the modest monument to Bouna Traoré and Zyed Benna in Aulnay-sous-Bois. We return to the statue a little later when, during the demonstration against the state of emergency imposed after the attacks, we see the shrine being trampled by the police as they fight a pitched battle with demonstrators in the square. Through a montage within the shot, the statue's permanence is set against contemporary protests against the state's action (Figure 6.5). There is a shot of a helicopter hovering over the demonstration. Shortly afterwards, another shot pans across a mural which reads 'Paris, je t'aime', to frame the serried ranks of riot police in the square. Later, a series of shots show an improvised refugee encampment in the same location before a long shot frames the tents with the plinth of the statue in view behind them. Later again, we return to the square to see the encampment being removed. Finally, we come back to the same location, now occupied by the Nuit Debout protestors, with the statue of Marianne in the background. After a fade to black, we see the film's final demonstration, the march on the prime minister's residence which ends with a festive dance in the square. One shot shows a banner reading 'Démocratie, t'es où?' ('Democracy, where are you?') draped across the plinth of the statue. The sequence closes on a slow-motion close-up of a bonfire.

The repeated production of Benjaminian constellations across the film takes its cue from the demonstrators themselves as, in time-honoured fashion, they protest in locations dense with historical resonances and seek to reinvigorate a radical tradition. But George also uses his own montage to bring contradictions and potentially productive historical alignments

**Figure 6.5** The spontaneous montage of political tradition and present-day struggle (*Paris est une fête*, Sylvain George, 2017)

into view. His film begins by evoking the preferred public narrative of a France, secure in its culture and values, standing united in the face of an external threat. It complicates that narrative by bringing its elements into collision with what it occludes: conflict; mounting precarity; repression and surveillance; lives considered less worthy of commemorating (Traoré and Benna) or protecting (the migrants and refugees). But, at the same time, it reawakens the elements of French history embedded in the square by bringing them into alignment with the present and challenging us to think what freedom, democracy, liberty or equality might mean now, not as handed down through a pacified tradition, but as framed in the context of contemporary mobilities, inequalities and exclusions.

The fire we see at the end of the film is an element that recurs in George's work. With a clear allegorical charge beyond any merely realist function, it suggests that, even as things are consumed or destroyed, something new may be being forged. More generally, across *Vers Madrid*, *Paris est une fête* and the Calais migrant films, George is repeatedly drawn to shots of statues, urban monuments, discarded consumer goods, clothing, bedding or natural forms (plants, water) which, when placed next to other shots, can deliver an allegorical charge. In the Calais films, for example, he repeatedly includes shots of abandoned clothes or food containers on waste or scrubland. A trace left behind by migrants as they move or are moved on, these objects speak of precarious lives exposed to the elements and, beyond that, the gross inequalities and unequal mobilities that characterise the contemporary world. This use of objects which achieve great eloquence precisely when they become detritus is profoundly Benjaminian in its spirit.

## Filming the occupation and its plural semiosis

The Benjaminian dimension of George's filmmaking underscores how, when the grip of narrative is broken and the individual human voice loses its centrality, cinema's plural semiosis is unshackled and normally subordinated things (objects, spaces, the gaps between images) can speak. It is this unleashed power of plural semiosis in its conjunction with the demonstration as site of political enunciation that we will now consider. Although marches and occupations are prominent in *L'Impossible* and *Paris est une fête*, it is in *Vers Madrid* that they are given the most developed treatment. As is well known, Occupy movements typically enacted a form of direct democracy that sought consensus through non-hierarchical discussion involving turn-taking and general participation. Hand gestures were used to indicate assent or disagreement. In addition, typically occurring in prominent, symbolically resonant public locations, the occupation's relationship to space was itself a kind of collective utterance, a refusal to accept marginalisation or silencing. In its choice of shots and editing, and its attention to groups, gestures and bodies in specific spaces and places, George's film observes and extends these underlying dynamics. The film is not uninterested in individual faces and voices and often frames particular speakers but, with the exception of Bader, the Tunisian migrant, only ever follows them briefly, quickly moving from one voice to the next, folding them into the occupation as a site of collective reflection and enunciation. Underscoring this process, the framing of shots and the construction of sequences ensures that we are aware of the occupation's machinery of enunciation: we note the managing of turn-taking, the stage and microphone as well as the audience's response as it indicates agreement, disagreement or uncertainty. By attending to the facial expressions, bodily disposition and hand signals of the crowd, the film tracks the emergence of a collective self-positioning that is not simply based on the spoken word but brings a richer semiotics into play. This semiotic breadth is further extended by the attention paid to the many posters and banners which the occupation generates and the different creative and expressive activities to which it gives rise (Figure 6.6). The posters are sometimes framed alongside speakers and sometimes shown in montage sequences, and bring together the written word and visual art. There are also sequences of singing, dancing and improvised street theatre. We see, on two occasions, mass drumming by the occupiers on the kind of corrugated iron fence used to close off building sites.

As constructed through the interaction of the machinery of the occupation and George's own cinematic machinery, the Spanish movement thus becomes the site of a rich, plural semiosis associated with the emergence of a new collective subject. In Lazzarato's Guattari-inspired terms, the film brings together signifying semiotics (the spoken and written words) and symbolic semiotics (art, music, dance and gesture) in an egalitarian interaction which undoes the usual predominance of the spoken

**Figure 6.6** Capturing the occupation's rich semiosis (*Vers Madrid: the Burning Bright*, Sylvain George, 2012)

word and is orchestrated by the rhythms, spacings and juxtapositions of montage, cinema's own primordial asignifying semiotics. This semiotic richness means that what the film shows emerging from the occupation is not simply a political discourse or set of convictions but an affectively charged, embodied and creative collective movement. Referencing the great anti-colonial theorist Frantz Fanon, George suggests he is seeking to capture the occupation as a Fanonian festival of the imagination (Speno 2017). As summarised by Achille Mbembe, such a festival mobilises the body, the intelligence and memories of past sufferings. Through intense work on objects and forms and through dance and song, it restructures the perceptions of an oppressed people, thereby undoing the sense that the existing world is all there is and that they are trapped in existing forms (Mbembe 2016: 121–2). To the extent that the Spanish movement could be seen as a similar festival of the imagination, *Vers Madrid* provides a vehicle for its reflexive self-perception, its montage and semiotic richness allowing it to capture the occupation's complex unfolding. Things are more complicated, however.

Montage challenges us to make connections, yet in its assembly of things that do not seem immediately or organically connected, it can reveal non-, partial or failed encounters. The demonstrations and occupations that George tracks across his films address, in their different ways, a rising precarity and mounting repression and surveillance. The migrants he shows in his films, individually or as a group, are also shown to be precarious and subject to police harassment. The toehold both groups have on urban space is unsure. By using montage to move back and forth between the two, the films ask us to make connections between situations and find visual echoes between shots. This connective drive is mirrored by the occupation in *Vers Madrid* when there is a working group discussion about how their movement must be 'mestizo' to be meaningful. All this contributes to the films' continued probing of foundational European political values as underscored by their repeated incorporation of politically emblematic spaces, building and statues in their sequences. Yet, in their montage, *mise-en-scène* and choreography of bodies and spaces, the films also suggest that the connections between different groups and struggles still remain to be made. In *Vers Madrid*, Bader joins the group discussing how to open the movement to non-nationals but, tellingly, says nothing. Repeatedly, in the rest of the film, we see shots of him walking alone and framed in lonely nocturnal spaces that are very different to shots of the crowded, vibrant spaces of the occupation in their symbolically resonant location in the heart of the capital. Similarly, in *Paris est une fête*, we often see Mohamed alone in nocturnal space, sometimes tracking him in long takes, sometimes watching him as he makes a bed for the night in some isolated, non-descript or rubbish-strewn location, away from the symbolic resonance of the Place de la République, and the collective strength, vibrant unruliness or concentrated collective attention of the demonstrators. While the film pushes us to make connections, these variations in its editing patterns, *mise-en-scène* and treatment of bodies in space constitute an implicit acknowledgement of the enormous differences that still exist between experiences. As Ronaldo Munck persuasively argues, European mobilisations around precarity developed in a specifically Western context in which the relative security of employment and welfare associated with Fordism was increasingly under threat. Precarious employment and a lack of other welfare protections has long been the experience in other parts of the world. It is an error to think that different experiences and histories can simply be folded into each other (Munck 2013).

Despite this risk of unwitting Eurocentrism, Occupy movements do signal a potentially major shift in the framing of political claims. As Judith Butler notes, they brought embodied needs for sustenance, shelter and care out of the private domain to which they have often been relegated and into the public sphere. These needs appeared not simply as abstract political claims but as the physical grounds of the mobilisation itself in its need to nourish and protect its inter-dependent participants (Butler 2015: 66–153). With their close attention to bodies, their need for care and their claim on urban spaces, George's films are particularly well-equipped to respond to these emergent forms of political mobilisation and the new types of demand they make. The films' refusal to centre on individuals, and their constitution of a collective body through montage, also resonates with the Occupy movement's aspiration towards direct democracy and horizontal, non-hierarchical organisation. Yet, at the same time, the films point towards the failure of Occupy to create the durable structures and forms achieved by the old party systems they so strongly rejected (Dean 2018). As they progress, and despite their refusal of anything like a conventional narrative, they move through moments when the movement is active, creative or combative to conclusions marked by the movement's absence and the return of routines. This progression is as implicit and eloquent a comment on the movement's limits as was the formally very different treatment of migrants and occupiers discussed above.

In the fourth of his famous *Theses on the Philosophy of History*, Benjamin (1940) wrote, 'just as flowers turn their heads towards the sun, so too does that which has been turn, by virtue of a secret kind of heliotropism, towards the sun which is dawning in the sky of history'. The flower's solar tracking thus becomes an allegory of the way the past can turn towards an emergent present, as in a Benjaminian constellation. George signals his debt to Benjamin by his recourse to the sunflower motif in both *Vers Madrid* and *Paris est une fête*. In *Vers Madrid*, the sunflowers are seen in a short sequence with two fast pans, a tracking shot and a still shot framing them against the sky. In *Paris est une fête*, they are shown in a longer, more confusing nocturnal sequence with disorienting tracking shots, fast cutting, strange barking noises and discordant music. George seems to be pointing to both the need to connect historical aspirations to contemporary struggles and the challenging difficulty of those connections. Unless, of course, a sun which we cannot yet see is about to pierce the nocturnal sky.

## Conclusion

This chapter has sought to give a sense of cinema's machinic powers and semiotic richness and its capacity to engage with both the omnipresence of machinic subjection under contemporary capitalism and with the demonstration or occupation as oppositional socio-political machineries. I make no claim here to have carried out some systematic or representative coverage. Rather, I have sought to establish a range of types of response. The two broadly social realist films considered are, I would suggest, typical of many similar films within which, rather than being used to explore the increasing prevalence of machinic enslavement in our lives, cinema's machinic powers and semiotic diversity are subordinated to cause-effect narratives and centred subjects, except for around the film's edges, in title and montage sequences or in the blurred background of images, where they are available to deliberately *ex-centric* readings of the sort I have practised here. *Lucy*, the contemporary action blockbuster examined, is also reasonably typical of similar films. It showcases cinema's digital powers, as blockbusters routinely do, and uses them to bring a range of forms of semiosis into apparent view, but all the better to re-centre the human perceptual apparatus. At the same time, and like other superhero or enhanced-human films, it plays on the fantasy of surmounting, through its superhuman protagonist, the radical contradiction between our cog-like disempowerment and the power of the socio-technical machineries we are inserted into.

In contrast to these films, and the broader categories they belong to, George's films give free rein to cinema's machinic powers and plural semiotics by liberating them from their habitual self-erasing subordination to narratives centred on individual subjects. These qualities, as we noted, enable them to track the emergence of the collective bodies of the Occupy and anti-austerity movements as they expressed themselves in their semiotic richness and through their relationship to space and place. This might seem to indicate a perfect synergy between the machinery of the movements and that of cinema. Yet, as we saw, the films implicitly signal the difficulty of aligning the situation and struggles of paperless migrants with those of the European movements shown while also pointing to the failure of the latter to establish themselves as durable presences. Although, in their proximity to the migrants and the movements, these films are clearly committed, they are also critical and interrogative. Their montage seeks alignments between experiences of precarity or between past and present struggles without assuming that the connections already exist or will automatically occur. In this, the films are contemporary of a moment where a progressive way forward often remains uncertain. At the same time, in their very specific use of the machinery of cinema and in their difference to the other films discussed, they remind us of the fluidity within the cinematic machine itself, its capacity for dis- and re-assembly.

# Conclusion

This book began by suggesting that crisis was a complex, multi-dimensional topic because of its association with the long-term crises neoliberalism generates, a specific period of systemic crisis which began in 2007, and an ongoing mode of neoliberal governance. It went on to argue that any fixation on a singular crisis, even as a potentially liberatory moment, and no matter how cataclysmic it seemed, risked blinding us to its connections to, and functioning in, a broader context.

If one were temporarily to disregard such an argument and look for a cinema of the crisis as a singular event, one could surely find it. Assuming that there is an inevitable time lag between any given occurrence and cinematic responses to it, we might reasonably begin to look for crisis films from about 2010 onwards. I have discussed a number of these in each chapter of this book. While few directly reference the global financial crisis, they do develop what one might call a thematics of crisis: rising precarity and debt; workers becoming disposable and driven to suicide; social isolation and a murderous competition for productive places expressed in the collisions of individual bodies. The same films suggest a closing in of temporal horizons: a past whose memories of collective resistances can only be accessed nostalgically or not at all; a future foreclosed by debt or by the profoundly asymmetric nature of the forces in play; characters trapped in an oppressive present, their bodies defeated or exhausted, running to stand still. As I argued across several chapters, patterns in these films often converge around a sense of the neoliberal subject in crisis: a crisis contained in Audiard's films where the threat of precarity and murderous competition was put to work for narratives of triumphant entrepreneurial flexibility; a crisis refusing containment in the debt and worker-suicide films discussed and within which the neoliberal entrepreneur of the self, shedding any heroic veneer the figure might have, was forced to manage their own insolvency or disposability and inevitably failed to do so; a crisis, finally, of individual agency within which, becoming mere cogs, subjects were torn apart, their attributes, affects and gestures inserted into the complex machineries that structure our lives but with which so much mainstream cinema struggles to engage. And, at the same time, a cinema whose own resources seemed to be breaking down as it clung to an impotent left moralism (Brown 2001: 30) or struggled to convince itself and its audience of the promise of the future or the possibility of private happiness.

Under closer scrutiny, however, this over-neat account of a cinema of the crisis breaks down. As the range of films discussed shows, the features we might associate with such a cinema can also be found in works which were released or in gestation before the effects of the crisis began to be felt. The precarity and murderous competition that drive Audiard's characters to flexible entrepreneurship are already present in the pre-crisis films, while *Un prophète*, shot in 2008, could only problematically be seen as a response to the crisis. Similarly, the Dardennes' films turn their focus to the ruthless struggle for secure or productive places from *La Promesse* (1996) onwards. Their *Deux jours, une nuit*, with its attempted worker suicide is from 2014 but, released in 1999, *Rosetta* already had a similar act and, as I have discussed elsewhere, was far from the only worker-suicide film from around that time (O'Shaughnessy 2019). Continuing the pattern, there was certainly a significant cluster of debt-centred films released in 2011, as we saw in Chapter 2, but the more interesting and original films we considered came out between 2001 (Cantet's *L'Emploi du temps*) and 2009 (Hansen-Løve's *Le Père de mes enfants*), the latter having been shot in 2008. Certainly, the films from around 2010 onwards do register crises of the subject, the future, and the belief films have in their own inherited narrative conventions. But the presence of similar concerns in earlier films suggests that these different types of crisis were already there and associated with neoliberalism more broadly. Given that, as discussed in the introduction, neoliberalism's governmental machinery knowingly nurtures a constant sense of individualised crisis, lived as precarity, to procure docility (Gentili 2021: xviii), this is unsurprising.

To the extent that, no longer able to persuade or seduce, neoliberalism has increasingly made itself punitive in this way, the capacity of cinema to render systemic violence visible risks impotence unless it is accompanied, not by a fully elaborated politics, but by a reawakened sense of possibility, of unpredictably transformative encounters, and of bodies, gestures, human connections, and relations to objects that bear a promise of the new. This sense of possibility, I have suggested, is what the important body of films discussed here provides. There is a risk, of course, of celebrating an empty utopianism, a generic, frictionless becoming that is at best consolatory and at worst easily folded back into a neoliberal cult of flexibility and self-fashioning. But, aware of this, the more interesting films balance their sense of possibility with an awareness of material constraints, of the limits of bodily energy, of hurt, of connections yet to be made or which may fail, of the hard work required for self-enfranchisement and the limits of any individual transformation without a broader social mobilisation to sustain it. Refusing the foreclosure of the future, its capture by a present that promises only a decaying version of the same, they invite us to be aware of alternatives constantly bubbling under and provide not a politics already made but raw materials for the political imagination. In the process, they also remind us of the powers of cinema itself. Despite all the institutional and financial constraints that hem it in, and to which the films discussed here bear witness, knowingly and unknowingly, it retains the capacity to question and renew its own forms and help us see afresh.

# Bibliography

Althusser, Louis (2006), *Philosophy of the Encounter: Later Writings, 1978–87* (trans. G. M. Goshgarian), London and New York: Verso.
Arendt, Hannah (1970), *On Violence*, San Diego, New York, London: Harcourt Brace Jovanovich.
Béghin, Cyril (2015), 'Quelle politique se dessine à travers les personnages du cinéma français: le sujet qui fâche', *Cahiers du Cinéma*, 714, September, 20–4.
Belot, Sophie (2012), 'Céline Sciamma's *La Naissance des pieuvres* (2017): seduction and be-coming', *Studies in French Cinema*, 12: 2, 169–84.
Benjamin, Walter (1940), *On the Concept of History (Theses on the Philosophy of History)* (trans. Dennis Redmond), available at: <https://www.marxists.org/reference/archive/benjamin/1940/history.htm> (last accessed 7 September 2021).
Berardi, Franco 'Bifo' (2015), *Heroes: Mass Murder and Suicide*, London and Brooklyn, NY: Verso.
Berlant, Lauren (2011a), *Cruel Optimism*, Durham, NC and London: Duke University Press.
Berlant, Lauren (2011b), 'Austerity, precarity, awkwardness', available at: <https://supervalentthought.files.wordpress.com/2011/12/berlant-aaa-2011final.pdf> (last accessed 7 September 2021).
Bernasconi, Robert (1997), 'What goes around comes around: Derrida and Levinas on the economy of the gift and the gift of genealogy', in Alan D. Schrift (ed.), *The Logic of the Gift: toward an Ethic of Generosity*, New York and London: Routledge, 256–73.
Bhandar, Brenna and Jonathan Goldberg-Hiller (2015), 'Interview with Catherine Malabou', in Brenna Bhandar and Jonathan Goldberg-Hiller (eds), *Plastic Materialities: Politics, Legality, and Metamorphosis in the Work of Catherine Malabou*, Durham, NC and London: Duke University Press, 287–99.
Boltanski, Luc and Eve Chiapello (1999), *Le Nouvel Esprit du capitalisme*, Paris: Gallimard.
Bourdieu, Pierre (1997), 'Marginalia: some additional notes on the gift', Alan D. Schrift (ed.), *The Logic of the Gift: Toward an Ethic of Generosity*, New York and London: Routledge, 231–41.
Brown, Wendy (2001), *Politics out of History*, Princeton, NJ: Princeton University Press.
Buck-Morss, Susan (1991), *The Dialectics of Seeing: Walter Benjamin and the Arcades Project*, Cambridge, MA and London: MIT Press.

Butler, Judith (2015), *Notes towards a Performative Theory of Assembly*, Cambridge, MA and London: Harvard University Press.
Caygill, Howard (2006), 'Walter Benjamin's concept of allegory', in David S. Ferris (ed.), *The Cambridge Companion to Walter Benjamin*, Cambridge: Cambridge University Press, 241–53.
Cederström, Carl and Peter Fleming (2012), *Dead Man Working*, Winchester (UK) and Washington: Zero Books.
Châtelet, Caroline (2015), 'Stéphane Brizé: *La Loi de marché*, un film qui parle de notre monde', *Regards*, 20 May, available at: <http://www.regards.fr/archives/web/Stephane-Brize-Exceptionnel-de> (last accessed 7 September 2021).
Châtelet, Caroline (2017), 'Désormais, tu es corporate ou tu ne l'es pas', *Regards*, 20 March, available at: <http://www.regards.fr/archives/web/article/desormais-tu-es-corporate-ou-tu-ne-l-es-pas> (last accessed 7 September 2021).
Chion, Michel (1999), *The Voice in Cinema* (trans. C. Gorbman), New York and Chichester: Columbia University Press.
Cooper, Melinda (2017), *Family Values: Between Neoliberalism and the New Social Conservatism*, Brooklyn, NY: Zone Books.
Cowan, Bainard (1981), 'Walter Benjamin's theory of allegory', *New German Critique*, 22, Winter, 109–22.
Dardenne, Luc (2005), *Au Dos de nos images (1991–2005)*, Paris: Seuil.
Dardot, Pierre and Christian Laval (2010), *La Nouvelle Raison du monde: essai sur la société néolibérale*, Paris: La Découverte.
Dardot, Pierre and Christian Laval (2016), *Ce Cauchemar qui n'en finit pas: comment le néolibéralisme défait la démocratie*, Paris: La Découverte.
Dean, Jodi (2018), *Crowds and Party*, London and New York: Verso.
Débordements (2014), 'Ne pas savoir d'où cela vient, où cela va', *Débordements*, 6 November, available at: <https://www.debordements.fr/Sylvain-George> (last accessed 7 September 2021).
Dejours, Christophe (1998), *Souffrance en France: la banalisation de l'injustice sociale*, Paris: Seuil.
Delépine, Benoît and Gustave Kervern (2012), *De Groland au grand soir: entretien avec Hervé Aubron et Emmanuel Burdeau*, Editions Capricci.
Deleuze, Gilles (1990), *Expressionism in Philosophy: Spinoza* (trans. Martin Joughin), New York: Zone Books.
Deleuze, Gilles (1992), 'Postscript on the societies of control', *October*, 59, Winter, 3–7.
Delorme, Stéphane (2007), '*La Graine et le mulet* d'Abdellatif Kechiche: Bateau ivre', *Cahiers du Cinéma*, 629, December, 11–13.
Delorme, Stéphane (2015a), 'Editorial: Vide politique', *Cahiers du Cinéma*, 714, September, 5.
Delorme, Stéphane (2015b), 'La loi de la jungle: Audiard & co', *Cahiers du Cinéma*, 714, September, 6–13.
Delorme, Stéphane and Dork Zabunyan (2015), 'Le reste, c'est à vous de l'inventer: entretien avec Jacques Rancière,' *Cahiers du Cinéma*, 709, March, 84–94.
Derrida, Jacques (1992), *Given Time: I. Counterfeit Money* (trans. Peggy Kamuf), Chicago and London: University of Chicago Press.
Diprose, Rosalyn (2002), *Corporeal Generosity: On Giving with Nietzsche, Merleau-Ponty and Levinas*, Albany NY: State University of New York Press.

Dobson, Julia (2008), 'Jacques Audiard: contesting filiations', in Kate Ince (ed.), *Five Directors: Auteurism from Assayas to Ozon*, Manchester: Manchester University Press, 38–58.

Dolphijn, Rick and Iris van der Tuin (2012), 'Interview with Rosi Braidotti', in Rick Dolphijn and Iris van der Tuin (eds), *New Materialism: Interviews and Cartographies*, Ann Arbor, MI: Open Humanities Press, 19–37.

Fabre, Clarisse (2013), 'Des techniciens racontent le tournage difficile de *La Vie d'Adèle*', *Le Monde*, 24 May.

Fevret, Christian and Jean-Marc Lalanne (2007), '*La Graine et le mulet*: entretien avec Abdellatif Kechiche', *Les Inrockuptibles*, 11 December, available at: <https://www.lesinrocks.com/cinema/entretien-abdellatif-kechiche-la-graine-et-le-mulet-1207-7827-11-12-2007/> (last accessed 7 September 2021).

Foucault, Michel (2010), *The Birth of Biopolitics: Lectures at the Collège de France, 1978–1979* (trans. Graham Burchell), Basingstoke: Palgrave Macmillan.

Foucault, Michel (2011), *The Courage of Truth: The Government of Self and Others II: Lectures at the Collège de France, 1983–1984* (trans. Graham Burchell), New York: Picador.

Gallard, Pauline (2013), '*La Vie d'Adèle*: Julie Maroh amère contre Kechiche', *Gala*, 28 May, available at: <https://www.gala.fr/l_actu/culture/la_vie_d_adele_julie_maroh_amere_contre_kechiche_291036> (last accessed 7 September 2021).

Gentili, Dario (2021), *The Age of Precarity: Endless Crisis as an Art of Government*, London and New York: Verso.

Gheoghe, Cezar (2014), '"Give me a body then": Abdellatif Kechiche and the cinema of the flesh', *Ekphrasis*, 12: 2, 159–66.

Graeber, David (2001), *Towards an Anthropological Theory of Value: The False Coin of Our Own Dreams*, New York and Basingstoke: Palgrave.

Graeber, David (2011), *Debt: The First 5000 Years*, Brooklyn, NY: Melville House.

Haraway, Donna (1991), 'A Cyborg Manifesto: science, technology, and socialist-feminism in the late twentieth century', in *Simians, Cyborgs and Women: The Reinvention of Nature*. New York: Routledge, 149–81.

Hardt, Michael (1997), 'Prison Time', *Yale French Studies*, 91, 67–94.

Harvey, David (2010), *The Enigma of Capital and the Crises of Capitalism*, London: Profile Books.

Immelen, Cathy (2017), 'L'interview de Nicolas Silhol, à propos de *Corporate*', rtbf.be, 18 May, available at: <https://www.rtbf.be/culture/cinema/realisateurs/detail_l-interview-de-nicolas-silhol-a-propos-de-corporate?id=9609504> (last accessed 7 September 2021).

Irigaray, Luce (1997), 'Women on the market', trans. Catherine Porter, in Alan D. Schrift (ed.), *The Logic of the Gift: Toward an Ethic of Generosity*, New York and London: Routledge, 174–89.

Jameson, Fredric (1979), 'Reification and utopia in mass culture', *Social Text*, 1, Winter, 130–48.

Kakogianni, Maria and Jacques Rancière (2013), 'A precarious dialogue' (trans. Olivia Lucca Fraser), *Radical Philosophy*, 181, 18–25.

Kearney, Richard (1999), 'On the gift: a discussion between Jacques Derrida and Jean-Luc Marion', in John Caputo and Michael Scanlon (eds), *God, the Gift, and Postmodernism*, Bloomington and Indianapolis: Indiana University Press, 54–78.

Koutsourakis, Angelos (2020), 'The resurgence of modernism and its critique of liberalism in the cinema of crisis', in Thomas Austin and Angelos Koutsourakis (eds),

*Cinema of Crisis: Film and Contemporary Europe*, Edinburgh: Edinburgh University Press, 60–75.

Lazzarato, Maurizio (2008), *Le Gouvernement des inégalités: critique de l'insécurité néolibérale*, Paris: Editions Amsterdam.

Lazzarato, Maurizio (2011), *La Fabrique de l'homme endetté: essai sur la condition néolibérale*, Paris: Editions Amsterdam.

Lazzarato, Maurizio (2014), *Signs and Machines: Capitalism and the Production of Subjectivity* (trans. Joshua Jordan), Los Angeles: Semiotext(e).

Lazzarato, Maurizio (2015), *Governing by Debt* (trans. Joshua Jordan), South Pasadena: Semiotext(e).

Lazzarato, Maurizio (2019), *Videophilosophy: The Perception of Time in Post-Fordism* (trans. Jay Hetrick), New York: Columbia University Press.

Lévi-Strauss, Claude (1967), *Les Structures élémentaires de la parenté*, Paris and the Hague: Mouton.

Lordon, Frédéric (2018), 'En guerre – pour la préemption salariale', *Le Monde Diplomatique*, 21 May, available at: <https://blog.mondediplo.net/en-guerre-pour-la-preemption-salariale> (last accessed 7 September 2021).

Lorey, Isabell (2015), *State of Insecurity: Government of the Precarious* (trans. Aileen Derieg), London, New York: Verso.

Magubane, Zine (2001), 'Which bodies matter? Feminism, poststructuralism, race, and the curious theoretical odyssey of the "Hottentot Venus"', *Gender and Society*, 15: 6, 816–34.

Mai, Joseph (2010), *Jean-Pierre and Luc Dardenne*, Urbana, IL: University of Illinois Press.

Malabou, Catherine (2015), 'Whither materialism? Althusser / Darwin' in Brenna Bhandar and Jonathan Goldberg-Hiller (eds), *Plastic Materialities: Politics, Legality, and Metamorphosis in the Work of Catherine Malabou*, Durham, NC and London: Duke University Press, 47–60.

Mallard, Grégoire (2011), 'The Gift revisited: Marcel Mauss on war, debt, and the politics of reparations', *Sociological Theory*, 29: 4, 225–47.

Masson, Alain (2009), '*Un prophète*: un début dans la vie', *Positif*, 583 (September), 14–16.

Mattoscio, Mara (2017), 'What's in a face?: Sara Baartman, the (post)colonial gaze and the case of *Vénus Noire* (2010)', *Feminist Review*, 117, 56–78.

Mauss, Marcel [1925] (2012), *Essai sur le don: forme et raison de l'échange dans les sociétés archaïques*, Paris: Presses Universitaires de France.

Mauss, Marcel [1934] (1973), 'Techniques of the body' (trans. Ben Brewster), *Economy and Society*, 2: 1, 70–88.

Mbembe, Achille (2016), *Politiques de l'inimitié*, Paris: la Découverte.

Monaghan, Whitney (2019), 'Not just a phase: queer girlhood and coming of age on screen', *Girlhood Studies*, 12: 1, Spring, 98–113.

Munck, Ronaldo (2013), 'The Precariat: a view from the South', *Third World Quarterly*, 34: 5, 747–62.

Niang, Mame-Fatou (2019), *Identités françaises: banlieues, fémininités et universalisme*, Leiden and Boston: Brill-Rodopi.

O'Shaughnessy, Martin (2007), *The New Face of Political Cinema: Commitment in French Film since 1995*, Oxford: Berghahn.

O'Shaughnessy, Martin (2019), 'Putting the dead to work: making sense of worker suicide in contemporary French and Franco-Belgian film', *Studies in French Cinema*, 19: 4, 314–34.

Oscherwitz, Dayna (2015), 'Monnet changes everything? Capitalism, currency and crisis in Jacques Becker's *Touchez pas au grisbi* (1954) and Jacques Audiard's *Un prophète* (2009)', *Studies in French Cinema*, 15: 3, 258–74.

Palmer, Tim (2017), 'Fine arts and ugly arts: *Blue is the Warmest Color*, Abdellatif Kechiche's corporeal state of the nation', in Lindsay Coleman and Carol Siegel (eds), *Intercourse in Television and Film: The Presentation of Explicit Sex Acts*, Lanham, MD: Lexington Books, 3–23.

Pensky, Max (2006), 'Method and time: Benjamin's dialectical images', in David S. Ferris (ed.), *The Cambridge Companion to Walter Benjamin*, Cambridge: Cambridge University Press, 177–96.

Rubin, Gayle (1975), 'The Traffic in women: notes on the "political economy" of sex', in Rayna Reiter (ed.), *Toward an Anthropology of Women*, New York and London: Monthly Review Press, 157–210.

Rutsky, R. L. (2007), 'Walter Benjamin and the dispersion of cinema', *symplokē*, 15: 1–2, 8–23.

Sarratia, Géraldine (2018), 'Dans le genre de Jacques Audiard', Radio Nova, May 6, available at: <https://podcloud.fr/podcast/dans-le-genre-de-dot-dot-dot/episode/publication-sans-titre-5af0d5c0a9b4971323000002> (last accessed 15 March 2019).

Scully, Pamela and Clifton Crais (2008), 'Race and erasure: Sara Baartman and Hendrik Cesars in Cape Town and London', *Journal of British Studies*, 47: 2, 301–23.

Sellier, Geneviève (2016), '*De battre mon coeur s'est arrêté (Audiard, 2005)*: la masculinité comme souffrance', *Studies in French Cinema*, 16: 3, 205–14.

Speno, Joffrey (2017), 'Paris est une fête – un film en 18 vagues: entretien avec Sylvain George', *Diacritik*, 27 March, available at: <https://diacritik.com/2017/03/27/paris-est-une-fete-un-film-en-18-vagues-entretien-avec-sylvain-george/> (last accessed 11 September 2021).

Stern, Marlow (2013), 'The stars of *Blue is the Warmest Color* on the riveting lesbian love story', *The Daily Beast*, 1 September, available at: <https://www.thedailybeast.com/the-stars-of-blue-is-the-warmest-color-on-the-riveting-lesbian-love-story> (last accessed 7 September 2021).

Streeck, Wolfgang (2009), *Flexible Employment, Flexible Families, and the Socialization of Reproduction*, MPIfG Working Paper 09/13, Cologne: Max Planck Institute for the Study of Societies.

Toscano, Alberto and Jeff Kinkle (2015), *Cartographies of the Absolute*, Winchester and Washington: Zero Books.

Van der Linden (2012), 'On the violence of systemic violence: a critique of Slavoj Žižek', *Radical Philosophy Review*, 15: 1, 33–51.

Vincendeau, Ginette (2008), 'Southern Discomfort', *Sight and Sound*, 18: 7, available at: <http://old.bfi.org.uk/sightandsound/review/4371> (last accessed 7 September 2021).

Waters, Sarah (2020), *Suicide Voices: Labour Trauma in France*, Liverpool: Liverpool University Press.

Wilkens, Matthew (2006), 'Towards a Benjaminian theory of dialectical allegory', *New Literary History*, 37: 2, 285–98.

Williams, Linda (2017), '*Blue is the Warmest Colour*: or the after-life of "Visual pleasure and narrative cinema"', *New Review of Film and Television Studies*, 15: 4, 465–70.

Wilson, Emma (2012), 'Precarious lives: on girls in Mia Hansen-Løve and others', *Studies in French Cinema*, 12: 3, 273–84.

Wilson, Emma (2017), 'Scenes of hurt and rapture: Céline Sciamma's *Girlhood*', *Film Quarterly*, 70: 3, 10–22.

Žižek, Slavoj (2000), *The Fragile Absolute, or Why is the Christian Legacy Worth Fighting for?* London, New York: Verso.

Žižek, Slavoj (2008), *Violence: Six Sideways Reflections*, London: Profile Books.

# Filmography

*L'Avenir/Things to come*, dir. Mia Hansen-Løve. France, Germany: Les Films du Losange, 2016.
*Bande de filles/Girlhood*, dir. Céline Sciamma. France: Hold Up Films, Lilies Films, Arte France Cinéma, 2014.
*Corporate*, dir. Nicolas Silhol. France: Kazak Productions, Auvergne Rhône-Alpes Cinéma, Canal+, 2017.
*De battre mon coeur s'est arrêté/The Beat that My Heart Skipped*, dir. Jacques Audiard. France: Why Not Productions, Sédif Productions, France 3 Cinéma, 2005.
*De bon matin/Early One Morning*, dir. Jean-Marc Moutout. France, Belgium: Les Films du Losange, Need Productions, France 2 Cinéma, 2011.
*De rouille et d'os/Rust and Bone*, dir. Jacques Audiard. France, Belgium, Singapore: Why Not Productions, Page 114, France 2 Cinéma, 2012.
*Deux jours, une nuit/Two Days, One Night*, dir. Jean-Pierre and Luc Dardenne. Belgium, France, Italy: Les Films du Fleuve, Archipel 35, BIM Distribuzione, 2014.
*Dheepan*, dir. Jacques Audiard. France: Why Not Productions, Page 114, France 2 Cinéma, 2015.
*Les Eclats (ma gueule, ma révolte, mon nom)/The Fragments (My Mouth, My Revolt, My Name)*, dir. Sylvain George. France: Noir Production, 2012.
*L'Emploi du temps/Time Out*, dir. Laurent Cantet. France: Haut et Court, 2001.
*L'Enfant/The Child*, dir. Jean-Pierre and Luc Dardenne. Belgium, France: Les Films du Fleuve, 2005.
*En guerre/At War*, dir. Stéphane Brizé. France: Nord-Ouest Films, France 3 Cinéma, France Télévisions, 2018.
*L'Esquive/Games of Love and Chance*, dir. Abdellatif Kechiche. France: Lola Films, Noé Productions, CinéCinéma, 2003.
*La Faute à Voltaire/Poetical Refugee*, dir. Abdellatif Kechiche. France: Flach Film, 2000.
*La Fille Inconnue/The Unknown Girl*, dir. Jean-Pierre and Luc Dardenne. Belgium, France: Les Films du Fleuve, Archipel 35, Savage Films, 2016.
*Le Fils/The Son*, dir. Jean-Pierre and Luc Dardenne. Belgium: Archipel 35, Les Films du Fleuve, Radio Télévision Belge Francophone, 2002.
*Le Gamin au vélo/The Kid with the Bike*, dir. Jean-Pierre and Luc Dardenne. Belgium, France, Italy: Les Films du Fleuve, 2011.

*The Godfather*, dir. Francis Ford Coppola. USA: Paramount Pictures, Alfran Productions, 1972.
*La Graine et le mulet/Couscous*, dir. Abdellatif Kechiche. France: Pathé Renn Production, Hirsch, France 2 Cinéma, 2007.
*Le Grand Soir*, dir. Benoît Delépine, Gustave Kervern. France, Belgium, Germany: GMT productions, No Money Productions, Panache Productions, 2012.
*Un héros très discret/A Self Made Hero*, dir. Jacques Audiard. France: Alicéléo, Cofimage 7, Lumière, 1996.
*I Feel Good*, dir. Benoît Delépine, Gustave Kervern. France: No Money Productions, JD Prod, Arte France Cinéma, 2018.
*L'Impossible, pages arrachées*, dir. Sylvain George. France: Noir Production, 2009.
*La Loi du marché/The Measure of a Man*, dir. Stéphane Brizé. France: Nord-Ouest Films, Arte France Cinéma, Canal+, 2015.
*Louise Wimmer*, dir. Cyril Mennegun. France: Zadig Productions, Arte France Cinéma, Canal+, 2011.
*Louise-Michel*, dir. Benoît Delépine, Gustave Kervern. France: MNP Entreprise, No Money Productions, Arte France Cinéma, 2008.
*Lucy*, dir. Luc Besson: France, Germany, Taiwan, Canada, USA, UK: Europacorp, TF1 Productions, Grive Productions, 2014.
*Ma part du gâteau/My Piece of the Pie*, dir. Cédric Klapisch. France: Ce Qui Me Meut Motion Pictures, Studio Canal, France 2 Cinéma, 2011.
*Mektoub, My Love: Intermezzo*, dir. Abdellatif Kechiche. France: Quat'sous Films, Pathé, Futurikon, 2019.
*Naissance des pieuvres/Water Lilies*, dir. Céline Sciamma. France: Balthazar Production, Lilies Films, Canal+, 2007.
*Near Death Experience*, dir. Benoît Delépine, Gustave Kervern. France: No Money Productions, Canal+, Ciné +, 2014.
*L'Outsider/Team Spirit*, dir. Christophe Barratier. France: Galatée Films, France 2 Cinéma, Le Pacte, 2016.
*Paris est une fête (un film en 18 vagues)/Paris is a Moveable Feast (a Film in 18 Waves)*, dir. Sylvain George. France: Noir Production 2018.
*Le Père de mes enfants/The Father of My Children*, dir. Mia Hansen-Løve. France, Germany, Belgium: Les Films Pelléas, 27 Films Production, Arte France Cinéma, 2009.
*Portrait de la jeune fille en feu/Portrait of a Lady on Fire*, dir. Céline Sciamma. France: Lilies Films, Arte France Cinéma, Hold Up Films, 2019.
*La Promesse/The Promise*, dir. Jean-Pierre and Luc Dardenne. Belgium, France, Luxembourg, Tunisia: Les Films du Fleuve, 1996.
*Un prophète/A Prophet*, dir. Jacques Audiard. France, Italy: Why Not Productions, Chic Films, Page 114, 2009.
*Qu'ils reposent en révolte (des figures de guerre)*, dir. Sylvain George. France: Noir Production, 2010.
*Regarde les hommes tomber/See How They Fall*, dir. Jacques Audiard. France: Bloody Mary Productions, Centre Européen Cinématographique Rhône-Alpes, France 3 Cinéma, 1994.
*Rosetta*, dir. Jean-Pierre and Luc Dardenne. Belgium, France: Les Films du Fleuve, 1999.
*Le Silence de Lorna/Lorna's Silence*, dir. Jean-Pierre and Luc Dardenne. Belgium, France, Italy, Germany: Les Films du Fleuve, 2008.
*Sur mes lèvres/Read My Lips*, dir. Jacques Audiard. France: Canal+, Centre National du Cinéma et de l'Image Animée, Ciné B, 2001.

*Tomboy*, dir. Céline Sciamma. France: Hold Up Films, Arte France Cinéma, Lilies Films, 2011.
*Tout va bien*, dir. Jean-Luc Godard, Jean-Pierre Gorin. France, Italy: Anouchka Films, Vieco Films, Empire Films, 1972.
*Toutes nos envies/All Our Desires*, dir. Philippe Lioret. France: Fin Août Productions, Mars Films, France 3 Cinéma, 2011.
*Vénus Noire/Black Venus*, dir. Abdellatif Kechiche. France, Belgium: MK2 Productions, France 2 Cinéma, CinéCinéma, 2010.
*Vers Madrid: the Burning Bright/Towards Madrid: the Burning Bright*, dir. Sylvain George. Spain, France: Noir Production, 2012.
*La Vie d'Adèle/Blue is the Warmest Colour*, dir. Abdellatif Kechiche. France, Belgium, Spain: Quat'sous Films, Wild Bunch, France 2 Cinéma, 2013.
*Une vie meilleure/A Better Life*, dir. Cédric Kahn. France: Les Films du Lendemain, Cinémaginaire Inc., Maia Cinéma, 2011.

# Index

*All Our Desires* (Lioret) see *Toutes nos envies*
Althusser, Louis
   and the materialism of the encounter, 7, 10, 99–102, 115–16
Arendt, Hannah
   on violence, 79
*At War* (Brizé) see *En guerre*
Audiard, Jacques, 11–12, 192
   and the critics, 12–15
   and the flexible family, 6, 35–7
   and gender, 6, 29–33
   and neoliberal subjectivity, 6, 11–12, 14–21, 24–5
   and precarity, 6, 11, 14, 25–9, 37
   see also *De battre mon coeur s'est arrêté; De rouille et d'os; Dheepan; Un héros très discret; Un Prophète; Regarde les hommes tomber; Sur mes lèvres*
austerity, 1–3, 40, 57, 161, 170, 178–80, 191
*L'Avenir* (Hansen-Løve), 52

*Bande de filles* (Sciamma), 99, 125–30
Benjamin, Walter
   and the constellation, 183–4, 190
   and divine violence, 79
   and history, 182–3, 190

Berardi, Franco (Bifo)
   on suicide waves, 96
Berlant, Lauren
   on the crisis, 1
   and cruel optimism, 7, 40, 57–9, 61–2, 67
   and impasse, 40–1, 58, 61–3
*A Better Life* (Kahn) see *Une vie meilleure*
*Blue is the Warmest Colour* (Kechiche) see *La Vie d'Adèle*
Boltanski, Luc and Chiapello, Eve
   on the connexionist hero, 23–4, 25
   on the new spirit of capitalism, 22–3
   on the precarious family, 34
Bourdieu, Pierre
   on the gift, 142–3
Brizé, Stéphane, 7, 80, 89; see also *En guerre; La Loi du marché*
Brown, Wendy
   on left moralism, 7, 77, 83, 193
Butler, Judith
   as criticised by Lazzarato, 169
   on political claims of Occupy, 189
   on precarity, 26

*Les Cahiers du Cinéma*
   on Audiard, 12–14, 24, 28, 38
   on Kechiche, 102, 106

Cantet, Laurent, 45; see also *L'Emploi du temps*; *Ressources humaines*
Cederström, Carl and Fleming, Peter
  on worker suicide, 7, 70, 80–3, 88
*Company Men* (Wells), 65
Cooper, Melinda
  on the neoliberal family, 34–5, 37
*Corporate* (Silhol), 71, 86–9, 97
*Couscous* (Kechiche) see *La Graine et le mulet*
crisis
  and neoliberal governance, 4–5, 192
  of the neoliberal subject, 5–7, 9–10, 40–1, 63, 65–6, 68, 73, 96–7, 160–1, 170, 192–3
  origins of, 2–3, 57, 168–9
  as theorised, 1, 3–6, 192

Dardenne, Jean-Pierre and Dardenne, Luc
  debt in the films of, 6–7, 42
  and ethics, 71, 89, 138–9, 143, 144, 149–50, 151, 152, 156–7, 158
  and film style, 41, 45, 96, 153, 159
  and the gift, 7–8, 132–59
  influences on, 132, 138
  suicide in the films of, 7, 71
  see also *Deux jours, une nuit*; *L'Enfant*; *La Fille inconnue*; *Le Fils*; *Le Gamin au vélo*; *La Promesse*; *Rosetta*; *Le Silence de Lorna*
Dardot, Pierre and Laval, Christian
  on neoliberal governance, 4–5, 24–5, 34
debt, 1, 27, 28, 29–31
  and the crisis, 2–3, 8, 168–9, 192–3
  and debt forgiveness, 139, 141
  as infinite, 55, 138–9, 144, 156–7
  and the neoliberal subject, 5–7, 40–69, 70, 72–3, 96, 160, 164, 170

Delépine, Benoît and Kervern, Gustave, 71, 92–3; see also *Le Grand Soir*; *I feel good*; *Louise-Michel*; *Near Death Experience*
Deleuze, Gilles, 100
  on control societies, 54
  on Spinoza, 116
  see also Deleuze, Gilles and Guattari, Félix
Deleuze, Gilles and Guattari, Félix
  and the assemblage, 167–8, 170–1
  on debt, 55–6
  on machinic enslavement, 8, 167
*De rouille et d'os* (Audiard), 11, 12, 28, 33, 35–6
Derrida, Jacques
  and Althusser, 100–1
  on the gift, 8, 141–3
  and Malabou, 101
*Deux jours, une nuit* (Dardenne and Dardenne), 7, 71, 89–92, 97, 148–50, 153, 193
*Dheepan* (Audiard), 11, 12, 27–8, 33, 36–7, 71
Dobson, Julia
  on Audiard and film form, 13–14
  on Audiard and gender, 13–14, 24, 29, 35, 38

*Early One Morning* (Moutout) see *De bon matin*
*L'Emploi du temps* (Cantet), 6, 40, 45–51, 59, 61–2, 68–9, 193
*L'Enfant* (Dardenne and Dardenne), 42, 144–7, 150
*En guerre* (Brizé), 7, 70–1, 74–7, 82–3

*The Father of My Children* (Hansen-Løve) see *Le Père de mes enfants*
*La Fille inconnue* (Dardenne and Dardenne), 153, 156–8
*Le Fils* (Dardenne and Dardenne), 144, 150, 151–3, 154–5

Foucault, Michel
    on neoliberal governance, 22, 24, 25, 34, 54, 167
    on parrhesia, 7, 70, 94–5

*Le Gamin au vélo* (Dardenne and Dardenne), 148, 150, 153–5
Gentili, Dario
    on the crisis of neoliberal subjectivity, 5–6, 193
    on precarity, 5–6, 193
George, Sylvain, 8–9, 161, 178–9
    and migrants and refugees, 8–9, 178–80, 182, 184–6
    and Occupy movements, 8–9, 179, 186–9, 191
    and Walter Benjamin, 182–6, 190
    see also *L'Impossible, pages arrachées*; *Paris est une fête, un film en 18 vagues*; *Vers Madrid: the Burning Bright*
*Girlhood* (Sciamma) see *Bande de filles*
Graeber, David
    on debt, 56
    on Marcel Mauss and the gift, 140, 144
*La Graine et le mulet* (Kechiche), 99, 102–9
*Le Grand Soir* (Delépine and Kervern), 7, 71, 93–5, 97
Guattari, Félix
    on semiosis, 167, 169, 171, 187
    see also Deleuze, Gilles and Guattari, Félix

Hansen-Løve, Mia, 52; see also *L'Avenir*; *Le Père de mes enfants*
*Un héros très discret* (Audiard), 11, 15–21, 24–5, 31, 33
Haraway, Donna
    and the cyborg, 177
Hardt, Michael
    on prison, 38
Harvey, David
    on the crisis, 2

*I feel good* (Delépine and Kervern), 92–3
*L'Impossible, pages arrachées* (George), 178, 186

Jameson, Fredric
    on *The Godfather*, 21

Kakogianni, Maria
    on the crisis, 3–4
Kechiche, Abdellatif, 7, 12, 98–9, 101–2, 130–1
    and criticisms of his work, 102, 111, 114–15, 129, 131
    and his style, 106–7, 115, 116
    see also *La Graine et le mulet*; *Vénus noire*; *La Vie d'Adèle*
*The Kid with the Bike* (Dardenne and Dardenne) see *Le Gamin au vélo*

Lazzarato, Maurizio
    on cinema's semiotic pluralism, 8, 161, 171–4, 187–8
    on crisis as neoliberal governmentality, 5
    on debt, 6, 40, 54–7, 59–61, 63
    on the machinic, 8, 10, 160–1, 167–71, 173–4
    on the neoliberal subject in crisis, 5–6, 40, 170
    on precarity, 26, 28
    on semiosis, 160–1, 169–70
Levinas, Emmanuel
    on the ethical obligation to the Other, 138–9, 150–1
    and the gift, 138–9, 143, 149, 151
*La Loi du marché* (Brizé), 7, 70–4, 76–7, 81–3, 161–4, 167, 172, 174
Lorey, Isabell
    on precarity, 26, 28
*Louise-Michel* (Delépine and Kervern), 92

*The Measure of a Man* (Brizé) see
    *La Loi du marché*
*My Piece of the Pie* (Klapisch) see
    *Ma part du gâteau*

*Naissance des pieuvres* (Sciamma), 99,
    123–5, 130
*Near Death Experience* (Delépine and
    Kervern), 93
neoliberalism
    and the crisis, 1, 4–6, 192–3
    and the family, 34–8
    and governance, 22, 24–5, 26,
        192–3
    and neoliberal subjectivity, 5–7,
        9, 11–12, 14–15, 22–5, 27, 29,
        31, 33
    *see also* debt and the neoliberal
        subject; Lazzarato on the
        neoliberal subject in crisis
Niang, Mame-Fatou
    on *Bande de filles*, 129
Nietzsche
    and debt, 54–5
*Nuit debout*, 2–3, 9, 184; *see also*
    Occupy

Occupy, 2–3, 9, 186–8, 189, 191; *see
    also* Toma la Plaza, Nuit debout
*L'Outsider* (Barratier), 71, 83–6,
    88–9

*Paris est une fête, un film en 18 vagues*
    (George), 178–9, 180–2, 184–6,
    189, 190
*Le Père de mes enfants* (Hansen-Løve),
    6–7, 40, 49–54, 59–63, 69, 193
*Portrait de la jeune fille en feu*
    (Sciamma), 98–9, 119–23, 126,
    130
precarity, 3, 5–6, 9, 11, 14, 24, 25–9,
    34, 36–7, 179–80, 185, 188–9,
    191, 192–3; *see also* Lazzarato,
    Maurizio on precarity; Lorey,
    Isabell on precarity

*La Promesse* (Dardenne and
    Dardenne), 42, 61, 63, 133–9,
    143–4, 146, 147, 148–50,
    154–5, 193
*Un Prophète* (Audiard), 11, 13, 15–21,
    24–5, 26–7, 31, 33, 35, 38–9,
    193

Rancière, Jacques
    on the crisis, 3–5
    as criticised by Lazzarato, 169
    on the politics of cinema, 9
*Read My Lips* (Audiard) see *Sur mes
    lèvres*
*Regarde les hommes tomber* (Audiard),
    13–14, 29–33
*Rosetta* (Dardenne and Dardenne),
    71, 89–92, 97, 150–1, 193
*Rust and Bone* (Audiard) see *De rouille
    et d'os*

*See How They Fall* (Audiard) see
    *Regarde les hommes tomber*
*A Self-Made Hero* (Audiard) see *Un
    héros très discret*
Sciamma, Céline, 7, 98–9, 101–2,
    115, 116, 130–1; see also *Bande
    de filles*; *Naissance des pieuvres*;
    *Portrait de la jeune fille en feu*;
    *Tomboy*
Sellier, Geneviève
    on Audiard and gender, 13–14, 29,
        33, 38
*Le Silence de Lorna* (Dardenne and
    Dardenne), 6–7, 40–5, 49,
    59–63, 69, 89, 144, 150
*The Son* (Dardenne and Dardenne)
    see *Le Fils*
Spinoza, Baruch
    as philosopher of immanence,
        115–16
Streeck, Wolfgang
    on the flexible family, 34–5
*Sur mes lèvres* (Audiard), 27, 29,
    32–3

*Team Spirit* (Barratier) see *L'Outsider*
*Things to Come* (Hansen-Løve) see *L'Avenir*
*Time Out* (Cantet) see *L'Emploi du temps*
Toma la plaza, 9, 179; *see also* Occupy
*Tomboy* (Sciamma), 99, 116–19, 126, 130
*Toutes nos envies* (Lioret), 41, 64–7
*Tout va bien* (Godard), 52–3
*Two Days, One Night* (Dardenne and Dardenne) see *Deux jours, une nuit*

*The Unknown Girl* (Dardenne and Dardenne) see *La Fille Inconnue*

*Vénus noire* (Kechiche), 99, 108–10
*Vers Madrid: the Burning Bright* (George), 9, 178–80, 181, 185–90
*La Vie d'Adèle* (Kechiche), 98–9, 102, 111–15
*Une vie meilleure* (Kahn), 41, 64–7

*Wall Street* (Stone), 86
*Water Lilies* (Sciamma) see *Naissance des pieuvres*
*Wolf of Wall Street* (Scorsese), 86

Žižek, Slavoj
    as criticised by Lazzarato, 169
    on suicide, 80
    on violence, 1, 7, 70, 77–80, 82–3, 96

EU representative:
Easy Access System Europe
Mustamäe tee 50, 10621 Tallinn, Estonia
Gpsr.requests@easproject.com

www.ingramcontent.com/pod-product-compliance
Lightning Source LLC
Chambersburg PA
CBHW070353240426
43671CB00013BA/2489